Creating the Premodern in the Postmodern Classroom:

Creativity in Early English Literature and History Courses

MEDIEVAL AND RENAISSANCE TEXTS AND STUDIES

VOLUME 537

Creating the Premodern in the Postmodern Classroom:

Creativity in Early English Literature and History Courses

Edited by

Anna Riehl Bertolet
Carole Levin

ARIZONA CENTER FOR MEDIEVAL
ACMRS
AND RENAISSANCE STUDIES
Tempe, Arizona
2018

THE ARIZONA CENTER FOR
MEDIEVAL & RENAISSANCE
STUDIES

Published by ACMRS (Arizona Center for Medieval and Renaissance Studies)
Tempe, Arizona

∞
This book is made to last. It is set in Adobe Caslon Pro,
and printed on acid-free paper to library specifications.
Printed in the United States of America

For my mother, and also for Clark Hulse and Peach Friedman,
the three teachers who opened the depths and horizons of my life in so many directions
Anya

For the three Pamelas in my life,
all wonderful and committed teachers, all great and loving friends
Carole

Contents

Illustrations *ix*

Essays by Topic *xi*

Acknowledgments *xiii*

Introduction *xvii*
Anna Riehl Bertolet and Carole Levin

The Prelude: The Pleasure of the Product

Of Giant, Bloody Fleas and Duct Tape Dragons: Flights of Fancy in the Renaissance Classroom 1
Nancy Hayes, *St. Ambrose University*

Quick Practical Takes: Creative Projects Menu

1. By Indirections Finding Directions Out: Creative Points of Entry to Shakespeare's Problem Comedies and Sonnets 13
Regina Buccola, *Roosevelt University*

2. From the Trial of Charles I to Comic Scenes of *Hamlet*: Using Creative Projects in Small Classes and Large Ones 23
Carole Levin, *University of Nebraska, Lincoln*

3. Very Simple Classroom Performance Exercises That Work (Usually) Even for Non-Actors of Shakespeare 33
Mary Ellen Lamb, *Southern Illinois University Carbondale*

4. Performing Interpretive Interventions in the Shakespeare Survey Classroom 43
Nathanial B. Smith, *Central Michigan University*

5. Shakespeare and Service-Learning 55
Matthew C. Hansen, *Boise State University*

6. Shakespeare and the Experimental Classroom 65
Jonathan P. Lamb, *University of Kansas*

7. Applicability in Chaucer's *Miller's Tale* and Virgil's *Aeneid* 83
Craig E. Bertolet, *Auburn University*

8. *Hare We Go!*: Deploying Films as Historical Texts in the Freshman Classroom 95
Charles Beem, *University of North Carolina at Pembroke*

9. Putting Sir Gawain on Trial 103
Kimberly Jack, *Athens State University*

10. Talking with the Dead: Teaching Early Modern History with Social Media 113
Renee Bricker, *University of North Georgia*

11. Experimenting with the Use of Wiki Projects in the Postmodern Classroom 123
Elena Woodacre, *University of Winchester*

Full Courses Designed Around Creative Projects

12. Reshaping, Refilling, Reimagining: Teaching Shakespeare through Intertextuality 135
Anna Riehl Bertolet, *Auburn University*

13. Teaching Global Shakespeares: All the World's His Stage 151
Jo Eldridge Carney, *The College of New Jersey*

14. What Would Helen of Troy Say?: Premodern Schoolroom Practices and Modern Students' Creative Projects 163
Linda Shenk, *Iowa State University*

15. Is There an Editor in This Text?: Renaissance Drama and Bibliographical History 179
Jonathan Walker, *Portland State University*

16. The Issue of Relevancy: Contemplative, Subjective, Affective 193
Karolyn Kinane, *Plymouth State University*

Selected Bibliography 215

Notes on Contributors 223

Illustrations

Cover Image: *Juliet and Romeo.*
Painting by Andie Perez. Class of Anna Riehl Bertolet.

Figure 1: Giant, bloody flea (John Donne's "The Flea").
Photo by Craig DeVriese, St. Ambrose University. Class of Nancy Hayes.

Figure 2: Duct tape dragon (Edmund Spenser's *The Fairie Queene*, book 1, canto 11).
Photo by Craig DeVriese, St. Ambrose University. Class of Nancy Hayes.

Figure 3: Elizabeth I look-alike necklace based on the *Rainbow Portrait.*
Photo by Craig DeVriese, St. Ambrose University. Class of Nancy Hayes.

Figure 4: Errour (Edmund Spenser's *The Fairie Queene*, book 1, canto 1).
Photo by Craig DeVriese, St. Ambrose University. Class of Nancy Hayes.

Figure 5: Elementary students perform *Twelfth Night* as part of "Shake It Up After School."
Class of Matthew Hansen.

Figure 6: Elementary students perform *Twelfth Night* as part of "Shake It Up After School."
Class of Matthew Hansen.

Figures 7, 8: PowerPoint Presentation about *Hamlet*, act 1.
Class of Jonathan Lamb.

Figure 9: Sample of Lear Family Tumblr.
Class of Jonathan Lamb.

Figure 10: Sample of Lear Family Tumblr.
Class of Jonathan Lamb.

Figure 11: Hippolita and Theseus.
Drawing by Shelby Hancock. Class of Anna Riehl Bertolet.

Plate 1: Photo of King Charles I on his knees.
Class of Carole Levin.

Plate 2: Queen Elizabeth Retelling.
Cartoon by Simran Sohi. Class of Carole Levin.

Plates 3, 4, 5: Elementary students perform *A Midsummer Night's Dream* as part of "Shake It Up After School."
Class of Matthew Hansen.

Plate 6: *Othello* Cupcakes, featuring the Othello cupcake (left), the Iago cupcake (center), and the Desdemona cupcake (right).
Class of Jonathan Lamb.

Plate 7: *Paradise Lost*: The cake of Eden.
Caitlin Sheridan and Scott Dukes. Class of Anna Riehl Bertolet.

Plate 8: *Paradise Lost*: Book XI Quilt.
Spenser R. Keel. Class of Anna Riehl Bertolet.

Plate 9: "Cookham" (based on the poem by Aemilia Lanyer).
Anna Mehta. Class of Anna Riehl Bertolet.

Plate 10: "A Dialogue Between Two Shepherds" (based on the poem by Mary Sidney Herbert).
Jordan Mollineux. Class of Anna Riehl Bertolet.

Essays by Topic

Ancient and Medieval Literature

Applicability in Chaucer's *Miller's Tale* and Virgil's *Aeneid*
Craig E. Bertolet, *Auburn University*

Hare We Go!: Deploying Films as Historical Texts in the Freshman Classroom
Charles Beem, *University of North Carolina at Pembroke*

Putting Sir Gawain on Trial
Kimberly Jack, *Athens State University*

The Issue of Relevancy: Contemplative, Subjective, Affective
Karolyn Kinane, *Plymouth State University*

Shakespeare

From the Trial of Charles I to Comic Scenes of *Hamlet*: Using Creative Projects in Small Classes and Large Ones
Carole Levin, *University of Nebraska, Lincoln*

Very Simple Classroom Performance Exercises That Work (Usually) Even for Non-Actors of Shakespeare
Mary Ellen Lamb, *Southern Illinois University Carbondale*

Performing Interpretive Interventions in the Shakespeare Survey Classroom
Nathanial B. Smith, *Central Michigan University*

Shakespeare and Service-Learning
Matthew C. Hansen, *Boise State University*

Shakespeare and the Experimental Classroom
Jonathan P. Lamb, *University of Kansas*

Reshaping, Refilling, Reimagining: Teaching Shakespeare through Intertextuality
Anna Riehl Bertolet, *Auburn University*

Teaching Global Shakespeares: All the World's His Stage
Jo Eldridge Carney, *The College of New Jersey*

What Would Helen of Troy Say?: Premodern Schoolroom Practices and Modern Students' Creative Projects
Linda Shenk, *Iowa State University*

Using Technology

Talking with the Dead: Teaching Early Modern History with Social Media
Renee Bricker, *University of North Georgia*

Experimenting with the Use of Wiki Projects in the Postmodern Classroom
Elena Woodacre, *University of Winchester*

Using Film

Hare We Go!: Deploying Films as Historical Texts in the Freshman Classroom
Charles Beem, *University of North Carolina at Pembroke*

Reshaping, Refilling, Reimagining: Teaching Shakespeare through Intertextuality
Anna Riehl Bertolet, *Auburn University*

Staging Trials and PR Campaigns

From the Trial of Charles I to Comic Scenes of *Hamlet*: Using Creative Projects in Small Classes and Large Ones
Carole Levin, *University of Nebraska, Lincoln*

Applicability in Chaucer's *Miller's Tale* and Virgil's *Aeneid*
Craig E. Bertolet, *Auburn University*

Putting Sir Gawain on Trial
Kimberly Jack, *Athens State University*

Poetics and Rhetoric

By Indirections Finding Directions Out: Creative Points of Entry to Shakespeare's Problem Comedies and Sonnets
REGINA BUCCOLA, *Roosevelt University*

What Would Helen of Troy Say?: Premodern Schoolroom Practices and Modern Students' Creative Projects
LINDA SHENK, *Iowa State University*

Textual Genealogies

Reshaping, Refilling, Reimagining: Teaching Shakespeare through Intertextuality
ANNA RIEHL BERTOLET, *Auburn University*

Teaching Global Shakespeares: All the World's His Stage
JO ELDRIDGE CARNEY, *The College of New Jersey*

Is There an Editor in This Text?: Renaissance Drama and Bibliographical History
JONATHAN WALKER, *Portland State University*

Acknowledgments

The concept for this book, as for many others, was born at a conference: a group of old friends gathered for an annual breakfast where the conversation quickly turned to using creative projects in our teaching. As we shared the assignments and described the imaginative projects produced by our students, we contemplated the profound impact of teaching through creativity. Since little had been published on the subject relative to medieval and early modern studies, we resolved to reach out to talented teachers who work with early English literary and historical materials and ask them to share their ways of engaging students with creativity in their classrooms.

We deeply appreciate the contributors to this volume for their passion for teaching, and we want to acknowledge our wonderful students, who participated so joyously in the creative projects we assigned and who surprised us, and often even themselves, with their originality, bravery, and playfulness as they took on the material at hand and made it their own. For her support and friendship, we are grateful to Margaret Hannay, who participated in the initial conversation.

The editors are most grateful to Dean Joseph Francisco and Associate Dean Aaron Dominguez and to the office of the Dean of Arts and Sciences at the University of Nebraska-Lincoln for a generous subvention. We also thank Roy Rukkila, our editor at ACMRS, for working with us on this collection.

Introduction

Anna Riehl Bertolet and Carole Levin

When a colleague who specializes in contemporary American poetry observed Anna Riehl Bertolet's class on British Literature before 1789, she sympathetically reported a renewed awareness of the difficulties faced in teaching early literature, difficulties she saw as rooted in pesky linguistic barriers. But these difficulties, of course, go beyond the puzzling language, and the challenges extend across all disciplines dealing with the premodern periods. In Carole Levin's History of England class, students have difficulty understanding how privacy and exact time are both modern constructs, that many family members shared rooms and beds and thought events took place "around sunset." Until students grasp the cultural context of literary texts or historical documents, they struggle with understanding the mentality encoded in the texts and events that both reflect and comprise the premodern world. As L. P. Hartley famously stated, the past is indeed a foreign country, and in the premodern lands the cultural beliefs can be especially difficult for students of the twenty-first century.[1] Conversations among teachers of the premodern often center on the difficulties of engaging students with what they initially perceive as the unfamiliar. While we need them to understand that some belief systems and ways of living are radically different from contemporary life, we also have to help them recognize that other stories, concerns, and tenets of the premodern are intrinsically connected to twenty-first-century life. Here and now, across the postmodern world, the accounts, concerns, and values are actively recollected and responded to, modified, and built upon in an effort to emulate or reject or at least truly understand the past.

While the texts discussed by our contributors are overwhelmingly medieval and early modern, we chose the spacious term "premodern" to describe the scope of the material explored in this book. This decision highlights the juxtaposition of premodern and postmodern as a jarring contrast between what has long passed and what has already moved beyond modernity. And yet the mirrored similarity in these terms points to the common ground, the essential continuity that we help our students discover as a result of the courses we teach.

---

[1] The opening sentence of his 1953 novel, *The Go-Between*.

The "premodern" in the title is also left intentionally untied to a particular subject matter, to indicate the interdisciplinarity of this collection. The contributors include scholars of history and literature, and their teaching interests reach into cultural studies, literary theory, performance studies, gender studies, modern technology, and so much more. Many of the contributors routinely collaborate with scholars in other disciplines, and the practice of sharing multiple scholarly perspectives on the premodern period is one of the delights of our academic lives that informs our research as well as our teaching.

Creative engagement is the key methodology that unites all the essays in this collection. This body of work differs from many other volumes discussing teaching techniques in that our explicit focus is on making the premodern come alive by eliciting thoughtful and sustained student responses through creative assignments that combine elements of scholarly research, personal experience, critical thinking, and freedom. As one contributor, Regina Buccola, puts it, "to play a little, experiment a little, dream a little, say something important." In dedicating the entire collection to creative pedagogical methods, we seek to supplement existing volumes that occasionally offer creative assignments among their chapters. Among these publications are numerous excellent Modern Language Association of America (MLA) collections (the *Options for Teaching* and *Approaches to Teaching World Literature* series), The Folger Shakespeare Library series *Shakespeare Set Free*, such useful books as Derval Conroy and Danielle Clarke's *Teaching the Early Modern Period*, and many additional resources listed in this volume's bibliography. Some of the principles and objectives of student engagement informing this collection tap into the same pedagogies as those harnessed in the role-immersion games in the rapidly expanding series *Reacting to the Past*. But while the reacting games brilliantly motivate and educate the students by plunging them into the past, the methods shared in this collection are intentionally diverse, and most of them are informed by the modern ways of understanding the premodern.

In a wide range of disciplines there is a growing awareness that students learn more thoroughly and can use what they learn more effectively when they are actively engaged in the course subject. As Craig Lambert points out, "Active learners take new information and *apply* it, rather than merely taking note of it. Firsthand use of new material develops personal ownership." Assignments that allow students to connect course material to their own experiences can help them care more about the material they are seeking to master. Candyce Reynolds, Dannelle D. Stevens, and Ellen West argue for the importance of creative projects in management classes: "There is significant evidence from multiple disciplines that suggests that the use of activities and assignments that engender student creativity can facilitate the types of outcomes we want our students to graduate with." Eric Jurgens writes that in all his classes his goal is "to foster a collaborative environment by stressing discovery." He decided, especially in humanities classes, that the best way to meet this goal was to ask his students to complete a creative project.[2] What all the authors in this collection share is a commitment to the use of creative projects to thoroughly engage their students in premodern studies.

We offer this book first and foremost as a toolbox for teachers of the premodern, to adapt and use in college courses of all levels; many of the assignments are also adaptable for a high school classroom. But this volume goes beyond sharing excellent projects and reaches into broader questions of pedagogical methodology, philosophy, and theory. The contributors reflect on the value and necessity of creative teaching and learning, on using nontraditional classroom activities to tether students to the material in a more intimate, more deeply conceived, and often transformative engagement. Thus students own the experience and course material in a deeply personal way and remember it for years after the class has ended.

The collection opens with a prelude, Nancy Hayes's lyrical journey through a decade of her students' creative projects. We begin with this essay not only to entice readers with the wonderful rewards for opening up students' creativity in the classroom, but also to provide examples that can be cited when introducing a creative project to a class that will provide tangible potential outcomes. Other contributors also eagerly describe some of the more outstanding creative products their students have prepared, and these examples could also be shared with students to set a standard for emulation.

We present the material in two parts: the first section entitled Quick Practical Takes: Creative Projects Menu is followed by Full Courses Designed Around Creative Projects. While every essay in this book is guided by its contributor's teaching philosophy, we found it useful to identify the essays that contain at least one easily adoptable specific project that could be used on short notice because it does not require an extensive engagement across the entire semester. We call this part of the book a menu because one can draw from it to add creative flavoring to an already established course. The second part of the book contains accounts of courses developed organically around creative projects, or courses in which creative projects are integrated on a systemic level. Individual assignments are still fully adaptable and could be disengaged from the rest of the course and used as "quick takes." Likewise, the content of each of these courses could be adjusted to accommodate different texts or pursue a different line of inquiry. However, these

---

[2] Craig Lambert, "Twilight of the Lecture," *Harvard Magazine* (March–April 2012), http://harvardmagazine.com/2012/03/twilight-of-the-lecture; Candyce Reynolds, Dannelle D. Stevens, and Ellen West, "'I'm in a Professional School! Why Are You Making Me Do This?' A Cross-Disciplinary Study of the Use of Creative Classroom Projects on Student Learning," *College Teaching* 61, no. 2 (2013): 52; Eric Jurgens, "Finding the Artist Within: Student Projects in the Humanities," *Tribal College Journal of American Indian Higher Education* (May 1, 2014), http://tribalcollegejournal.org/finding-artist-within-student-projects-humanities/.

essays also offer the convenience of an articulated course layout that could be used as a template for different material or followed exactly as presented.

In Quick Practical Takes, the reader will find a range of creative projects that include constructing public relations campaigns for clients who are characters from Chaucer's *The Miller's Tale,* or using embedded reporters to make sense of the battles in Virgil's *Aeneid* (Craig Bertolet); staging a mock-trial of Sir Gawain (Kimberly Jack); involving an entire large lecture course in a staged trial of Charles I or reworking fairy tales and scenes from *Hamlet* (Carole Levin); reimagining *Much Ado about Nothing* where Benedick would present Shakespeare's Sonnet 130 to Beatrice, constructing the missing dialog between Mariana and Isabella in *Measure for Measure,* or imagining how Mariana from *Measure for Measure* could be the same person as Mariana in *All's Well That Ends Well* (Regina Buccola); performing simplified scenes or even just one-liners to highlight multiple interpretations through acting (Mary Ellen Lamb); performing a scene in a way that deliberately seeks to disrupt conventions (Nathanial B. Smith); coaching elementary school students in staging a play (Matthew Hansen); incorporating self-assessment and reflection into projects (Jonathan Lamb); analyzing films in relation to history (Charles Beem); interviewing, blogging, and tweeting on behalf of historical figures (Renee Bricker); and creating wiki projects (Elena Woodacre).

In part two, Full Courses Designed Around Creative Projects, the five courses, while nuanced in their methodology, feature three broad approaches to the premodern: intertextuality highlighted through retelling by new voices in new contexts (Jo Eldridge Carney, Anna Riehl Bertolet); textuality in relation to rhetorical devices and printing culture (Linda Shenk, Jonathan Walker); and the use of contemplative pedagogy to inform the fundamental principles of approaching premodern texts (Karolyn Kinane). These approaches are echoed and diversified in the other essays in this collection: the creative exercises described by Regina Buccola are thoroughly intertextual; Mary Ellen Lamb, Matthew Hansen, and Nathanial Smith are explicitly advocating new ways of teaching through performance; and Renee Bricker, Charles Beem, and Elena Woodacre base their creative projects on student engagement of postmodern media.

The joy (and, admittedly, also the woe) of teaching is the ever-changing cast of characters, each term different students with varying personalities, interests, and abilities, which also means that no course plan or assignment will ever yield identical subsequent results, even at the hands of the same teacher. What we offer here is an opportunity to experiment. This volume is an invitation to foster learning through creativity, but it is also an encouragement for creative teaching. We hope that you find the experience and reflections shared on these pages invigorating, thought provoking, and inspiring.

Giant, Bloody Fleas and Duct Tape Dragons: Flights of Fancy in the Renaissance Classroom

Nancy Hayes, St. Ambrose University

Ten years ago in the English Department hallway at St. Ambrose University, I first encountered the concept of a creative final project while sliding my finger over the glazed, green surface of a student's life-sized ceramic U.S. Army "helmet" on display for a Vietnam War Literature class. Moved by the poignancy of that fragile, heavy objet d'art and the empathy as well as the wit it demonstrated, the very next semester I changed the routine final paper assignment in my Renaissance Literature course to a "final project." This came at a time when I was encountering an epidemic of plagiarized final papers in my survey classes, partly due to tantalizing new online sources such as Spark Notes and Grade Saver, but partly also, I think, to my own too conventional topic descriptions and relative inexperience in the classroom. The success I had with the final project in Renaissance Literature that spring led me to introduce it to my survey class the following fall, and I have been assigning it in those classes, as well as in Medieval Literature, ever since. During the final exam session I began holding a final "banquet" where students present their projects while we feast on period specialties, the more elaborate of which also constitute projects. In my office today, I am surrounded by many of those projects, the non-perishable ones of course, "gifted" to me by talented and generous undergraduate students. A semester of intense focus on difficult texts now culminates joyously rather than desperately, and many of the beautiful and meaningful objects and writings enjoy impressive afterlives as classroom visitors to subsequent sets of learners.

Here I will provide descriptions of a number of the more original final projects I have received. The simple rubric I created for the last formal task of the semester asks students to satisfy three out of four categories: historical relevance, creativity, knowledge of the literature of the time period, and personal relevance, and to account for having fulfilled those in an explanatory paper. Proposals must be presented for approval in advance, and credit is awarded for effectiveness of expression, depth of understanding, and enthusiasm. Since some students shy away from the notion of a "creative" final project, I dub the last assignment rather

Figure 1: Giant, bloody flea (John Donne's "The Flea").
Photo by Craig DeVriese, St. Ambrose University. Class of Nancy Hayes.

flatly the Final Project, yet most of the students do end up exercising a high degree of originality, higher in many cases than they would have thought themselves capable of achieving. From the first day of class, to which I bring a few notable examples, I encourage students to be thinking of ideas they might want to pursue for their projects. Throughout the semester, I bring in or wear past creations and cajole students into thinking outside the box and following up on particular talents or interests they possess or might want to develop. In addition to sharing some of the more memorable individual flights of my students' fancy, I will describe a couple of the creative writing assignments students work on as a class earlier in the semester, and out of which some final projects grow.

As I sit here contemplating ten years' worth of semester-end projects, a foot-and-a-half-long, foot-wide, dull brown, hand-stitched cotton pillow with large googly eyes and eight pipe cleaner legs (an anatomical inaccuracy by two) is perched on a chair peeking up at me. It is rather worse for wear, this giant flea, as brick-red paint has dried and clotted along its lower left jaw, and when I flip its poor torso over, I see the "blood" spread out over half its belly. This sad creature breathes no longer, having suffered death on a table in a Renaissance classroom in the spring of 2008. As the student read aloud the first two stanzas of John Donne's "The Flea," she held up the brown blob and made it seem to bite her and then nip one of her classmates:

Mark but this flea, and mark in this,
    How little that which thou deny'st me is;
    It sucked me first, and now sucks thee,
    And in this flea our two bloods mingled be,
    Thou know'st that this cannot be said
    A sin, nor shame, nor loss of maidenhead,
        Yet this enjoys before it woo,
        And pampered swells with one blood made of two,
        And this, alas, is more than we would do.

Lifting a hand to wave off an impending swat, the student read on:

Oh stay, three lives in one flea spare,
    Where we almost, nay more than married are.
    This flea is you and I, and this
    Our marriage bed and marriage temple is;
    Though parents grudge, and you, we're met,
    And cloistered in these living walls of jet.
        Though use make you apt to kill me,
        Let not to that, self-murder added be,
        And sacrilege: three sins in killing three.

At this point she instructed her classmate to slap the flea, but the classmate did not whack it strongly enough. Taking it into her own hands, the student struck the innocent creature wildly with the palm of her own hand until a red liquid from a plastic bag inside the pillow finally burst open, making a "bloody" mess all over the table. Some of the bystanders spoiled the tense scene by breaking out in guffaws, but the unfazed student read stalwartly on, peering angrily into her partner's face:

Cruel and sudden, hast thou since
    Purpled thy nail in blood of innocence?
    Wherein could this flea guilty be,
    Except in that drop which it sucked from thee?
    Yet thou triumph'st and say'st that thou
    Find'st not thy self nor me the weaker now;
        'Tis true, then learn how false, fears be:
        Just so much honor, when thou yield'st to me,
        Will waste, as this flea's death took life from thee.

The silent interlocutor had no retort. I cannot remember her name now, but I venture to say, she was probably scarred for life by that experience. Lucky for me, the flea's creator allowed as how she would never need the flea again and that it was mine to keep. In time its "blood" dried, and I stashed its stiffened corpse between my dictionary stand and the wall. The flea is resuscitated, however,

Figure 2: Duct tape dragon (Edmund Spenser's *The Fairie Queene*, book 1, canto 11).
Photo by Craig DeVriese, St. Ambrose University. Class of Nancy Hayes.

every other spring, and in fact will bring John Donne's little drama of seduction back to life again in a couple of weeks.

As my title promises, I shall also write of dragons, this one with a four-foot tail and three-foot wingspan, fashioned of duct tape and painted metallic emerald green, except for the gold along the front edges of its sail-like triangular wings and the tip of its spindly tail. Its maker had taken to heart the first three lines of stanza 10 in book 1, canto 11 of Edmund Spenser's *The Faerie Queene*:

His flaggy wings when forth he did display,
    Were like two sayles, in which the hollow wynd
    Is gathered full, and worketh speedy way:

Ruby red sequin eyes gleam hatefully and a wee white sword made of white duct tape has been lodged in its left armpit. Its maker presented it to the class at the final banquet, reading stanza 20 from book 1, canto 11:

He so disseized of his gryping grosse,

    The knight his thrillant speare againe assayd
    In his bras-plated body to embosse,
    And three mens strength unto the stroke he layd;
    Wherewith the stiffe beame quaked, as affrayd,

> And glauncing from his scaly necke, did glyde
> Close under his left wing, then broad displayd.
> The percing steele there wrought a wound full wyde,
> That with the uncouth smart the Monster lowdly cryde.

We could almost visualize the Redcrosse Knight, maybe two inches tall, having just thrust his trusty sword into the most vulnerable spot on the powerful beast's body, reeling backwards, barely escaping thrashing tail and grasping talons. We could almost see a tiny Una trembling from a hillock on the computer monitor table near the window, almost hear the anguished wail of the injured creature. Since the green dragon's classroom debut, it has flown around half a dozen British Literature classes, gliding full tilt over anxious students, who disguise their fear with stifled giggles. As each student reads a stanza, Big Green lands on his or her head, threatening to lift the student into the air. Sometimes it swoops down on the student's table, a wing covering the page of poetry as it trains a beady red eye on the startled reader. Whether supersized or miniaturized (we determine that Spenser's dragon is the size of nearby Vander Veer Park plus the adjacent city block to the south that holds St. Paul's Lutheran Church), such sculptural tours de force, which spring from students' imaginations, enliven not only the maker's experience of the literary text, but the classroom itself.

The decorative arts have also graced our classroom, notably in the form of Queen Elizabeth I look-alike pearl necklaces. A grateful recipient of these cast-off jewels, I usually wear one on the first day of class, and when we read aloud some of Elizabeth's poetry, letters, and speeches, I allow readers to wear the jewels, as well as Burger King crowns. In the meantime, a student has responded to my call for a higher quality crown by fashioning a stunning red felt and bejeweled gold duct tape crown worthy of the Queen herself. The designer of the most elaborate of the pearl necklaces based hers on the Rainbow Portrait, emulating the pendant with a fancy topaz-encrusted brass cross from Hobby Lobby. The authors of these projects research period dress, and have written about class differences and sumptuary laws. Several collages have been produced on the subject of Elizabethan fashion, and one student read aloud Robert Herrick's "Upon Julia's Clothes" when presenting hers:

> Whenas in silks my Julia goes,
> Then, then, methinks, how sweetly flows
> That liquefaction of her clothes. . .

In her paper the student analyzed Ben Jonson's "Still to be Neat" and Herrick's "Delight in Disorder" as well. Perhaps the most memorable decorative item was a life-sized Elizabethan ruff mounted on the torso of a seamstress's mannequin. The student's father had helped her to weld a wire frame, and her mother to starch and pleat the linen fabric before she glued it to the frame. With the help

Figure 3: Elizabeth I look-alike necklace based on the *Rainbow Portrait.*
Photo by Craig DeVriese, St. Ambrose University. Class of Nancy Hayes.

of fellow students, she was able to lift the large ruff off the mannequin and onto her shoulders for photos. Her accompanying paper detailed the rise of the ruff fashion, from a male accouterment to the elaborate high-backed queenly model, whose weight required a rabato, or stiff support. While impressive, and perhaps even seductive, these heavy contraptions surely cramped an early modern aristocratic woman's mobility.

Another project in this category was a stained-glass rendition of the Tudor Rose, made by a hobbyist who was smitten by the Tudor glamor of film and TV series. She sought her stained-glass master's help to model an eight-inch diameter stylized flower after a sixteenth-century image she had found online. She managed to cut and grind the red and white pieces of colored glass herself, but sought her teacher's help in soldering the petals together into the pattern. I run into this student occasionally, and she tells me the stained-glass rose hanging on her living room window often makes her think of our Renaissance class two years ago.

My literature students are often artists and poets, as well as budding literary critics. A student titled the paper she wrote to accompany her relief print of a white doe in a forest of birch trees, "Whoso List to Print." Of course, she read Sir Thomas Wyatt's sonnet aloud as she displayed her print: "Whoso list to hunt, I know where is an hind. . .." She chose the relief print process, for which she carved three separate blocks (but using linoleum, not wood), because the technique was coming into vogue in the sixteenth century. She brushed thin horizontal lines of red gouache across her printed white birch trunks "to symbolize the eventual and violent fate of Anne Boleyn," and applied a "white shimmery powder" to the doe "to help it give off a more ephemeral feel to strengthen the unattainability of the deer." Finally, she wrote, "I only hope I managed to do the beauty of this sonnet justice."

A simple charcoal drawing of Spenser's Errour from book 1, canto 1, stanzas 14 and 15 of *The Faerie Queene* depicts a naked, weeping woman rising up like a cobra from her coiled snaky bottom half. Her right arm is raised in anguish to her face, throwing a dark shadow over her right cheek and eye, but it is her wide, almost rectangular black mouth, which makes the viewer wince in horror. The following lines were read about the Redcrosse Knight's encounter in Errour's den:

> But forth unto the darksome hole he went,
> And looked in: his glistring armor made
> A little glooming light, much like a shade,
> By which he saw the ugly monster plaine,
> Halfe like a serpent horribly displaide,
> But th'other halfe did womans shape retaine,
> Most lothsom, filthie, foule, and full of vile disdaine.
> And as she lay upon the durtie ground,
> Her huge long taile her den all overspred,

Figure 4: Errour (Edmund Spenser's *The Fairie Queene*, book 1, canto 1).
Photo by Craig DeVriese, St. Ambrose University. Class of Nancy Hayes.

> Yet was in knots and many boughtes upwound,
> Pointed with mortall sting.

This student thought a charcoal drawing on white paper would effectively portray the character of Errour, whom she describes as "the embodiment of darkness, while the Redcrosse Knight is light personified." She refers to the knight's bringing light into the cave, "to which the monster is wholly unable to acclimate itself." The artistic caliber of these students' visual work has deepened their teacher and classmates' appreciation for the early modern poets' imaginative constructs.

Students are drawn to George Herbert's emblem poems, not a surprising response in today's strongly visual culture, where images seem to catch the attention before words. When we read Herbert's "Easter Wings" aloud, students register the urgency of his spiritual need in the single iambs, "Most poor" and "Most thin," which form the upper pieces of the literal hinges holding the two sets of wings together. Students get that the answer to the need is calling for God's help, made concrete in the buttressing of each of those single iambs with "With thee" to complete the two-line fulcrum of each stanza. Several students have fashioned their own pattern poems, and we have worked as a class to create one in the shape of a cross:

The day he died
His mother cried.
Along the winding path the cross us led.
His life seemed lost upon the cruel bed.
But then a hope
To help all cope:
It took three days
For him to rise.
The devil he slays;
He claims his prize:
Eternal life!
Now ends the strife.

In that same class, another student created one titled, "The Hourglass":

Time goes so quick, like sand through a big hourglass.
It's hard to understand how the days pass,
When a year is like a long day,
Not a moment will stay.
Youth goes by fast,
Sunrise-sunset,
No day will last,
So don't regret.
Take every last chance,
Take in the world and its expanse.
If minutes fly in the blink of an eye,
Hold close to the day and don't let time pass you by.

Written by a senior in the last half of her spring semester, this poem expressed the poignant realization that the final days of her college experience were running out. Perhaps conventional when viewed through a poet's critical eye, but from the perspective of this teacher, who also sees a student thoroughly assimilating her assigned reading, this poem registers classroom success.

As mentioned above, I have had a number of budding poets in my classes and have numerous examples of miniature sonnet cycles composed for the final project.

A nontraditional student in the first Renaissance Literature class where I assigned final projects dedicated her "Brief English Sonnet Series" to her granddaughter, Emma Rose Holden, on her fourth birthday. I would like to know Emma's thoughts as a twelve-year old today reading her grandmother's sonnet:

Shall I compare thee to a springtime day?
  Thou art more lovely than the summer's rose,
  Sweet Emma Rosebud, brimming with repose
As you are turning four, this fourth of May.
Your bright blue eyes flash like a May day's sun,
  Not hot, but warm, assured, so pure and fair;
  They look 'neath curls of berry sunshine hair
And see beyond years, since your life's begun.
You're full of promise, like the season, date;
  At four years old, no others can compare
  To all you are, and those whose hearts you snare
Declare you, Emma Rose, God's gift, complete.
  So long as people breathe or eyes can see
  Longer, forever more, I will love thee.

As with the hourglass poem above, this sonnet may not really compare poetically to its famous model, but its topical, personal context endows it with lasting value, and again, from the perspective of a teacher, represents the depth of the student's learning.

Some of the many sonnets composed for the Final Project transcend a sentimental or technical approach to sonneteering, and express a Hamlet-like existential angst. The example I share here is the first in "a short sonnet cycle inspired by the classical four elements," and further prefaced by the poet's statement, "I create and destroy myself often in poetry, like Prometheus, like fire."

Sonnet One: Carbon on Paper
If I could write myself into a page
And look out at myself, pen gripped in hand
To feel the pressure of my ball-point rage
Indent myself again, these canyons grand
Would I know myself better than before?
Insight, metaphysical division
Only to find me, yellowed leaf of yore
In a notebook, forgotten revision
Or published and read by other masses

Me facsimiled, spread thin over bread
Misrepresented to diff'rent classes
Tasted by the willing, understood dead
"Things like this could make you immortal, kid"
Somber, undone, consider what I did.

An intensity of tone and the relentless enjambment obscure an underlying conventional metrical structure and rhyme scheme. These sonnets do not seem like quaint throwbacks, but rather startlingly contemporary. In the second sonnet of the series, the student demonstrates that he has taken his course work seriously with the line, "Reaping the harvest of Petrarch's lover," as well as in the third of the series, when he steals a line from Elizabeth I's "On Monsieur's Departure":

What love can do for inspiration's gait
A stride striking and long, rife with candor
Or shaking with, "Inwardly do I prate"
A hot mess, the ultimate endeavor. . ..

These allusions to assigned readings which have been so gracefully embedded in the student's own lyrical idiom suggest that a uniquely creative form of learning has taken place, one which cannot be described simply as an analytical process, but rather a more elemental, emotional, or poetical one. The student has internalized the material, and has been changed by the experience of reading and writing early modern poetry. I do not think the students would have learned in this radical, transformative way had they not been asked to complete this kind of final project.

One final example of a creative assignment in my Renaissance Literature survey course is the class booklet of Spenserian Stanzas, assigned mid semester as we are reading *The Faerie Queene*, and compiled by a student or two for their final project. Our work on book 1 includes the students' first experience with scanning poetry, when each is asked to count the beats of a particular stanza, and to read it aloud emphasizing the stressed syllables. Then students are required to compose a stanza of their own in strict adherence to the nine-line form, with its two iambic pentameter quatrains and additional final hexameter line. They can write about any subject, and may also include artwork or clip art on their respective page. Cover art is solicited, and we have had some marvelous drawings and watercolors of gigantic dragons and diminutive Redcrosse Knights on the front and back of our coiled booklets. The editors are responsible for working with their classmates on the meter and rhyme, and for ordering the pages. The booklets are handed out as gifts at our final banquet.

While there are dozens of wonderful stanzas to choose from, one of the more unusual ones was composed by a nontraditional student about her three children:

Three bounding tots maned with wild golden heads
Stalk quick from shadows and race through halls
Roaring to spoil sweetly my silent bed
Linen lions my body come to maul
And dawn's light cast a play by waking suns
Shows fierce the savage attack against me
For these lions use their teeth just for fun
Collective numbers take their prey aptly
    Then lions lie o'er me ignoring their kill hap'ly.

By learning to conform their stories, ideas, and images to the metrical parameters of *The Faerie Queene* stanza, students can better appreciate Spenser's technical accomplishments. The complex thought processes required to make sentences adhere to metrical patterns and rhyme may cause frustration at first, but eventually trigger creative activity in order to satisfy the formal demands. That creative effort generates a personalized and lasting kind of academic learning experience.

As I gathered materials to write this overview of the substantial creative production of my many students over the past decade, I was virtually reunited with many wonderful individuals who have graced my rosters and peopled my classrooms. Reviewing and rereading meant revisiting the essential task of teaching as I see it—to make learning a joyful experience. My expectation of creative expression, coming especially at the end of the semester when students are exhausted and under maximum pressure to be mentally agile, seems to have the outcome of lifting spirits as well as fostering student achievement. Since students are prompted from the get-go and throughout the semester in class discussions or conferences to plan for their final projects, the assigning and development of these projects infuse the classroom with a thoughtful, buoyant kind of learning that not only develops a sense of community, but finally inspires original work of lasting value. This work registers a more rigorous and personal encounter with early modern culture than conventional scholarship usually allows, particularly in the undergraduate classroom.

By Indirections Finding Directions Out: Creative Points of Entry to Shakespeare's Problem Comedies and Sonnets

Regina Buccola, Roosevelt University

My professional appointments afford me numerous opportunities to collaborate with other educators dedicated to helping students—ranging from middle school to graduate level—engage with Shakespearean texts. As a professor at an urban liberal arts institution, I routinely encounter students in my Introduction to Shakespeare course who are pursuing degrees in English literature, education, or theater. Many of them go on to join me in upper-division courses dedicated to topics such as Teaching Shakespeare, Shakespeare and Film, and the other course to which I will refer in this essay, Shakespeare: Comedies and Problems.

Like many of our neighbor colleges and universities in Chicago, Roosevelt University maintains a close working relationship with the Newberry Library. In addition to teaching undergraduate seminars there from time to time, I also facilitate workshops for area middle- and high-school teachers. We discuss resources in the Newberry's archival holdings that may be useful to them, along with best practices for active work with Shakespearean-era texts in the classroom. Finally, in my role as Scholar in Residence at Chicago Shakespeare Theater, I collaborate with theater practitioners, professors of education, and area teachers to achieve similar objectives grounded, in this case, in the theater's own productions and excellent self-published pedagogical resources. All of us, as educators, learn from our students every day. In my case, I also have the luxury of routinely learning from other educators. Thus, all my suggestions about creatively engaging students in the study of Shakespeare are the product of much collaborative work with colleagues from throughout the Chicago metropolitan area.[1]

In all of my courses, one of my main objectives is to get students to apply what we have learned to their own written work. I have found creative assign-

[1] For a discussion of how to learn to teach Shakespeare as literature by learning to study Shakespeare as an actor, see Marshall Gregory, "From Shakespeare on the Page to Shakespeare on the Stage: What I Learned About Teaching in Acting Class," *Pedagogy: Critical Approaches to Teaching Literature, Language, Composition, and Culture* 6, no. 2 (2006): 309–25.

ments to be one of the most effective ways to accomplish that, in part because such assignments tend to "trick" students into engaging texts that they might otherwise regard as intimidating. I often find that students will embark on a creative assignment operating under the assumption that because it involves creativity it will be less difficult than an assignment overtly based in close reading of the text, or in research. However, if they effectively work to meet the criteria of the assignment, they will quickly find themselves driven back to the text to justify their "creative" choices. Here, I will describe three separate creative writing exercises that I have given to students in three different contexts with the goal of getting them to explore characterization and plot in the case of plays, and verse structure relative to a poem's content in the case of the sonnets.

Before I describe these assignments, a cautionary note to my readers. Do not be deceived into thinking that a creative assignment is any easier to assess than a more conventional one, as some students are deceived into thinking that it will be an easier assignment to complete. You may find it more enjoyable as a grading task, but it will not be any less onerous. For example, in my experience, students are more likely to exceed the specified parameters of the assignment in creative assignments than in conventional ones.

I bring up the verbosity of some responses to creative assignments in order to raise the larger issue of the lived reality of those of us who teach literature throughout North America and in the United Kingdom. As Kate McLuskie notes of her experience teaching Shakespeare:

> Changes to the funding system in the UK have put pressure on universities to maximize their student-based income by overrecruiting [*sic*] in areas of high student demand and transferring the funds to expensive student facilities or high prestige research areas. The resulting large classes in English departments with high ratios of students to staff have imposed instruction-based pedagogy that leaves less scope for a creative challenge to students' assumptions.[2]

Less scope, perhaps, but still a powerful need. Over the course of my fourteen years at the institution where I teach, I have watched my class sizes balloon from a cap of twenty-five (seldom reached when I was first hired) to a maximum of forty (in courses that are frequently closed, with students wait-listed). Last year I dodged an attempt to push this to seventy-five students, with one undergraduate teaching assistant to help with grading. Any substantive written work—creative

[2] Kate McLuskie, "Dancing and Thinking: Teaching 'Shakespeare' in the Twenty-First Century," in *Teaching Shakespeare: Passing It On*, ed. G. B. Shand (Malden, MA: Blackwell, 2009), 137.

or otherwise—in such circumstances becomes a challenge, but it is a challenge we owe it to our students to meet head on.[3]

I hold this viewpoint because I remain a specimen of the dying breed that believes instruction in the arts and humanities is vital to the production of young people with critical thinking skills, the ability to empathize with others, and the imaginative range to find solutions to the myriad challenges that will face them in the twenty-first century. Slowing our entropic rush toward the visions of dystopia dancing in the heads of writers ranging from Aldous Huxley to Margaret Atwood will rest with them. As a counterpoint to my own earnest belief in the power of art, consider the reflections of Russ McDonald, who cedes the field to those who would dismiss the power of the humanities too readily, in my view. He writes:

> There are more efficacious ways of achieving social change than the study of imaginative literature. Strictly speaking, the humanities are useless, and that is as it should be. Useless, but not worthless: the Shakespearean text, for example, is a source of limitless pleasure, and my aim as a teacher is to identify and pass along strategies for allowing others to partake of that pleasure.[4]

I think I am doing far more when I teach Shakespeare than preparing students to enjoy Shakespeare on page or stage as a pleasurable form of relaxation after they have finished their "useful" work. I will go further still: I think that the skills in critical thinking, assessment of character, and extrapolation from a given plot scenario to likely ramifications (or precursors) of that sequence of events help students to hone skills that they can deploy in more obviously "useful" contexts over the course of their lives.

The first example of a creative assignment that I have given more than once is actually an exam question.[5] In an introductory, undergraduate-level Shakespeare course in which we have read both *Much Ado about Nothing* and a selection of the sonnets, I have posed the following short essay question on the exam:

---

[3] See Carole Levin's essay in this volume for a full discussion of how to cater creative projects to varying class sizes and types.

[4] Russ McDonald, "Planned Obsolescence or Working at the Words," in Shand, *Teaching Shakespeare*, 31.

[5] On the subject of exams, Barbara Hodgdon says: "Exams test whether students have 'done the reading': they imply completion, closure. . .. I'm not convinced that the examination situation invites them to do their best thinking." Perhaps I can persuade her by proposing an appealing invitation to do their best thinking in response to an exam question that delves more deeply than conventional types of exam instruments do in posing, for instance, true/false questions about who does what to whom. See Barbara Hodgdon, "The Last Shakespeare Picture Show or Going to the Barricades," in Shand, *Teaching Shakespeare*, 116.

Imagine that Benedick presents Sonnet 130 ("My Mistress' Eyes Are Nothing Like the Sun") to Beatrice in *Much Ado about Nothing.*[6]

a. What aspects of Beatrice's character, as we know her from the play, does this sonnet capture?

b. At what point would she have to stop reading the sonnet in order to fail to realize the poem's true import?

c. What *is* the poem's true import? How can you tell?

d. Given what you recall of the play's plot, when might Beatrice have occasion to receive/read this sonnet?

While students tend to be amused by this set of questions and have, in fact, gone so far as to draw smiley faces in the margins of their exams, among other things, they are actually being called upon to demonstrate their command of both the plot and characterization of *Much Ado* as well as the melding of form and function in sonnet structure. The strongest answers consider the indictment of Petrarchan conceits common to Shakespeare's sonnet and to Benedick and Beatrice's acerbic commentaries on romantic love. Sonnet 130, like many of Shakespeare's sonnets, is structured as three quatrains and a closing couplet, with its volta occurring in the transition into the closing couplet. So, Beatrice could read a full twelve lines of the poem, her level of outrage escalating with every line, before she would encounter the volta's reversal, its turn from apparent insult into loving praise.

Obviously, this essay question sets up a task for which students are equipped inequitably: I supply the text of the poem to them, while they are relying on their memories to respond to the questions focused on Beatrice and Benedick. Their work with the text of the sonnet offers them opportunities to perform directed close reading of the text, while they will need to be more general in their discussion of the play. I have prepared them for the task of working closely with the text of the sonnet by administering a quiz that asks them to work through the melding of form and content in a sonnet. On this quiz, given in class prior to the exam with the question about Sonnet 130 as applied to *Much Ado*, I ask them to bracket each of the quatrains and the closing couplet, to draw an arrow to the volta, and then to explain what is being discussed in each quatrain and in the closing couplet. Finally, I ask them how the shifts in rhyme scheme relate to the shifts in topic, imagery, sensory detail, et cetera. The quiz teaches them not merely to divide a sonnet into its constituent parts, but also to consider how the

6 I provide the text of the sonnet on the exam; in the interests of space, it is not reproduced here.

form of the sonnet directly correlates to its content, and the ways in which that content is being presented.

The questions posed on the exam about Sonnet 130 and *Much Ado* also give students the opportunity to reflect on the love/hate relationship of Beatrice and Benedick throughout *Much Ado*, and the fact that, like the sonnet's closing couplet shift, they make an eleventh-hour turn into full romantic commitment to one another, and to love (and marriage) itself in the play's final moments. Moreover, both of them are publicly contemptuous of the conventions of romantic courtship for much of the play (although they do privately confess in soliloquy and to one another their susceptibility to lovesickness); the questions posed give students opportunities to point out these character details and the evolution of Beatrice and Benedick's relationship over the course of the play. The most studious will remember details such as Benedick's reference to Beatrice as "my dear Lady Disdain," or her reference to any man she might be matched with as "a piece of valiant dust" (1.1.97 and 2.1.52).[7]

Miriam Gilbert notes that, "for many students, questions begin with characters. . .what grabs students—and what bothers them—is what the characters are like, and why they are behaving as they are."[8] The other two assignments I will discuss also offer students opportunities to delve into characterization, a task that drives them back into the text to hunt for clues—evidence—to support what they claim about the characters and the creative decisions they take, founded on Shakespeare's own, about how to depict their extra-textual conduct.

These next two assignments are short essay prompts typically given in my Shakespeare: Comedies and Problems course. I offer this course at the advanced undergraduate and at the graduate level, and I have made these assignments in both contexts. The first example is an essay assignment in which students must write the dialogue between Mariana and Isabella in act 4, scene 1 of *Measure for Measure,* when Isabella persuades Mariana to perform the bed trick with the corrupt deputy, Angelo, in an abortive attempt to save Isabella's brother from execution.[9] Since Shakespeare offers no details of this conversation, students may use their imaginations; however, the students' characterization and plotting must be consistent with the plays' representation of the two women, and their experiences.[10] The conversation may be written in prose, but students interested in trying

[7] All references to and quotations from Shakespeare's plays will be from *The Norton Shakespeare,* ed. Stephen Greenblatt et al., 2nd ed. (New York: W.W. Norton, 2008); parenthetical in-text citations will be to act, scene, and lines.

[8] Miriam Gilbert, "A Test of Character," in Shand, *Teaching Shakespeare*, 92.

[9] Linda Shenk's essay in this volume also discusses the productivity of asking students to compose letters never sent, or the speech of advice never delivered in Shakespeare's plays.

[10] Dan Mills takes a similar tack in teaching *Othello.* He starts by pointing out to students that *Othello* begins in medias res. He suggests having students write cre-

their hand at producing a script are encouraged to do so. The most adventurous will actually respond to the assignment in free verse. Regardless of the mode students choose, they all must write eight to ten typed, double-spaced pages at the undergraduate level, or twelve to fifteen pages at the graduate level. They also must indicate, via citations and explanatory footnotes or introductory apparatus, the relationship between their construction of this conversation and the play text from which they have extrapolated it.

When I have made this assignment at the graduate level, I have added the wrinkle of asking the students to address a textual crux. Both the Oxford and Norton anthologies of Shakespeare's plays have, for a number of years now, accepted the possibility that the Duke's soliloquy in act 3 and the soliloquy that "covers" Mariana and Isabella's offstage conversation in act 4 may have been switched. There are a number of valid reasons for this conjecture, which students may read about in the Introduction, Textual Note, and Additional Passages in *The Norton Shakespeare,* and in *William Shakespeare: A Textual Companion.*[11] In addition to asking them to write the conversation itself, I also ask them to explain which version of the Duke's soliloquy they imagine being delivered during this conversation, and why.

Anthony Dawson points out that "the business of the 'script' can start us talking about how we know, or rather how we don't exactly know, what Shakespeare actually wrote; about how the theatre, from his own time till now, has collaborated with, and yes, even at times contaminated, what he wrote."[12] Dawson goes on to provide examples of working with the variant texts of *Hamlet*; similar strategies work with *Measure for Measure*, conjectured to have been revised for publication in the First Folio (1623) by Thomas Middleton. These possible revisions matter, because they impact the length of the soliloquy Shakespeare assigned to the Duke to "cover" Isabella's conversation with Mariana about the bed trick, a textual moment I invite students to write. In theatrical terms, they

ative pieces establishing the backstory for characters encountered in the first act. How did Othello woo Desdemona? What occurred in the courtship scene in which Othello presented Desdemona with his handkerchief? How do Cassio and Othello know one another? How did he contribute to Othello's courtship of Desdemona, exactly? Why did he get promoted, rather than Iago? See "Mind the Gap: Teaching *Othello* through Creative Responses," *Pedagogy: Critical Approaches to Teaching Literature, Language, Composition, and Culture* 8, no. 1 (2008): 154–59. Mills discusses the prompts I describe on pages 155–56.

[11] William Shakespeare, *Measure for Measure*, 305–74; Katharine Eisaman Maus wrote the textual introduction to the play; Stanley Wells and Gary Taylor, eds., *William Shakespeare: A Textual Companion*, rev. ed. (1987; repr., Oxford: Oxford University Press, 1997), 468–75. For a fuller treatment of the authorship questions posed by *Measure*, see Gary Taylor and John Jowett, *Shakespeare Reshaped, 1606–1623*, Oxford Shakespeare Studies (Oxford: Oxford University Press, 1993).

[12] Anthony B. Dawson, "Teaching the Script," in Shand, *Teaching Shakespeare*, 79.

are doing method work here, constructing the conversation Isabella and Mariana have in act 4, which informs their collaborative humiliation—and recuperation—of Angelo in the play's long final scene. I point out to them that they really need to take into account what they know about Mariana and Isabella from the play in its entirety in order to accurately represent them in this crucial, closing scene.

Since the lengths of these soliloquies differ, that is one obvious opportunity for student commentary. If they believe that Mariana would be difficult to persuade to the ignoble task at hand, they might choose to have the longer of the two soliloquies cover Isabella's attempt to persuade her. Conversely, if they imagine that Isabella finds Mariana apt, they might opt for the shorter soliloquy. The truly ambitious among the graduate students construct some sort of interplay between what the Duke is saying as Mariana and Isabella discuss their plot and the terms in which they present that conversation. The potential reversal of the Duke's soliloquies in acts 3 and 4 is of relevance here since, for example, if students want to forge a connection between his ominous assertion that:

> With Angelo tonight shall lie
> His old betrothèd but despisèd.
> So disguise shall, by th'disguised,
> Pay with falsehood false exacting,
> And perform an old contracting. (3.1.498–502 in First Folio)

and the arguments that Isabella makes in persuading Mariana to the bed trick task, they will also have to propose that the Duke's soliloquies be reversed from the order in which they appear in the First Folio.

I should note at this point that the majority of students who take my courses at the graduate level are actually master of fine arts candidates in our creative writing program. They are required to take literature courses in addition to writing workshops, and they tend to be up for almost any creative challenge I pose to them. Both graduate and undergraduate students are encouraged to exercise ingenuity in the presentation of their ideas. I assign *The Norton Shakespeare* at all levels, and encourage students to use the introductory essays, marginal glosses, and footnotes in their text as a model for how to present explanatory notes linking their representation of Mariana and Isabella's conversation to what we know of them and of their interactions in the text of *Measure*. At the undergraduate level, I also have a number of students from our theater conservatory in my classes, and they, too, are often leaders on assignments that involve a creative component. Their leadership comes in handy in the second assignment I will describe, which involves group work.

The group work assignment assumes an upper-level undergraduate or graduate-level course in which students read both *Measure for Measure* and *All's Well*

That Ends Well (in that order).[13] Working in small groups of four to five people, students are asked to imagine that the Mariana of act 3, scene 5 of *All's Well* is the Mariana of *Measure for Measure*. The questions that I direct them to consider within their small groups are:

a. What are the details of Mariana's biography since we met her last? How did she get from Vienna to Florence?

b. How did Mariana go from wife of a high-ranking member of the Viennese leadership (Angelo) to surly servant of a Florentine widow (mother to Diana)?

c. What clues does Mariana's brief appearance in *All's Well* offer to fill out this biographical sketch?

d. What do you know about Mariana from her more substantive appearance in *Measure* that helps you to imagine that she and her *All's Well* counterpart might be one and the same?

After small group discussion, the entire class convenes to develop a composite narrative using preferred details from each group's brainstorming session.

In addition to the fact that each of them is party to a bed trick, Mariana of *Measure* and Helena of *All's Well* have a number of points of commonality, many of which emerge in these class discussions. Some of the points that students have emphasized in these group exercises are:

- Both are married to men who are scornful or dismissive of them. For the brunt of *Measure*, Mariana is betrothed to Angelo, who has thrown her over under false pretenses. Helena spends almost the entirety of the plot of *All's Well* pursuing her spouse Bertram, who prefers the threats of military life to married life with her.

- Both Mariana and Isabella lack familial support; indeed, a key part of the plot in *Measure* concerning Angelo's jilting of Mariana is the loss of her brother—and her dowry—at sea. Helena has come to know Bertram by living as the orphaned ward of his mother, the Countess of Roussillon.

- Mariana and Helena are compelled to navigate the ostentatious, self-aggrandizing lies of the foppish Lucio (of *Measure*) and the sycophantic coward Parolles (of *All's Well*) who serve, in their respective plays, as foils to Angelo and Bertram. In essence, Angelo and Bertram, odious

[13] Mary Ellen Lamb's contribution to this volume also discusses teaching *All's Well That Ends Well* and *Measure for Measure* in tandem, with a performance studies focus.

though they might be, seem less despicable when set off by the well-nigh irredeemable Lucio and Parolles (though I do grant that Parolles ends *All's Well* in a greater state of self-abnegating chagrin than Lucio seems capable of mustering).

- Both Mariana and Helena (as well as their counterparts, Isabella and Diana) must publicly defend one of their most private attributes, their chastity. Many students point out that the Mariana of *Measure for Measure* would have equal cause to say, with the Mariana of *All's Well*, "The honour of a maid is her name, and no legacy is so rich as honesty" (3.5.11–12).

Notice even in this brief round-up of some of the kinds of things that have emerged from these in-class brainstorming sessions how consistently the effort to elucidate Mariana's character in an extra-textual context drives students to consider her in the context of the plays in which she appears as well as that of other characters from *Measure for Measure* and *All's Well That Ends Well.*

Once we have done this exercise, we are well positioned to consider the similarities between the bittersweet endings of both *Measure for Measure* and *All's Well That Ends Well.* In particular, students often note the riddling nature of Mariana's confrontation with Angelo in act 5 of *Measure for Measure*, and Diana and Helena's similar riddling confrontation of Bertram after a similar bed trick in *All's Well.* In *Measure for Measure*, Mariana enigmatically informs the Viennese citizenry assembled to welcome the Duke home: "My lord [the Duke], I do confess I ne'er was married, / And I confess besides, I am no maid. / I have known my husband, yet my husband / Knows not that ever he knew me" (5.1.182–185). In *All's Well*, Helena's "factor," Diana, offers a similar riddling explanation of the bed trick that has been played upon Bertram: "He [Bertram] knows himself my bed he hath defiled, / And at that time he got his wife with child. / Dead though she be she feels her young one kick. / So there's my riddle; one that's dead is quick" (5.3.297–300). These arch revelations of sexual treachery offer rich fodder for students eager to construct twenty-first-century, empowered versions of Mariana (and, often by association, Isabella, Helena, and Diana).

Carol Chillington Rutter writes about the recent (2005) shift in England to privilege creativity, fostering it in students and future teachers. For Rutter, such creativity is grounded in the performative nature of the early modern drama she teaches, but her appraisal applies equally well to the assessment tools I have proposed here, although none of them includes an expressly performative component. In a proposal Rutter wrote to the Higher Education Funding Council for England, she analogized good teaching and good rehearsal, on the grounds that "both rely on 'the arts of imagining other minds, role-play and improvisation, trust and teamwork, discovery through the creative process.'"[14] The group exercise with *Measure* and *All's Well* encourages students to imaginatively place themselves in the minds of others, and to collaborate with the other members of their group, who might imagine different outcomes for the same characters. Like all group work, this task requires students to consider the perspectives of others—whether characters in Shakespeare's plays or their classmates—as well as their own.

Alexander Leggatt notes that:

> Shakespeare was an actor, and wrote for actors. In the end, actors have to make choices about moments readers can leave open. But there is a stage of rehearsal where the choices are open, and free exploration takes place. A class needs to be like that kind of rehearsal, a place where ideas can live and grow, not a place where they are frozen and stored, never to stir again.[15]

In a similar vein, Barbara Hodgdon characterizes her pedagogy as leaning "towards (loosely) Socratic dialogue, building not from a proposition, but from a question that spurs a train of thought—one that (ideally) leads, not to the 'right answer' but to a response that provokes another question (finding questions trumps knowing answers. . .)."[16] Even if they fill fifteen pages in response to an essay assignment that called for only ten, my students also often find that they are left with more questions than answers about Mariana and her fellow Shakespearean characters.

I agree with Hodgdon, however, that there is much virtue in questions that keep the train of inquiry chugging steadily forward. Despite the invocation in my title of the proto-Orwellian Polonius of *Hamlet*, with his creepy red herring approach to investigating the conduct of his son Laertes at university, I do not intend my questions to yield information of the "gotcha" variety about my students' reading habits and levels of comprehension. Rather, I intend to pose questions that will require them to meet Shakespeare's characters face-to-face, calling into question, perhaps, their assumptions about these characters and, ultimately, the people around them. It is, in the end, a far more courageous task than Polonius delegates to Reynaldo. It involves a deep dive into the best and worst of which people are capable: blind devotion, appalling self-centeredness, and the abiding grace of forgiveness.

---

[14] Carol Chillington Rutter, "Playing Hercules or Laboring in My Vocation," in Shand, *Teaching Shakespeare*, 227.

[15] Alexander Leggatt, "Questions That Have No Answers," in Shand, *Teaching Shakespeare*, 72.

[16] Hodgdon, "The Last Shakespeare Picture Show," in Shand, *Teaching Shakespeare*, 107.

From the Trial of Charles I to Comic Scenes of *Hamlet*: Using Creative Projects in Small Classes and Large Ones

Carole Levin, University of Nebraska, Lincoln

I teach history and directed the Medieval and Renaissance Studies Program at the University of Nebraska-Lincoln (UNL). In November 2013, I was delighted to attend an Elton John concert here in town. I had a wonderful time and he played with a passion that had concertgoers dancing in the aisles. As great as the music was, what I valued most was when Elton said he felt so blessed to be doing work he loved, and that the older he got the more appreciative he was of that. I thought to myself how that is just what I feel about my work—my teaching, research, and program planning. And, I also realized how completely intertwined these three segments of my job are, each making the others better. Just as the audience enjoyed the concert so much more because of how interactive it was, classes where students are truly involved are also the ones where they learn more.

One example of this confluence is work I have done on Joan of Arc. Once, years ago, I was reading Shakespeare's *Henry VI, Part I* as I was preparing the unit on Joan of Arc for my Pre-Modern European History through Biography course. In the final act, after Joan has been captured by the English, she is brought on stage but claims she is pregnant, saying that as a result they cannot execute her. Joan is executed anyway, and the editor's gloss stated simply that Joan was "pleading pregnancy," without explaining what that meant. In order to clarify this for the class, I began doing research, learning that in medieval and early modern England if a woman could prove that she was quick with child she would not be executed, at least not until the child was born. This information not only became a significant part of the class discussion of Joan, but some years later became part of a whole chapter on Joan of Arc and early modern women pleading pregnancy in the book I coauthored with John Watkins, *Shakespeare's Foreign Worlds*.[1]

In the fall of 2012, which was the six-hundredth anniversary of Joan of Arc's birth, the Medieval and Renaissance Studies Program presented a student cel-

[1] Carole Levin and John Watkins, *Shakespeare's Foreign Worlds: National and Transnational Identities in the Elizabethan Age* (Ithaca, NY: Cornell University Press, 2009).

ebration of Joan. Music students in UNL's Chamber Singers sang songs about Joan of Arc; a UNL graduate who had double-majored in history and English read poems she had written about Joan of Arc; a history graduate student doing the graduate minor in Medieval and Renaissance Studies gave a short, illustrated lecture on early modern English attitudes toward Joan; and a master of fine arts graduate student specializing in directing and also doing the Medieval and Renaissance Studies minor arranged for theatre students to do scenes from several plays about Joan of Arc.[2] In addition, a journalism student attended and put together a short video of the event. We had an audience of more than sixty people, with students from many different classes and majors. Indeed, audience response to the event was very enthusiastic. Some of those in the audience were students from my classes who enjoyed the evening a great deal and saw the connections between what went on in our classroom and what had happened that evening.

One great joy about teaching at the University of Nebraska is being able to teach a broad range of courses that includes Western Civilization and an English history survey for beginning students; a course for undergraduates on women in European history; advanced undergraduate-graduate courses such as Tudor/Stuart England, Pre-Modern European History through Biography, and Saints, Witches, and Madwomen; and graduate seminars in such topics as queenship in Renaissance Europe, readings in early modern European history, and how to teach history. My students range from first semester freshmen to doctoral students, and it is a pleasure and honor to work with all of them. All my classes share certain things: a passionate engagement with the subject matter; readings that include primary texts, modern historiography, and often drama and fiction from the period being studied; a great deal of writing in a range of modes from informal in-class free writes to formal research papers; and the possibility for students to engage with the course material in creative ways. Every second or third year I teach a course I developed—Historic/Literary Retellings—as an upper-level seminar for juniors and seniors for the University Honors Program. I have had significant success in devising a range of assignments in my various courses that have fostered critical reading of primary and secondary sources and effective modes of writing and thinking about history.

Students acquire knowledge in a variety of ways and have different strengths when demonstrating what they have learned. My courses employ out-of-class essays, in-class essay exams, informal writing, and the opportunity to do creative projects. Creative projects are a way to challenge students to engage more thoroughly in the subject matter and make it their own. It is also a way for a student to work hard and do well who might be less successful at taking in-class essay tests or writing research or analytical essays outside of class. Students who

---

[2] These students were Jillian Boston, Andrea Nichols, and Dennis Henry. I am very proud of all of them.

actively engage with material are more able to understand and retain what they learn, and I believe this is even more true if they also enjoy the engagement.

I have used creative projects in the many courses I have taught. Here I will discuss using creative projects in three very different courses: a large lecture class with mostly first- and second-year students, a medium sized course with advanced undergraduate and graduate students, and an upper-level honors course limited to fifteen students. One of the largest classes I teach is History of England from Roman Britain to 1688, and it frequently has eighty to one hundred students. It is often easier to do creative assignments in a seminar, but it is of great value to provide them in larger classes as well. In fact, creative assignments can add something that personalizes the potential anonymity of a large lecture course. Creative project assignments do not replace in-class examinations and out-of-class essays, but rather supplement them.

In my large enrollment class each fall, I make a particular effort to learn all the students' names. I believe that they will be more committed to doing well if they do not feel they are simply a nameless face in the crowd. One way I learn student names is to take photos the first day of class and study them. I also do "coffee with the professor" once a week. It is purely optional, but I send around a sign-up sheet and meet with groups of four students each week outside of class where I treat them to coffee and we chat. We may talk about the class, but other times we discuss where they are from, what their majors or career goals are, or what movies they have seen recently.

I try to make the class challenging and interactive. As I lecture I ask students questions based on readings and lectures and encourage them to ask questions and respond to each other. In addition to two one-hour essay exams, early in the semester students write an essay based on their interpretations of Stephen Knight's *Robin Hood: A Mythic Biography*, which leads to a very active discussion. Another book I assign is *The Trial of Charles I: A Documentary History*, edited by David Lagomarsino and Charles T. Wood, which contains a thorough collection of primary documents.

I assign each student a participant from Charles I's trial, and to assure that they are prepared, students must write a paper about their person that is due the day we reenact the trial in class. Papers must include background information on the person, if they were a juror whether they voted to convict or not, and, if possible, what happened to the person after the trial, in other words, that person's fate. If the student was assigned someone who was not a public figure, the background paper needs to examine the life of a person of that social status and what life might have looked like for them. Students are graded on both the paper and their participation in the trial. The paper can be an essay or a creative piece written in the first person as either a journal entry or a letter.

I assign someone to be Charles I; John Cooke, the Solicitor General; John Bradshaw, President of the Court and head juror; and such well-known figures as Oliver Cromwell, Cromwell's son-in-law Henry Ireton, and Colonel Thomas

Pride, who organized the purge of Parliament so that those who remained would agree to the trial and many would serve as jurors. Many of the students are jurors—called judges in the trial—such as John Blakiston, Michael Livesey, John Hewson, William Purefoy, Edward Whalley, Daniel Blagrave, Simon Mayne, Thomas Waite, or Robert Lilburne, all of whom signed the death warrant, or John Lisle, Edmund Harvey, Nicholas Love, or Gilbert Pickering, who refused to sign it. Others are witnesses, such as Richard Price, scrivener, or professional scribe: John Thomas, husbandman, or farmer; Samuel Lawson, maltster: John Bennet, glover; and Thomas Rawlins, gentleman. The testimony of all the jurors appears in the assigned text. I also assign someone to be Anne, Lady Fairfax, wife of Commander and Chief of the army Thomas Fairfax, who opposed the trial. Although called as a juror, Fairfax refused to attend. However, Lady Fairfax did attend, and as the masked lady in the gallery called Oliver Cromwell a traitor. The trial was public so other students are assigned to be Londoners who are either pro-Parliament or pro-king and are encouraged to comment throughout the trial. I also have several Scotswomen come to London to attend the trial. Some ghosts of historical figures we have already studied, such as Edward II, Henry VI, Mary Stuart, and Elizabeth I, also come to haunt the trial and respond at different moments.

In addition to the documentary material found in their text, students must do further research. If the assigned person was a juror, I encourage students to look them up in the *Oxford Dictionary of National Biography* as each has an entry. For those assigned to be a witness or spectator, additional information can be gleaned by watching a social history documentary that describes London life or the typical experience of a scribe, farmer, maltster, glover, or gentleman. For ghosts of a king or queen, it is easy for students to find further information, although since the person was already dead at the time of the trial, students do not really have to worry too much about what happened to them afterwards, unless they want to consider time in purgatory.

The trial begins with each juror being called and answering, explaining their background and briefly what will happen to them. Then Bradshaw and Cook, with the aid of Cromwell, present the evidence against Charles, with witnesses; spectators, whose comments are often raucous; the masked lady in the gallery; and an array of ghosts interacting. I keep the trial moving so that by the end of the class the jurors can find Charles guilty and the king can attempt to have his say. Students love participating in the trial—they find it the most valuable class of the semester [Color Plate 1]. Because of their excitement over the assignment, their written pieces are also usually of high quality.

Another creative option I offer is "t-shirt day," which is usually the class before Thanksgiving break in the fall semester and the class before spring break in the spring semester. I first devised it as an incentive for students not to cut the last class before a holiday. If students wear a t-shirt that in some way represents a theme of the class, they get bonus points. Some students buy t-shirts but many of them make their own. It is also fun because I usually dress very "professionally" when I teach, but on t-shirt day I also wear a t-shirt that expresses a class theme. In my history of England from Roman Britain to 1688, now called Revolutions and Misbegotten Monarchs, perhaps because the students know how much I love the Tudor reigns and especially Elizabeth I, many students wear t-shirts that have Elizabeth on them or refer to the Tudors. In the fall of 2013 one of my favorite t-shirts was created by a really excellent and very enthusiastic student. It read "The Tudors—cutting off heads for 118 years." The last time that I taught Women in European History, one of the few male students wore a t-shirt that stated "Real men take women's history from Professor Levin."

In virtually all my classes I offer students the chance to do part of their final as a creative project. They can do this singly or in small groups. In my English history survey if students choose to do creative projects, then on the in-class final they only have to do the identification section and not the essay. If they have gotten As on the hour exams and both essays and they do the creative project, they are exempt altogether from the in-class final. Projects have included complete books, PowerPoint presentations, poetry sequences, plays, songs, and a newspaper from a specific time. Some students have even made films, and in one case, the student played all the roles and said the twenty-minute film took sixteen hours of filming. One young man composed a song about all the rulers of England from William the Conqueror to James II. Often students work far harder on their creative projects than they would have simply studying for the final exam, which they do anyway as they still must take part of it. Students present their projects to the class during the last two class periods of the semester, which works as a review for everyone and gives students pride in their work as they share it.

A few years ago one student, Kelli Montey, wrote a script for a television show and convinced her friends to act in and film it. It was a shock talk show, called *The Maurine Show*, where the guest was Henry VIII. Maurine, wearing a blue wig, opens by interviewing Henry and as he mentions his marriages, she says, "Well, speaking of your wives; we have a surprise for you." When Henry responds, "I love surprises," Maurine assures him, "You're going to love this one. Ladies and gentlemen, please welcome our next guest, Catherine of Aragon." Soon Anne Boleyn joins them, and the women get into such a tussle that Maurine has to break for commercial. Eventually, the other four wives make their appearances, ending with Katherine Parr. The video had everyone laughing so hard we were in tears. Kelli wrote in her accompanying three-page essay, "As soon as our class began the section on King Henry VIII, I knew that this is what I wanted to do my creative final about. It upsets me to think of the way women were treated during the sixteenth century. I admire the strong women of that time who were brave enough to voice their opinions and stand up against the king, although they paid for it with their lives. They are truly an inspiration to women everywhere. While brainstorming ideas on the best way to portray

Henry and his six wives, I went through a series of ideas beginning with a dating game show or a reality television show and finally ending with the idea of a Jerry Springer talk show." Kelli ended her essay by stating, "I had a great time doing this project, although I ran into many complications, I am happy with the outcome of the video. I feel I have an even better understanding of this time period after completing the project and doing further research on each wife and Henry himself."

As Director of the Medieval and Renaissance Studies Program, I instituted two undergraduate contests, one for best essay and the other for best creative project. All the winners present their work at our annual spring celebration of students. Since many of those who submit material to the contest are my students, I have nothing to do with the judging. The graduate assistant to the program puts together a panel of graduate student judges. I was delighted that the year Kelli submitted her video she received second place.

My course Saints, Witches, and Madwomen explores historical stereotypes about women and men and examines women on the margins in Western Europe and America from the Middle Ages to the present. As well as teaching this course during the regular academic year, I also have had great success teaching it in the intense compacted summer session. In that context, with classes meeting for three hours a day, it is even more important to have activities and assignments that go beyond lectures and discussions.

The first day of class we discuss a range of historical ideas about women and madness. One theme is "gaslighting," which is when one person manipulates another—often a woman—by psychological means to make her doubt her own perception and memory and think she is insane. We begin by watching a scene from the 1940 film *Gaslight*, which gave the term its name, about a Victorian gentleman who attempts to make his wealthy wife believe she is crazy. To demonstrate that gaslighting was used creatively centuries earlier—although in comic form—I have students read aloud scenes 1 and 5 of act 4 of *The Taming of the Shrew,* where in the first scene Petruchio has meat served then sends it away as "burnt and dried away," though Kate knows the meat was perfectly fine, and now they have no dinner. In the second of the scenes, Petruchio insists Kate call the sun the moon and an old man a sweet young virgin; although Kate does this, she is clearly aware of what her husband is doing and how she must follow suit if they are to continue on their way to her father's house. Having some students act out the scenes makes the discussion far more lively.

Later in the course we read from Christine de Pizan's *The Book of the City of Ladies*, and after I lecture on Christine's life, I break the class into groups, giving each group sheets of construction paper and felt markers, explaining that the sheets of paper are their bricks on which to write names of women they admire, and that we are building our own city. Each group comes to the front of the class and explains about the women they have chosen. Then we tape the paper to the wall so at the end of the period we do indeed have our own city. It is fascinating to see what names students choose, ranging from women of today in politics and the arts, to historical figures, writers, composers, artists from long ago, and some students include their own mothers. The women chosen come from different ethnic backgrounds, different social classes, and a range of ages. It is always exciting for me, because in every class I learn about new, intriguing women.

We also read sections of *The Book of Margery Kempe* and I again break the class into groups. I assign each group a scene from Margery's life and give them about fifteen minutes to figure out how they are going to portray it. The scenes and their participants include: Margery after childbirth—Margery, devil, husband, women in household, and Christ; Margery in city streets having a very public fit of sobbing and weeping and then a vision of Christ in which they have a conversation to the discomfort of townspeople—Margery, townspeople, and Christ; Margery and her husband on a Friday midsummer eve when they return from the fair and John expresses his lustful feelings but Margery exclaims she would rather eat the ooze and muck of the gutter than be with him—Margery and John; Margery's pilgrimage to Norwich to consult with Julian—Margery and Julian; Margery with the pilgrims and their attempt to leave her behind—Margery and three or four pilgrims; and Margery tried for heresy—Margery, archbishop, clerk, witness, observers. Students not only enjoy presenting their own scenes and watching the others, but they have a far more vivid understanding of Margery's life and how she handled it. We also do scenes from *Macbeth* that include the witches or Lady Macbeth. Some years we also enact a witchcraft trial. The t-shirts students create for this class have been especially interesting, with a number celebrating Lady Macbeth.

In my honors seminar, Historical/Literary Retellings, we examine certain historical people and works of literature and discuss their significance within a particular historical-cultural context. We then look at the presentation of the same person or story in other periods and contexts to analyze different cultural meanings. The differences in narrations often allow us to focus on specific cultural themes and anxieties.

Since I am a scholar of late medieval-early modern England and Europe, the people and stories to be retold come from that period. I have used a wide range of pairings over the semesters that I have taught this course, including retellings of Shakespeare's *King Lear* and *The Tempest*, the Salem witch trials, the early medieval queen Emma—wife of both Ethelred and Cnut, and Joan of Arc. In addition, I always begin and end the course with fairy tales. The last few times I have taught this course, the units I used were *Hamlet*, *Romeo and Juliet*, and Queen Elizabeth I. While we watch brief cartoons or music videos and short clips from longer films in class, we do not have the time to watch an entire film. Five times during the semester we do "Sunday afternoon at the movies," where we watch an entire film and share pizza. The last time I offered the class we started with *Stardust* (2007). Our second film was the Ethan Hawke *Hamlet* set in the year 2000. *Shakespeare in Love* (1998) works as a retelling both for *Romeo and Juliet* and for

Queen Elizabeth I. We come back to fairy tales with *Pan's Labyrinth* (2006). I let the students choose the last film of the semester, and over the years we have watched such films as *Ten Things I Hate About You*, *Ever After*, and *Ladyhawke*.

Students keep a reading journal and all complete a research paper, but a number of the assignments in this course are also creative. For the first class, the group, including the teacher, breaks into teams of two, if possible with someone they do not yet know. Then each interviews the other and introduces them to the seminar. Afterwards we talk about how the introductions are retellings of what the interviewee had said and how much was accurately presented in the introduction and how much changed or was left out. I also tell them two fairy tales and give them written versions. Most recently the tales were Hansel and Gretel and Tam Lin. I chose these because one is very well known and the other is usually unknown to most of the students.[3] In the Scottish folk tale Tam Lin, Fair Janet saves Tam Lin from the queen of the fairies. Both stories also have strong women characters as heroes and villains. For the next class, each student needs to retell the fairy tale by changing the point of view—changing who is the hero and who is the villain or who is the more sympathetic character; putting the story in a different time period or setting; changing the gender, sexuality, or age of one of the main characters; or perhaps taking a minor character and telling the story from that person's perspective.

The retelling can be a story, a play, or a poem. Both original stories resonate strongly with students, and a number have created poignant retellings from the point of view of the witch in Hansel and Gretel or the queen of the fairies in Tam Lin, while others have produced comic riffs or satires. As well as the retelling, each student is asked to write an analysis of their retellings, explaining why the changes were made and how they are significant. In the next class, each student presents their retelling and discusses the process. Two years after I taught the seminar, one of my students used her Hansel and Gretel retelling as a basis for her senior honors thesis, which was in part an animated film of the version she had written.

One of the most enjoyable creative projects of the seminar is part of the *Hamlet* unit. The class is broken into three groups and each group is assigned one

[3] Tam Lin is a Scots ballad that dates to the sixteenth century. Fair Janet has to rescue her love, Tam Lin, from the queen of the fairies. Years earlier Tam Lin had been out riding and fallen from his horse and was captured by the queen of the fairies. Every seven years the fairies give one of their own as a tithe to Hell and Tam Lin fears he will be the next victim. He instructs Janet to wait until he and the fairies are riding by and then pull him from his horse and hold onto him no matter what the queen turns him into. Janet does as he asks and the queen turns Tam Lin into a snake but Janet holds on. Then the queen turns him into a fierce bear but Janet still holds on. Finally, the queen turns him into a burning coal, but even though Janet scorches her hands, she keeps holding onto him. Finally, the queen of the fairies gives up and turns Tam Lin into a naked man.

scene of *Hamlet*. They can do the original scene in a different setting or rework the scene as a retelling. The last time I taught the seminar the three scenes were all reworkings and all were outstanding. One group did their scene of the confrontation between Ophelia and Hamlet (act 3, scene 1) as a musical, breaking into contemporary popular songs. Another did the final scene of the play as a bedtime story for Hammy and Larry with the parents using light sabers. And the third did the confrontation scene between Hamlet and his mother in her bedchamber (act 3, scene 4) where Hamlet slays Polonius thinking he is the king, as a silent movie with captions. For the unit on Queen Elizabeth I, each student was asked to do a retelling, and again the results were impressive. One composed music, another did a drawing and wrote a poem. The most inventive, by Simran Sohi, was a comic strip interview of Elizabeth conducted by James Lipton in Inside the Actors Studio, Royalty Style. This demonstrated a real knowledge of Elizabeth and a very clever and engaging way of presenting it [Color Plate 2]. I was again delighted that a number of students from the seminar won awards from the Medieval and Renaissance Studies Program.

In the nineteen years I have been at the University of Nebraska-Lincoln, I have been fortunate to work with majors and non-majors, with undergraduates and graduate students. While I have taught them in a variety of classes, I have also learned much from them. I am no rock star, and my largest classes are approximately one hundred students, not the 14,000 fans of the Elton John concert. But I hope the students in my classes feel some of the same satisfaction of interacting with someone who loves what she does. Just as concert-goers got up to dance to the music, I want my classes to be interactive and joyous, as well as demanding. Sometimes I am privileged to teach History 990, the graduate seminar on how to teach history. While we work hard the entire semester, I think the best advice for being a good teacher is simple: love your subject and love your students.

Very Simple Classroom Performance Exercises That Work (Usually) Even for Non-Actors of Shakespeare

Mary Ellen Lamb, Southern Illinois University Carbondale

At first, it may seem that a dramatic engagement with Shakespeare's script does not provide historical context for teaching early modern literature. But I would claim that it does, by demonstrating the extent to which Shakespeare's plays, then as well as now, require choices to be made by directors and actors. The interpretive decisions made today may differ from those made in the sixteenth and early seventeenth centuries. Despite a flourishing discipline of theater history, which has restored so much understanding of Shakespeare's context as a dramatist, there is little information about the specific choices made in the performance of individual plays. The concept that a college textbook includes scripts ready for interpretation, rather than plays as already complete works of literature, is crucial, and students generally find it exhilarating, if sometimes a bit unsettling.

There are various ways to approach this idea of play-as-script. I am especially grateful for the opportunity offered by current technologies to juxtapose short scenes from different films as a stimulus for discussion. (This technique works splendidly for performances of Shylock and of Hamlet.) Some instructors require students to memorize and present a scene, and this also works well, especially for those bright lights of the class who are theatrically inclined. I have been working also with a third alternative, geared to student groups that include those unfamiliar or uncomfortable with dramatic presentations. This essay describes some performance-based exercises for which no preparation or memorization is required. The goal of these exercises is to provide insight into differences in what an interaction or encounter in a Shakespearean play can "mean," as it is performed by different small groups of students before the class. Through these exercises, I aim to unsettle single or simple readings of Shakespeare's plays in order to point to their richness of potential interpretation, so that no individual production (or even any reading) is like any other. My larger goal is to empower students to think creatively and personally about how to embody a choice, and have that choice matter. And they never forget a scene they have acted.

1. Taming of the Shrew

To show how these exercises work, I will start with an example from *Taming of the Shrew*. This is scene 5 in act 4, when Petruchio demands that Katherine agree with him that the sun is the moon.[1] I am especially intrigued by this scene because it seems to me to be a practice or dry run between them for Katherine's final speech. I have simplified the language to strip the text down to the interaction so students do not have to memorize more than a few words, and they can perform without any paper in front of them getting in the way. They are free to improvise if they wish, adding not only gestures but words.

Petruchio: It is the moon

Katherine: No, it is the sun.

Petruchio: It is the moon.

Katherine: All right, it is the moon.

At first, I just turned the four groups loose to see what they would come up with. Lately, I have been assigning groups their interaction, to be sure that we see real differences between the interpretations.

Here are the instructions:

Group 1: Play it for maximum laughs. Make it really funny.

Group 2: Play it for maximum romance.

Group 3: Play it with tension and hostility.

Group 4: Play it as the abused and the abuser.

By the time of the exercise, we will have talked quite a bit about possible perspectives on the relationship between Katherine and Petruchio and what this may mean for their interpretation of the play. Group 1: Is she exaggerating the role to enjoy its absurdity, and making it even more absurd, perhaps turning it back on Petruchio? Group 2: Is she showing her love this way, as totally bedazzled by Petruchio? Group 3: In this scene, is she angry and exasperated, and just going along? Group 4: Or is she submissive and even abused, perhaps a bit robotic? In

[1] Throughout, I am using Stephen Greenblatt et al., eds., *The Norton Shakespeare*, 1st ed. (New York: W.W. Norton, 1997). Abbreviated and parenthetical citations are to act, scene, and line.

2006, a performance at the Brooklyn School of the Arts played Katherine as abused, to represent a powerful statement against abuse. While it has been my position that the play is about sexism but not necessarily a sexist play, a performance might try out sexist possibilities, as a play recommending the taming of women. It was the most performed Shakespeare play in Hitler's Germany. The Nazis loved it. How might this work?

For the technicalities, the script with the directions is given to each student. In a class of twenty-four, I divide the students into four groups of six. Two students chosen by their group (or volunteers) have "speaking parts," but the other students also have an important role—to guide responses from the audiences with their own responses. Timing is up to the instructor. For me, it is always a balance between how much time to give to performance exercises and how much to class discussion. For the first activity they try out an exercise (they get faster with experience), they might have twenty to thirty minutes to prepare and about twenty minutes for the presentations by all four groups. I usually circulate among the groups to provide encouragement and sometimes suggestions if they want them. If one group finishes before another, they might try out directions from another group's prompt. Since the scenes are so short, even with repeated attempts, often it does not take the whole twenty minutes for performance. Afterwards we take some time to discuss what was done. After the first group performs their script (from memory with no paper in front of them), the class (and sometimes I) suggests ways to do it even better. Students sometimes need cues or perhaps permission to use their bodies—to kneel, to embrace, to pretend to hit. In the case of the first group, they might be encouraged to make it even funnier. The first group tries it again. The best interactions often happen in the second or third performance by a group. We all clap of course after each performance. Then on to Group 2. The last time we did this assignment, Group 4 stole the show. It was absolutely chilling.

As an alternative scene, or perhaps as an added scene if there is time, I have added an abbreviated version of Katherine's final speech, with directions to the four groups as above:

> K. Come, you forward and unable worms. (to Bianca and the widow)
> ...
> I place my hands beneath my husband's foot.
> P. Why, there's a wench. Come on and kiss me, Kate.

Since this is Katherine's final speech, the nonspeaking students might take on a specific persona—Bianca and the widow, obviously, but also Katherine's father, or another marriageable male in the audience. They announce these identities before the performance begins.

These performances lead to productive discussions about which scenes work best, and for what kind of audience. Often students come up with additional ideas about possible performances of the relationship between Petruchio and Katherine. Except for some of the very shy ones, most students enjoy this exercise, and it really does empower them to think for themselves in specific ways about the play.

2. *Twelfth Night*

Some performance exercises are much briefer and entirely individual. For *Twelfth Night* 3.4.18, Malvolio is given the precious line, "Sweet lady, ho, ho!" in which he packs in a great deal of meaning: "I have received your letter of love, and now you know that I know that you wish me to be your lover instead of a steward, and here I am, wearing yellow cross-garters and ready for you!" For this one, we chuckle over the potential for the line, and instead of dividing them up into groups, I just ask for a moment of silence, and then invite volunteers to try it. I always get a few. They will never forget that line.

3. *Merchant of Venice*

Similarly, Shylock's line at the end of his trial scene in *Merchant of Venice*, "I am content" (4.1.389), works very well with this briefer format. After a discussion of what Shylock's feelings might be, and why he might say he is content (when in most performances he is not), I ask for a moment of silence and then invite volunteers to say it according to their interpretation. Sometimes I might ask specifically if anyone thinks he might be angry, or broken, or threatened, or (perhaps—this one would need some explaining) actually content. This leads into what has been a continuing discussion of who Shylock is and what meanings his character gives to the play.

4. *Henry IV, part I*

With *Henry IV, part I*, we are back into the group format. For me, the conundrum at the core of this play is the relationship between Hal and Falstaff. In his soliloquy at the end of 1.2 ("I know you all…"), Hal reveals that his time in the tavern is a brilliant publicity move, and that he intends to cast off Falstaff and the others when it is time to step forward in his role as prince, as he will in the battle of Shrewsbury. What are his feelings for Falstaff? Is he just using him (cold Hal)? Or does he feel real affection (warm Hal) that he must then renounce when he is king? And what are Falstaff's feelings? Is he using Hal, as well, pretending fondness in a mistaken attempt to gain wealth and status when Hal becomes king? Or does he feel affection or even love, so that his betrayal at the end of *Henry IV, part 2* breaks his heart? What is at stake here, I argue, is not only an interpretation of

Hal, but also a concept of kingship, perhaps applicable to any political figure who must remain in the public eye. This script is very short:

> F: Banish plump Jack, and banish all the world.
> H: I do; I will
> The directions to the groups are:
> Group 1: Try a drunk, unappealing, unattractive Falstaff and cold Hal.
> Group 2: Try a political and self-interested Falstaff and a Hal who loves him.
> Group 2: Try an appealing and loving Falstaff and cold Hal.
> Group 3: Try an appealing and loving Falstaff and a Hal who really does love him.

The directions passed to each student are: Stage the emotion that your group is to convey for Falstaff and Hal. This emotion is to be expressed primarily through body language or "bits." There will be one person acting out Falstaff and one for Hal; other persons in each group will be tavern people reacting to what they see. On "stage," take your time. Slow it down to "do" something. How do you look/move/sit/stand when you pity someone? Feel contempt for someone? When you love someone deeply? When you are more concerned with your own self-interest than the other person—i.e., do not really care about the other person? What gestures do you use? If the emotion is not clear to us, we will work with you as a class. Tavern people—are you happy drunks (having fun and laughing), lonely drunks (deeply unhappy), or other? How do you fit in with this scene?

5. Hamlet

For Hamlet, we tried two exercises. The first exercise involves a third party reading 2.1.88–98, in which Ophelia describes to her father a very puzzling interaction with Hamlet:

> He took me by the wrist and held me hard,
> Then goes he to the length of all his arm,
> And with his other hand thus o'er his brow
> He falls to such perusal of my face
> As a would draw it. Long stayed he so.
> At last, a little shaking of mine arm,
> And thrice his head thus waving up and down,
> He raised a sigh so piteous and profound
> That it did seem to shatter all his bulk
> And end his being. That done, he lets me go,
> And, with his head over his shoulder turned,
> He seemed to find his way without his eyes,

> For out o'doors he went without their help,
> And to the last bended their light on me.

Here is the prompt: Experiment briefly as a class: one person reads it and two students do what it says. Then back in your groups, repeat this pattern, in which one student reads and two others enact, and this time decide on a meaning enacted in this interaction. (Ophelia, do not forget to react to whatever Hamlet is doing). Here are two possibilities:

> Group 1: Try a Hamlet who really loves Ophelia and is trying to figure out where she stands—perhaps in a pathetic "love me" sense?
>
> Group 2: Try a Hamlet who is suspicious of Ophelia, and possibly fed up (the great sigh of exasperation)—his enactment frightens her, for a reason.
>
> Groups 3 or more: Choose one of these two options or something else.
>
> Once enacted, which interpretation works best for you? What does this suggest about "your" Hamlet?

The second of these is actually not my original idea. A colleague, Miriam Gilbert, suggested it on an airplane ride back from a Shakespeare Association meeting. As she noted, the "gifts" that Ophelia returns are never described, and what they might be says a great deal about their relationship. Here *Hamlet* 3.4.93 is staged as a standard break up scene. Here is the prompt:

> In 3.1.93, Ophelia returns Hamlet's "remembrances" or gifts. You know the scenario—this is the "here's your stuff back" part of a breakup of a relationship. If Hamlet takes them, then he accepts the breakup. If he doesn't, then he doesn't. Initially, he seems to reject them "I never gave you aught." She tries again, "You know right well you did." Does he take them this time? Does Ophelia continue to carry them? Ophelia doesn't say what these gifts are—gifts say a lot about what kind of relationship they have: beautiful love letters? An old book? Expensive jewelry? What kind of gifts do you think Hamlet gave Ophelia? And what happens to them?

For this one, decide as a group what the gift(s) may be (maybe label them on a piece of paper for Ophelia to give Hamlet), and then enact the scene, without many words. Maybe something like (feel free to improvise):

> Ophelia: Here's your stuff.
>
> Hamlet: I don't want it back.
>
> Ophelia: Please, take your stuff.

> Hamlet: <what do you do? perhaps Hamlet and Ophelia pretend to talk awhile—walk around, gesticulate wildly—and then, what happens to the stuff?>

Students were very inventive with this exercise. In one performance, the gift was a small package of letters, and it was left on the floor, until Ophelia sneaked back in to retrieve it. In another, a student playing Ophelia stood on a table and threw her book on the floor shouting (screaming actually) "Here's your stuff!" Hamlet was at a total loss. It was a powerful moment. I talked to the student playing Ophelia afterward. She had just broken up with someone and it was very cathartic to play it this way. (I was initially a little worried about her, but she was fine.) I am not sure in this case that this performance was actually *Hamlet,* but it was unforgettable theater.

6. *Othello:* The Game of "Would it Work"

As I teach *Othello,* each semester several students lose all patience with Desdemona, claiming that she does not really defend herself. They are not usually swayed by my observation that she does not realize what she is accused of until 4.2, when Othello confronts her, saying that she is as "false as hell" (4.2.41). She responds with questions, "To whom, my lord? With whom? How am I false?" When Othello directly asks "Are you not a strumpet," she answers just as directly, "No, as I am a Christian" (4.2.84-85). Othello clearly does not believe her—I would claim that he has lost faith in anything she might say. But I invite interested students to write a scene in which Desdemona would be able to convince Othello of her loyalty.

Here is the prompt:

> In act 4, scene 2, Othello confronts Desdemona with the accusation of sexual infidelity. If you believe she could have prevented her death by being more forthright with Othello, write a dialogue that you think might have worked. What might she have said, that she didn't say in this scene?

Then, preserving anonymity, I distribute the scripts to willing pairs of students to act out. I open it out to the class to judge, "Would it work?" Very few of them in fact work. This exercise leads to a spirited discussion of Desdemona's character.

7. *Measure for Measure*

In *Measure for Measure,* Isabella's character may be performed in a range of ways. In this exercise, groups of students will perform both scripts, to show a relationship between them in the character of the Isabella for their group. The first is just a very odd line, that stretches an actor's skills to perform. The second represents a crux evident in performances of the last decades: after informing Isabella suddenly that her brother, who he claimed was dead, is actually alive, the duke proposes. There is no response in Shakespeare's text scripted for Isabella. As a comedy, one might assume that Isabella would gladly accept, as has been performed until recently. But this is a problem comedy, so really any response is possible.

Here is the prompt:

This exercise has two parts. Each group will do both of them. Which interpretation of Isabella works best for you?

1. Isabella has a difficult line (act 2, scene 4, lines 184–85):

   Then, Isabel, live chaste, and, brother, die:

   More than our brother is our chastity.

2. What does this Isabella (the one in #1) do in response to the Duke's proposal, "Give me your hand, and say you will be mine" (act 5, scene 1, line 495). She isn't given anything to say. What reaction does she have? How would she express it?

   Group 1: Play Isabella for maximum humor, of an admittedly dark kind. The test is this—can you get a laugh from either or both of these situations?

   Group 2: Play Isabella straight, as a very sincere person. There should be nothing funny or uncomfortable about #1. Make us absolutely sympathize. How does she respond to #2?

   Group 3: Play Isabella as very conflicted. Make us see her divided responses. What does she choose for #2?

   Group 4: This is Vienna, which would produce Freud a few centuries later. Play her as a very repressed neurotic, very uptight. Your Isabella should be very disturbing.

I have always suspected that dark humor lurks at the core of *Measure for Measure,* but I have not seen performances that exploited this possibility. I am interested in how students respond especially to group 1.

8. *All's Well That Ends Well*

As in *Measure for Measure,* the ending of *All's Well That Ends Well* raises challenging questions about the end of the play. In both plays, Shakespeare seems to be playing with complications to the standard ending for comedy in a happy marriage.

Here is the prompt:

In *All's Well That Ends Well* Bertram's response to Helena's fulfillment of his supposedly impossible tasks (to get his ring and to become pregnant with his child) is notably brief. Is he so moved he is at a loss for words? Or perhaps he feels tricked? In addition, his proposal to love Helena is preceded by an "if" and apparently not directed to her since he refers to her in the third person as "her" rather than in the second person as "you." When the King turns to the audience in his last lines, he uses the word "seems" in "All yet seems well." What may be made of this ending?

Bertram, Countess, King (and anyone else) stand as Helena enters. She goes to Bertram.

Helena to Bertram: I am only the shadow of a wife.
Bertram: O pardon!
Helena to King: Here is your ring.
Bertram—to king To Helena also?: If I can know this clearly, I'll love her dearly, ever dearly.
King: All yet seems well.
Does everyone exit here? Or leave B and H on stage? Your choice.
King to audience in abbreviated epilogue: now applaud for us!
(do we?)

- Group 1: Play it as a happy ending. (but not ridiculous)
- Group 2: Play it as open-ended—ambiguous. (is this possible?)
- Group 3: Play it for laughs. (is this possible?)
- Group 4: Play it dark as a play exposing the fault line in the happy ending of comedy

Which one works best for you?

9. *Winter's Tale*

The exercise for *Winter's Tale* has few words; it is primarily physical. Students may be divided into groups, but without special instructions. This is the scene at the end of the play when Hermione's "statue" becomes Hermione in the flesh.

Here is the prompt:

> As Hermione descends, various characters have very complicated feelings: Hermione herself, Leontes, Perdita, and Paulina. There is not much of a detailed script. She embraces Leontes (if this is the "him" that she embraces), and then she invokes the blessings of the gods upon her daughter. (Hermione can condense this to: "Oh bless you, daughter"). How might you express these complicated feelings on stage? One of you, as Hermione, might stand on a chair (carefully). Who comes to help you down? How do all of the characters express their complicated feelings in their bodies? Each character probably feels at least two emotions. How would each of you actors express them both, clearly enough for an audience to get them? For this assignment, you can't add words, but you can add sighs or other sounds. Gestures are good. What atmosphere do you want to create? One of miracle/holiness? One of an old tale? Be inventive, and do whatever feels right for your character, and have fun with it. On "stage," take your time—slow it down a bit to enable actors time to express their responses.

This is one of the more complicated exercises. There was a great diversity between groups as to how well it worked out. (But they will always remember it).

Conclusion

The purpose of acting exercises is not to produce great or even good theater, but to empower students to active engagement with a text, and to help them to understand that a script only gains meaning in performance. These exercises are especially appropriate for any moment, in other plays as well, when a character's emotions or motives may be interpreted in a range of ways. Exercises take up class time, but they are well worth doing. There are other exercises I have not tried out on a class. When an actor has a very long speech, the other actors must decide what to be doing. Are they uniformly attentive? The speeches in *Troilus and Cressida* are especially long in the Trojan war council. I would like sometime to ask one student to read a long speech and then experiment with how the others react—with boredom? With restlessness? Can they hold an attitude of interest in some convincing way? Finally, I aspire someday to bring an actual dog in the classroom for a scene between Launce and Crab the dog in *Two Gentlemen of Verona*, just to see what would happen.

Performing Interpretive Interventions in the Shakespeare Survey Classroom

Nathanial B. Smith, Central Michigan University

> Just as a script may be enacted in various ways, and just as the play requires both text and interpretation, so the gendered body acts its part in a culturally restricted corporeal space and enacts interpretations within the confines of already existing directives.[1]

On the day students in my Shakespeare course came ready to discuss the second half of *Macbeth*, two different groups of four students enacted an interpretation of the banquet scene for their classmates. The group project assignment to which they were responding, called the "Interpretive Intervention," uses performance to encourage creative and critical inquiries into plays. Groups of students choose a scene from the day's reading and craft a performance that both follows the language of Shakespeare's play texts precisely yet also (as the assignment sheet states) "disrupts an obvious or conventional rendition of the scene."[2] It was a happy coincidence that both *Macbeth* groups had selected the banquet scene, and even though performers from both groups spoke the same words and sat around the same long table on the same chairs, the two versions of the scene could not have been more different. The first group performed the scene with cross-gender casting, Macbeth with flowing red hair, Lady Macbeth sporting a goatee. A woman in a formal white dress took the role of the ghost, eerily drumming her

---

[1] Judith Butler, "Performative Acts and Gender Constitution: An Essay in Phenomenology and Feminist Theory," *Theatre Journal* 40, no. 4 (1988): 526.

[2] As I discovered during my research for this essay, James C. Bulman uses the idea of performance as a kind of "intervention" in an audience's experience of a dramatic text: "A dramatic text, therefore, acquires meaning depending on the questions one asks of it. But performance adds another layer, for an audience at a play interacts not just with a dramatic text, as a reader might with a novel, but with interpreters of that text—middlemen: directors, actors, designers—who intervene in an audience's experience of the play and create what Marco De Marinis calls the 'performance text,' which can be decoded in much the same way words on a page can be." James C. Bulman, "Shylock, Antonio, and the Politics of Performance," in *Shakespeare in Performance: A Collection of Essays*, ed. Frank Occhiogrosso (Newark: University of Delaware Press, 2003), 27.

fingernails on the tabletop at opportune moments. Ignoring the editorial stage direction in their version of the play that has Lady Macbeth conversing "apart" with Macbeth, the bearded Lady sat and scolded Macbeth in front of the invited guests, who were nervously playing with their cups.[3] Lady Macbeth rendered her mocking question, "Are you a man?" (3.4.59), with a comic touch, and a slight abridgement of subsequent lines made a bold Macbeth seem but mildly concerned about the possibility that "charnel-houses and our graves must send / Those that we bury back" (3.4.72–73). The ghost, in this performance, merely annoyed rather than truly haunted; the scene focused audience attention on gender roles and the potential for discrepancies—and unlikely analogies—between external sex characteristics (like beards) and gendered performances, demonstrating that female characters can be more masculine than the men.

The second *Macbeth* group, like the first, began the performance immediately after Macbeth has spoken with Banquo's murderer. This group also played with depictions of gender: a strong and confident female Lady Macbeth lectured a tiara-wearing male Macbeth about his failure to "give the cheer" and entertain his guests properly (3.4.34). But the group also put its interpretive signature on other elements of the script, including its decision not to have an actor perform the role of the ghost. Following the Lady's belittling speech, where the Folio stage directions read "*Enter the Ghost of Banquo, and sits in Macbeths place*," the group concentrated on Macbeth's next line, the epithet "Sweet remembrancer," which conventionally refers to Lady Macbeth, who has just reminded her husband to be a good host and join his guests at table (3.4.38). The group decided, however, that the line could also refer to Macbeth remembering Banquo throughout the scene: as the actor playing Macbeth waxed sentimental over his absent guest—"Here had we now our country's honour roofed / Were the graced person of our Banquo present" (3.4.41–42)—he grabbed a dry erase marker and drew a Pac-Man-style ghost on the classroom whiteboard, directly behind a vacant chair at the table. From the audience's perspective—and Macbeth's, after he moved downstage—the table indeed appeared "full" (3.4.46) with the sketched ghost occupying the central chair. Lady Macbeth privately scolded her husband about his behavior: "This is the very painting of your fear; / This is the air-drawn dagger which you said / Led you to Duncan" (3.4.62–64); and as she spoke, she erased the image from the whiteboard, momentarily calming Macbeth. But at his next line, he rose again and retraced the ghost while toasting "our dear friend Banquo, whom we miss" (3.4.92), and again (mis)recognized his own drawing as Banquo: "Hence, horrible shadow, / Unreal mock'ry, hence!" (3.4.108–9). Through performance, the students in these two groups became

[3] Stephen Greenblatt et al., eds., *The Norton Shakespeare: Essential Plays / The Sonnets* 3rd ed. (New York: W.W. Norton, 2016), 3.4.59. References are to act, scene, and line of Shakespeare's plays from this edition and appear parenthetically in text. The Folio lacks stage direction for Lady Macbeth at this point in the scene.

what James N. Loehlin calls "co-creators of the play's meaning," reimagining the text according to their own analytical and creative interpretations and enacting their own interests and concerns.[4]

Witnessing these back-to-back performances inspired my students and me to spend the remainder of the class period debating the implications and larger significance of the groups' choices. If a director has a ghost appear on stage, visible to Macbeth and the audience alone (as in the first group and most productions),[5] does this deepen our identification with Macbeth's character? Do we think of Macbeth differently if no ghost appears, or if (as in the second version) the ghost appears in some simulated form? Is Lady Macbeth somehow implicated in the murder of Banquo if she is able to see the ghost, as she seemed to in the second group's rendition of the scene? What might these decisions imply about the role of the supernatural in the play and in early modern culture more generally? What is at stake in the decision to stage the quarrel between husband and wife "apart" or publicly? And how might we think of these characters differently if Macbeth's character is performed by a woman and Lady Macbeth by a man: does this decision uphold, subvert, or otherwise complicate gender roles, a central focus of the play? Do we villainize or sympathize with Macbeth or his wife more in one version of the scene than the other, and if so, why? Similar questions about character, cultural context, gender, and response emerge when discussing any complex literary text. But when students have ideas about a play, something more is possible: their ideas can quite literally be enacted, brought to life, in performance. When students perform scenes from a play, questions such as these are more concrete and in some sense, more pressing, given that choices—in the form of answers to interpretive questions—*must* be made in performance.[6]

Incorporating performance into the literature classroom is, of course, nothing new.[7] Introducing a 1984 special issue of *Shakespeare Quarterly*, "Teaching Shakespeare," John F. Andrews finds that "virtually everybody acknowledges

[4] James N. Loehlin, "Teaching Through Performance," in *A Companion to Shakespeare and Performance*, ed. Barbara Hodgdon and W. B. Worthen (Malden, MA: Blackwell, 2005), 634.

[5] Simon Forman's notes on a 1610 production of *Macbeth* assert that "the ghoste of Banco came and sate down in his cheirer behind him," Greenblatt et al., *The Norton Shakespeare,* Digital Edition.

[6] James P. Lusardi and June Schlueter, "'I have done the deed': *Macbeth* 2.2," in Occhiogrosso, *Shakespeare in Performance*, 71–83: "The actor acts under necessity: he or she is compelled to interpret the material provided by the playwright," 71.

[7] "Performance pedagogy," Ralph Alan Cohen asserts in his introduction to a 1990 special issue of *Shakespeare Quarterly*, "seems to have attained the status of a given," "From the Editor," *Shakespeare Quarterly* 41, no. 2 (1990): iii. See also Milla Cozart Riggio, ed., *Teaching Shakespeare through Performance* (New York: Modern Language Association of America, 1999).

the need to approach Shakespeare's plays as dramatic rather than literary works."[8] This stated privileging of "dramatic" over "literary" approaches to Shakespeare signaled a reversal of the narrowly text-centered approach to plays used by mid-century New Critics who privileged written language, the site of rich and ambiguous literary meaning, over the purportedly impoverished physical medium of the stage.[9] The Interpretive Intervention assignment I discuss in this essay, however, elides this distinction: student performances of dramatic texts emerge from careful and provocative "literary" reading. Students approach their chosen scene both as a script inviting action and also as an open-ended text containing what Wolfgang Iser calls "gaps left by the text. . .[that] may be filled in different ways."[10] Challenging students to fill these gaps in inventive and textually grounded ways, this assignment encourages students to use performance to stage scenes that, in the words of W. B. Worthen, "create an event, *play*, through practices—acting, direction, scenography—that don't merely sound the writing, but transform it."[11]

When I first began experimenting with performance pedagogy, students had difficulty "transforming" their scenes, worried as they were about language difficulties and not wanting to embarrass themselves in front of their peers. While there were exceptions, as a rule they were more likely to play their chosen scenes in highly conventional ways—restricting themselves to interpretations based on their perception of the play's genre or even unreflectively mimicking a filmed version of the scene. These highly iterative tendencies not only served to flatten the play text but also worked against the grain of Shakespeare's own theatrical practice of twisting and reworking sources, challenging orthodoxies, and raising questions about the conventions that structure and shape social performances. Many students, I came to think, were responding to Shakespeare much the way Judith Butler describes the iterative performance of conventional gender roles: "the more mundane reproduction of gendered identity takes place through the various ways in which bodies are acted in relationship to the deeply entrenched or sedimented expectations of gendered existence," expectations that result in the performance of "a set of corporeal styles which, in reified form, appear as the natural configuration of bodies into sexes which exist in a binary

---

[8] John F. Andrews, "From the Editor," *Shakespeare Quarterly* 35, no. 3 (1984): 515.

[9] See William B. Worthen, *Shakespeare and the Authority of Performance* (Cambridge: Cambridge University Press, 1997) for an excellent discussion of this history.

[10] Wolfgang Iser, "The Reading Process: A Phenomenological Approach," in *Reader-Response Criticism: From Formalism to Post-Structuralism*, ed. Jane P. Tompkins (Baltimore: Johns Hopkins University Press, 1980), 55.

[11] William B. Worthen, *Drama: Between Poetry and Performance* (Malden MA: Wiley-Blackwell, 2010), 11.

relation to one another."[12] For Butler, even the most conventional performances of gender, like the most conventional performance of a dramatic scene, involve individual choices made and not made: "the body is not passively scripted with cultural codes."[13] While she makes it clear that individual performances are restricted by a variety of social and cultural conventions, the very fact of gender performativity, for Butler, guarantees the potential for individual variations in the standard script, "the breaking or subversive repetition of that style" of gender performance, what she intriguingly calls "interpretations within the confines of already existing directives."[14] While Butler's sense of performativity can sit uneasily alongside notions of theatrical performance,[15] in the literature classroom short excerpts of her writing can encourage students to think anew about not only gender performances but also dramatic performances that make critical and creative interventions into the most mundane, conventional understandings of the Bard while operating within the richly polysemic confines of the Shakespearean script.

As a first step toward the group project, I routinely turn the classroom into a performance space. On the first day teaching *Taming of the Shrew*, for instance, I might bring students together into small groups to debate and perform a dozen or so lines of the initial meeting of Katherine and Petruccio, leaving it to students to make interpretive choices about how to play the lines and represent the characters. Often, several choose the section where Kate slaps her suitor, either as evidence that she resists his aggressive sexual advances or to represent Petruccio responding with a slap of his own. Students perform their selected lines without commentary, afterwards asking their peers in the audience to decipher the group's intended interpretation of the lines. This exercise makes the point not only about the ambiguities and multiplicities in Shakespearean language, but also about the indeterminacies of performance, the possibility that different audiences will react differently to similar events. Students start with Shakespeare's text, but once they perform it, that performance itself acquires meanings of its own.

Literary and dramatic interpretation, then, go hand in hand in my classroom.[16] After getting students accustomed to performing brief scenes and

---

[12] Butler, "Performative Acts," 524. See also Judith Butler, *Gender Trouble: Feminism and the Subversion of Identity* (New York: Routledge, 1990).

[13] Butler, "Performative Acts," 526.

[14] Butler, "Performative Acts," 520, 526.

[15] See, for instance, Andrew Parker and Eve Kosofsky Sedgwick, eds., *Performativity and Performance* (New York: Routledge, 1995). For an excellent discussion of the intersection of Shakespeare performance and Butler's conception of performativity, see Amy L. Smith, "Performing Marriage with a Difference: Wooing, Wedding, and Bedding in *The Taming of the Shrew*," *Comparative Drama* 36 (2002): 289–320.

[16] Harry Berger, Jr.'s *Imaginary Audition: Shakespeare on Stage and Page* (Berkeley: University of California Press, 1989) offers a compelling model of what he calls a "*literary*

analyzing short clips from film adaptations of Shakespeare plays that reveal differing interpretations, I assign a short essay asking students to use textual evidence to propose two different and plausible interpretations of a single scene of their own choosing from an assigned play. From the beginning of the semester, I stress to students that the strongest interpretive ideas develop from close and careful analysis of dramatic language, from the use of a dictionary to reveal potential ambiguities and multiple meanings, and by noticing and inquiring about formal elements like tropes, sounds, and images. Students use these techniques to gather evidence for their "Two Interpretations" essay. Some students write successful essays by imagining different motivations for a single character; others use a scene to demonstrate different potential approaches to a relevant topic (power, identity, emotion, desire, loyalty, or art) that the plays ask us to consider. Students often write on the abdication scene in *Richard II* (3.3), for instance, finding that the scene could be played such that Bolingbroke overwhelms Richard with superior military force or that Richard sadly and reluctantly gives Bolingbroke power, depictions that involve fundamentally different ideas about how political power works. The best among these essays imagine two interpretations that would each require its own performance to enact, with the lines delivered differently so that they tell different stories about the characters, situations, and the underlying significance of the scene.[17]

The Two Interpretations assignment demands that students approach dramatic texts as "an art of sights *and* sounds: what they *see* or imagine is as vital in interpreting a play as what they *hear* or read."[18] Part of the process of encouraging students to "*see* or imagine" a play involves introducing them to early modern stage conventions. Students read Holger Schott Syme's "The Theater of

---

model of stage-centered reading" that begins and ends with close reading, a "deceleration" of dramatic dialogue accompanied by the "reacceleration" of lines in order to capture how they would appear on stage in the reader's imagination. My Interpretive Intervention assignment in essence asks students to take Berger's literary approach and to perform the results; the performative element, I find, allows students to gain interpretive insight.

[17] This assignment was designed before the publication of the newest edition of the *Norton Shakespeare*, which includes considerable commentary on performance by Brett Gamboa, including a general "Performance Note" for each play and more specific footnotes with a "Performance Comment" at key moments. One such comment, at *Richard II* 3.3.183, notes that directors must decide whether "a tired and unstable Richard appears to cede the crown to Bolingbroke" or whether "Bolingbroke and Northumberland are predators moving in for the kill" (Digital Edition Performance Comment 2). These comments helpfully offer students specific examples of performative and interpretive choices; instructors might ask students to defend or evaluate these choices with textual evidence, to propose additional performative possibilities for a given moment, or to choose scenes without Performance Comments for analysis.

[18] Susan McCloskey, "Teaching Dramatic Literature," *College English* 46 (1984): 385.

Shakespeare's Time," from the *Norton Shakespeare*, and we spend several class periods near the beginning of the semester discussing how early modern stage conventions shape plays, how plays comment on these conventions, and how these conventions influence audiences. These conversations continue throughout the semester, not only during performance activities but also in our regular class discussion of plays. How might the practice of double casting influence our conception of Cordelia and the Fool in *King Lear*? When Petruccio and Kate debate whether it is day or night in act 4 of *Taming of the Shrew*, how might the realities of the day lit stage influence the audience's understanding of the scene? Such questions can be addressed both through discussion and also in impromptu classroom performances. Ralph Alan Cohen has shown how easy it is to transform a classroom into a model of an early modern playhouse: the lack of resources in the typical literature classroom can actually work to mimic the conditions of the bare, early modern stage.[19] Early modern plays required active imaginations from their audiences, and re-creating early modern theatrical practices in the classroom can invite students to hone their ability to imagine complex possibilities so central to creative and critical thinking.[20]

As students prepare for the group performance assignment, they also need practice imagining how Shakespearean language gets enacted in physical space, how movement and action, the speech and silence of bodies influence dramatic meaning. Students can benefit from imagining and then performing in small groups one character's wordless reactions to another's speech. Other exercises might ask them to consider how an actor can use gestures, movements, and pauses to add nuance and depth to spoken dialogue. James P. Lusardi and June Schlueter describe a brief moment from the 1955 Stratford-upon-Avon staging of *Macbeth* that demonstrates these corporeal elements of performance. In act 3, as Laurence Olivier's Macbeth begins speaking with the men he will enlist to kill Banquo, he utters three words that can easily be discounted: "Well then, now" (3.1.75). Olivier, however, added gesture, tone, and silence to his performance of these words:

[19] "With a little effort teachers can virtually put their students into an Elizabethan theater: the thrust stage can be desks arranged in a horse-shoe extending from three feet on either side of the central desk, the doors to the tiring-house can be the three feet space on either side of the central desk, the discovery space can be the area directly in front of the desk, the balcony above can be the top of the desk, and the columns holding up the heavens can be two desks or trash cans placed far downstage left and right." Ralph Alan Cohen, "Original Staging and the Shakespeare Classroom," in Riggio, *Teaching Shakespeare through Performance*, 80.

[20] My students are fortunate to be able to attend performances of the Pigeon Creek Shakespeare Company, a professional touring group based in Grand Haven, Michigan that employs original staging and theatrical practices: http://www.pcshakespeare.com/.

> Facing the murderers center stage, . . . he 'eyed them mockingly.' Then, he raised both hands and pointed at each murderer, putting 'Well' as a question—"Well?" Pausing, he crooked each index finger to invite them to come closer, with a peremptory 'then.' When the murderers hesitated, he dropped his hands to point to the floor on either side of him and turned the final word into a 'frightening imperative'—'Now!'"[21]

An actor could speak these lines any number of ways to communicate a different effect. So how did Olivier (or director Glen Byam Shaw) conceive the performance of these three words that lack any stage direction? Olivier's sense of Macbeth's character, his imagination of how this scene might be played out, seems to have guided his delivery of the words, rather than these particular words guiding his delivery. Analyzing a dramatic text with an eye toward performance is here exposed as a reciprocal process wherein the text generates interpretations, which then influence the performance of words, a kind of hermeneutic circle.[22] The performance of a single scene, then, requires the careful reading, analysis, and interpretation of the entire play.

These assignments and classroom exercises prepare students for their group Interpretive Interventions in the second half of the semester. The assignment undoubtedly exposes my bias toward literary interpretation, even though I demand that students take dramatic performance seriously. For example, it is explicitly *not* a requirement of the assignment that group members themselves act the parts. Rather, they are (to quote from the assignment sheet) "responsible for conceptualizing and directing the performance of one short scene or part of a longer scene of [their] choosing": group members can cast themselves (usually the case), talented theatrical friends, or, as in one case and in homage to the children's companies of early modern England, the students' younger brothers and sisters. Actors are not required to memorize lines, dress in period costume, or follow period stage conventions, although I do ask them to consider how the scene would be performed in Shakespeare's theater and to research the play's performance history. Ultimately, the quality of the acting and the polish of the performance is secondary for this assignment. More important for my purposes is the requirement that a group produce and turn in a "script" that records all spoken lines—groups can delete words and lines but cannot add new material to Shakespeare's language—and includes the group's own stage directions: instruc-

[21] Lusardi and Schlueter, "'I have done the deed,'" 71.

[22] Dudley Andrew applies the idea of the hermeneutic circle to describe adapting texts into films as "both a leap and a process": "The hermeneutic circle, central to interpretation theory, preaches that an explication of a text occurs only after a prior understanding of it, yet that prior understanding is justified by the careful explication it allows. In other words, before we can go about discussing and analyzing a text we must have a global conception of its meaning," Dudley Andrew, "Adaptation," in *Film Adaptation,* ed. James Naremore (New Brunswick, NJ: Rutgers University Press, 2000), 29.

tions for actors' gestures, expressions, vocal tone and intonation, intended emotion and effect, and so on. The emphasis, then, is on the imaginative acts of interpretation and direction rather than the quality of the final performance. Students can perform their scenes live or record them,[23] and following the performance, group members report on their research into performance history and ask the class a series of questions about interpretive choices. Students report that they feel a sense of ownership over the material in a way that is impossible to achieve by taking a test or writing a paper; they have become "co-creators" of Shakespeare's texts.[24]

Particularly delightful are groups that perform challenging interpretations skillfully. Just so, the two groups of students who performed the banquet scene from *Macbeth* combined careful textual analysis and imaginative thinking about bodies, movement, and performance. The first group's reverse gender casting "intervention" tested the gender ambiguities of Macbeth and his wife, the former accused by his wife of a lack of manhood, the latter wishing that spirits might "unsex" her and strip her of feminine traits (1.5.39). Embodying Macbeth as a woman, students thought, had an oddly proto-feminist effect, since a powerful woman was seen presiding over the banquet and boldly threatening the dinner guests while the man sat passively making excuses for the aggressive outbursts of his partner. The creepy ghost, students thought, made Macbeth seem less mad and worked to align Shakespeare with King James's beliefs in the reality of ghosts and spirits as opposed to skeptics like Reginald Scot.[25] The second *Macbeth* group's decision to depict Macbeth drawing the ghost at the very moments he is remembering Banquo and speaking about him to his guests, on the other hand, had the effect of making the play correspond more closely to Scot's skepticism. Here, ghosts, like witches and other spirits, are creatures of a diseased imagination, and students agreed that this Macbeth appeared gullible, weak, and unsympathetic. As the second group's reimagining of the phrase "Sweet remembrancer" testifies, the demands of performance can encourage the cultivation of analytical and close reading skills.

The assignment's emphasis on provocative interpretations, while creating some memorable scenes, also brings with it the possibility—perhaps even the inevitability—of anachronism, the imposition of a postmodern, twenty-first-century mindset onto premodern dramatic texts. As an example of the promises

[23] On the potential perils of YouTube postings of Shakespearean performance, see Ayanna Thompson, "Unmooring the Moor: Researching and Teaching on YouTube," *Shakespeare Quarterly* 61, no. 3 (2010): 337–56.

[24] Loehlin, "Teaching Through Performance," 634.

[25] I assign excerpts from Donald Tyson, *The Demonology of King James I: Includes the Original Text of Daemonologie and News from Scotland* (Woodbury, MN: Llewellyn Publications, 2011) and Reginald Scot, *The Discoverie of Witchcraft* (1584; repr., New York: Dover, 1989).

and perils of this sort of performance assignment, I would like to examine one key moment in one group's performance of the trial scene from *The Merchant of Venice.* At the conclusion of the trial, Portia-as-Balthazar, implored to take a gift for her services, requests a glove from Antonio and then turns to Bassanio, who of course does not recognize her as his betrothed: "And for your love I'll take this ring from you. / Do not draw back your hand. I'll take no more, / And you in love shall not deny me this" (4.1.425–27). Portia's demand, of course, is meant to test Bassanio's loyalty; she has earlier given him the ring with the ominous warning that "when you part from, lose, or give [it] away, / Let it presage the ruin of your love" (3.2.172–73). In this moment, Bassanio is asked to measure and weigh (like so much else in the play) his affection for Antonio against his "love" for and earlier pledge to Portia: "when this ring / Parts from this finger, then parts life from hence. / O, then be bold to say Bassanio's dead" (3.2.183–85). Portia's lines entangle Bassanio in a complex web and beg a number of interpretive questions about these characters' demeanor and motivations.

The dialogue in 4.1 offers some clues about how actors might perform the scene. For instance, Portia-as-Balthazar's request that Bassanio not "draw back [his] hand" registers an apparently verbal response to the character's (and actor's) physical movement not recorded in Quarto or Folio stage directions. When read, the language functions retroactively to create the appearance that Bassanio recoils from Portia in an attempt to protect the ring; in performance, these lines likely have offered actors cues to physical movement that gets enacted on stage. The verbal creation of Bassanio's physical reaction carries interpretive significance: in pulling back, he is signaling—to Portia, Antonio, and the audience—that his very first, impulsive allegiance is to Portia, his earlier oath, and the secure bonds of heteronormativity. Even if, from Portia's perspective, he subsequently fails the test, the implied backward movement assures the audience that Bassanio's heart, his "love," rests firmly with his betrothed.

One group of students who chose the trial scene for their intervention, however, had discovered textual evidence throughout the play that Bassanio and Antonio's "love" went beyond mere friendship. Group members learned during their research into the play's performance history that "playing Antonio as a gay man has moved center stage only since the 1970s," and this interpretation colored the way they performed the trial scene.[26] The intimacies exchanged between the two "friends" unsettled the group's disguised Portia to the extent that she

[26] Bulman, "Shylock, Antonio, and the Politics of Performance," 38. Bulman discusses a Royal Shakespeare Company production from 1971, where Portia (Judi Dench) "could claim that her Portia felt a neurotic rivalry with Antonio for the love of Bassanio, which drove her to despair during the trial scene. Tony Church, who played Antonio in this production, reported to me that the contest between Portia and Antonio over the ring that Portia has made Bassanio vow never to remove from his finger was regarded as pivotal to their conception of the play," 39.

considered rendering a verdict against Antonio to remove a potential rival before having a last-minute change of heart. In their staging, when Portia asked for the ring, Bassanio immediately removed it from his finger and started handing it over, making her admonition, "Do not draw back your hand," a delightfully ironic expression of her wish that Bassanio *would* value the ring and want to guard it. Delivering the line with a staccato melody and an icy stare, she seized Bassanio's forward-reaching arm and gently pushed it back into his body while telling him not to "draw [it] back"—eliciting a howl of laughter from classmates in the audience. Her subsequent line, "I'll take no more," emphasized "take" and metamorphosed into another command, demanding now that Bassanio—contrary to her earlier statement—*not* give her the ring to "take" back to Belmont. The group's confused Bassanio held on to the ring until Portia left the stage and only too happily parted with it when asked by Antonio. The group's interpretive intervention worked within the confines of Shakespeare's language, as the assignment required, while rendering the scene immediately relevant to queer theory and contemporary debates about same-sex marriage.

Writing on the twentieth-century performance history of *The Merchant of Venice* that records increasingly queer interpretations of Antonio, James C. Bulman admits that "Historians might object that Portia's understanding of the 'love' between her husband and his friend is anachronistic," and students from the *Merchant* group could certainly be accused of this.[27] In fact, the Interpretive Intervention assignment itself is open to the charge that it discourages fidelity to early modern theatrical practice and instead encourages performances that are overly concerned with being "relevant" to twenty-first-century audiences and applicable to newer theoretical concerns. Such interpretive choices may repel purists, and I certainly do not agree with all the decisions students make in their performances. But the benefits of allowing students the latitude to "enact interpretations within the confines of already existing directives," as Butler writes with regard to gender performance, far outweighs the drawbacks of infidelity. In addition to cultivating close reading, analysis, and creativity, Shakespearean performance pedagogy can serve as a springboard for classroom conversations about performative gender and social roles. Shakespeare's plays, after all, continually remind us of analogies between the theatrical and the social. Focusing on performance pedagogy in Shakespeare courses, then, need not result in anti-theoretical, conformist treatments, as Ann Thompson has observed,[28] but can allow students to pose strong literary, interpretive, and, inevitably, political questions about bodies, race, gender, sexuality, and the cultural contexts of these plays. Analyzing and performing Shakespeare's plays can also encourage in students an awareness of their own enactment of performative roles, allowing them to exper-

[27] Bulman, "Shylock, Antonio, and the Politics of Performance," 42.

[28] Ann Thompson, "'King Lear' and the Politics of Teaching Shakespeare," *Shakespeare Quarterly* 41, no. 2 (1990): 139.

iment not only with Shakespearean scripts but also with the social and cultural scripts we all perform—and sometimes deform and reform—in our own lives.

Shakespeare and Service-Learning

Matthew C. Hansen, Boise State University

William Shakespeare is among the best known literary and historical figures from the premodern era. The task of understanding his plays and, in particular, aspects of the ways in which his plays constitute part of the fabric of both the premodern and postmodern world is at once easy and daunting. It is potentially easy because there is an embarrassment of riches (especially in comparison with other early modern English playwrights and poets) in the form of teaching aids ranging from lesson plans, to full-length videos, video and audio clips, and an ever-growing bibliography of approaches to teaching and learning Shakespeare; these resources are easily accessed through libraries and, increasingly, online. That wealth also presents a challenge as the sheer volume of material is nearly overwhelming. This essay adds to that treasure trove but aims to do so with a difference. The approach I outline here describes my use of a service-learning project in which upper-division undergraduates teach Shakespeare to elementary-school students by helping them to learn, rehearse, and perform an abridged version of one of Shakespeare's plays.

Service-learning is a teaching and learning strategy that "seeks to engage individuals in activities that combine both community service and academic learning."[1] Academic content in a given course is reinforced and examined in immediate, hands-on ways through integrated community service that has relevance to course content. Students themselves are asked to articulate the connections they find between course learning and service through structured reflection. Student learning and growth through service-learning can be seen in three principal areas: enhanced understanding of academic content, personal growth, and civic engagement. I have written elsewhere about some aspects of how my use of service-learning in teaching Shakespeare improves students' skills as literary critics[2] and of the social justice and civic engagement underpinnings of this

---

[1] Andrew Furco, "Is Service-Learning Really Better than Community Service?," in *Service-Learning: The Essence of the Pedagogy*, ed. Andrew Furco and Shelley H. Billig (Greenwich, CT: Information Age Publishing, 2002), 25.

[2] Matthew C. Hansen, "Shake It Up After-School: Service Learning, Shakespeare, and Performance as Interpretation," in *Service Learning and Literary Studies in English*, ed.

project[3] but the approach I outline also offers unique opportunities to situate the words, ideas, and contexts of the premodern world in postmodern contexts by, in part, exploring the validity of Ben Jonson's infamous claim that Shakespeare was "not of an age, but for all time."

Since 2006 I have incorporated a service-learning project in my teaching of a 300-level Shakespeare course. I regularly offer this course each spring semester and, over time, planning and other coordination aspects of the project now span the entire academic year. However, it would (I hope) be easy to conceive a less-intensive and time-consuming approach than the one I outline here. My approach requires all students enrolled in my upper-division Shakespeare course in any given sixteen-week spring semester to collaborate on a single project—an after-school Shakespeare program for Title I elementary schools that I call "Shake It Up After-School" (SIUAS). Over the course of seven weeks, undergraduates enrolled in my course help elementary students to read, discuss, rehearse, and perform an abridged version of a Shakespeare play. I ask that each undergraduate student complete forty hours of service over the course of the semester, with the bulk of those hours being direct contact time teaching the elementary student performers. This is in some ways easy as the after-school program itself runs for seven weeks and meets after school for approximately two hours each day, Monday through Thursday. Additional student or alumni leaders—whom I recruit to return to the program as interns or volunteers after their initial semester in my course—take on directorial, teacher-planning, design, and textual editing responsibilities. The ways in which this aspect of the project has enabled a community of learners at various stages and levels of knowledge of Shakespeare and performance to coalesce has been truly remarkable. Reexamining this project as part of larger patterns of practice that bring the premodern into the postmodern classroom lets me see that what I have created is my own form of a guild workshop. With myself as the master teacher (craftsman) I have a team of apprentices who are gaining increasing mastery in their knowledge of Shakespeare, performance, and teaching, the three main knowledge areas the course and project explore.

As an adapted form of Team-Based Learning[4] and Project-Based Learning,[5] SIUAS approaches the teaching and learning of Shakespeare in ways that require deep immersion in the study and analysis of a single play text from which fruitful

---

Laurie Grobman and Roberta Rosenberg (New York: Modern Language Association of America, 2014), 104–15.

[3] Matthew C. Hansen, "'O Brave New World': Service-Learning and Shakespeare," *Pedagogy* 11, no. 1 (2011): 177–97.

[4] Larry K. Michaelsen, Arletta Bauman Knight, and L. Dee Fink, eds., *Team-based Learning: A Transformative Use of Small Groups* (Westport, CT: Praeger, 2002).

[5] Lillian G. Katz and Sylvia C. Chard, *Engaging Children's Minds: The Project Approach*, (Norwood, NJ: Ablex, 1989).

Figure 5: Elementary students perform *Twelfth Night* as part of "Shake It Up After School."
Class of Matthew Hansen.

comparative analysis with other specimens of Shakespearean drama can proceed. It also enables undergraduates to more fully explore both the early modern and postmodern contexts of the play. I frequently make extensive use of the Bedford/St.Martin's "Texts and Contexts" editions of the play as well as EEBO to help my undergraduate students to access voices and ideas from the early modern world. My undergraduates then explore ways to frame aspects of the play and its contexts that are important to them and to the elementary students participating in SIUAS. This happens in both formal and informal ways: undergraduates will occasionally plan and deliver a short lesson on, for example, sumptuary laws and the ways in which dress and other forms of expression were regulated (or regulation was attempted) in early modern England. When we are helping the

Figure 6: Elementary students perform *Twelfth Night* as part of "Shake It Up After School."
Class of Matthew Hansen.

elementary students to perform comedies such as *As You Like It* or *Twelfth Night* it is also often useful to explore the historical condition of Shakespeare's all-male acting troupes.

Frequently, we employ our own form of cross-gender or gender-blind casting as we seek to assign parts for performance that not only will yield an artistically successful production but, more importantly, one that challenges and enriches the elementary students' educational experience. At one of my partner schools (I currently run the program each spring at three different Title I elementary schools) we have a strong tradition of "girl power" casts. One year we cast a fourth-grade girl as Hamlet; the following year, as a fifth-grader, the same girl played the cross-dressing Rosalind in *As You Like It*. Both of these casts had several girls playing male characters.

Written undergraduate student reflections often comment on the deepened learning that occurs for them as they spend an extended period of time immersed in reading, rereading, performing and teaching a play. The year we produced *As You Like It* one of my students, Tanya, wrote:

> Having to go into so much detail explaining different relationships between characters and answering all the questions of why and how come, really tests your own knowledge and understanding of the material. I had a basic understanding of *As You Like It* as a whole when we started working with

> the kids but my own understanding of the relationships between characters has deepened as I have had to teach. It was easy to catch onto the comedy and irony of Rosalind being a woman, dressed like a man, being wooed as a woman on the first read through. It isn't until you have looked at this play over and over again for days or weeks on end that you start to ask questions and consider the implications of why she keeps her disguise until the end of the play. The forest turns out to be a seemingly peaceful and safe place, she is near her father, reunited with the man she loves so why keep pretending? This was a question many of the kids asked within the first two days and one I didn't consider much deeper until about the third week in. The answer seems obvious: it is funnier if she stays in disguise, but there are so many other reasons to continue the charade. I believe the main reason is the freedom and power that Rosalind is afforded in her disguise as a man that she'd lose were she to reveal her true identity. Another very plausible reason is the chance that it gives her and Orlando to interact without any of the previous awkwardness and shyness with which he'd approached her before. Seeing Rosalind as Ganymede, his equal, sets Orlando at ease and allows their relationship to grow. It is definitely a test of your own ability to analyze and understand these plays when you have to be able to teach the skills to someone else, it is also a great opportunity to gain new ideas and insights that would be missed without the open discussion that this program facilitates. A great example was when we asked the kids what the play was about and a few of them answered "girl power." At first it struck me as funny but it also has some truth to it and made me think about the play from an angle I hadn't previously considered.

In the turn near the conclusion of this long comment Tanya articulates in brief another significant, unique, and enriching feature of this program: it shakes up the expected, conventional dynamic of teacher and student and causes the learning dynamic to move beyond a standard two-constituency (student, teacher), two-role (student, teacher) learning structure and into a five-constituency (professor, undergraduate student, elementary school student, elementary school principal/teacher, elementary school parent) and three-role (student, student/teacher, teacher) structure.

Similarly, Elizabeth, a 2010 student who later became a leader and site director, observed that transferring the insights from readings and discussion in our college classroom to applicable reading and interpretive skills for elementary students allowed *The Tempest* (that year's production text) to "become more multifaceted and intriguing" than she felt it was on an initial reading. She observes: "This experience has challenged me to do the same type of rephrasing and re-communication with everything I read so that I can test my own understanding of a text." This same student, working closely with the elementary student playing Ariel, learned from her elementary-age collaborator about the power dynamics between Ariel and Prospero. The elementary student, in discussion with Elizabeth, proffered the paradoxical insight that Ariel, possessing magic and doing the actual magical work, is more powerful if submissive to Prospero. This led Elizabeth "to examine the text further and write my reading response on the support that I found that backed up [our Ariel's] initial interpretation" that "Ariel is the main source of power in the play." Through this approach, we all are teaching each other and learning from each other. While this is radically different from what we are led to believe the medieval and early modern classroom looked like—teacher-centered with some combination of threat (the switch) or reward (the apple) to motivate student learning—what I have constructed here is something far more democratic and, by extension, arguably more modern in its structure as we all work together to complete a difficult and highly complex project.

Incorporating performance in the teaching of Shakespeare is neither radical nor unique to me. Indeed, it seems as though many if not most college-level Shakespeare instructors incorporate some form of performance—be it the in-class performance of scenes or the viewing of films or video clips—to help deepen and enrich undergraduates' understanding of the play texts. However, in my structure of the course and especially its use of performance-focused service-learning, performance is the spine. I ask students to think about the plays as texts for performance, holding the whole scope of the story in mind as they are assigned the entire play—not segments—as the initial reading assignment when we begin to study a specific play. Throughout the semester I arrange optional, extra-credit group read-throughs of all the plays so that students can experience the texts in ways that draw on performance practice and honor the inherently collaborative and poly-vocal nature of dramatic texts.[6] Students are assigned to a performance troupe and work together in those teams throughout the semester, performing assigned scenes in class roughly every other week. As part of the in-class performances, we discuss and critique the performances as part of class discussion. Doing so enables students to consider the practicalities and implications of decisions related to blocking and movement, vocal intonation and facial expression. Class discussion of these performances explores the strengths and weaknesses of those performance choices and their implications as an interpretation of the text. Undergraduates also submit a written self-evaluation of their performance in which they assess their team's work overall, the insights gained from performing and discussing their performance, and their individual contribution to the performance.

I also incorporate the use of film clips to show and analyze the interpretive decisions at work in specific scenes. At times we will watch clips of some of the same scenes I ask students to perform in class, thus gaining a deeper perspective on that specific scene. At other times we will explore other scenes from the

[6] Matthew C. Hansen, "Learning to Read Shakespeare: Using Read-Throughs as a Teaching and Learning Strategy," *Working Papers on the Web 4: Teaching Renaissance Texts* (2002), http://extra.shu.ac.uk/wpw/renaissance/hansen.htm.

play, thus engaging in close-reading and analysis of still more of the play text as a whole. The process of watching peer performances, professional performances (on video), performing themselves and then teaching elementary students to perform grounds performance-as-interpretation as a central tenet of intellectual practice in the course. Textual interpretation in the moment of performance temporarily fixes the text in order to make concrete decisions about that particular performance; but by discussing performance choices and alternatives, we further explore the fluidity and indeterminacy of the text. This kind of intellectual flexibility then empowers the undergraduates to explore performance and interpretation options with elementary student-performers. I help to prepare undergraduates to shift from learning to teaching by discussing how their learning through performance will be extended when they begin to teach in the SIUAS program. For example, we discuss practical considerations such as how we can help the elementary students block scenes that keep their faces visible to the audience and their voices audible. Discussion of performance styles and choices also connects back to considerations of historical context. We read and discuss some of the limited audience accounts of sixteenth-century performances of Shakespeare and, by considering the ongoing life of Shakespeare in performance—on amateur and professional stages and on film—we likewise reconnect with an important aspect of Shakespeare's "timelessness."

I also seek to disrupt and unsettle certain aspects of this notion of Shakespeare's "timelessness." For, while Shakespeare is undeniably an important commodity appropriated and reproduced by high or elite culture, Shakespeare's origins are in and his works remain intertwined with popular and even low culture. At times, the elementary students' knowledge of Shakespeare and appropriations of Shakespeare drive this home. They will observe how certain character names, phrases, or story lines recur in movies, television shows, and cartoons that they know. For example, several years ago when producing *A Midsummer Night's Dream* as we explained the plot of the play to the elementary students, they immediately recognized it as central to an episode of the Disney Channel show "The Suite Life of Zach and Cody." My undergraduate students knew the show (I did not) but not the specific episode. In showing us how Shakespeare and *A Midsummer Night's Dream* were already a part of their world, the elementary students became our teachers, illuminating for us a specific example of how this premodern writer continues to influence dramatic entertainment in the postmodern world. A few weeks later, we watched this episode with them as a kind of reward for their hard work in rehearsals. As other students observed in their written analysis of *A Midsummer Night's Dream* and the other Shakespearean comedies we studied that semester, the happy resolution of conflict between generations is key to the resolution and closure of Shakespearean comedy. We explored this not simply as a literary construct, but in actual practice by empowering the elementary students to not simply be the recipients of knowledge and learning, but to be active co-creators of it and, in fact, to teach us. [Color Plates 3, 4, 5]

Considering such an approach—even a less extensive version of what I have developed—may necessarily cause instructors to redesign their course and to face the long-standing anxiety that incorporating experiential learning approaches like service-learning means that one will by necessity not be able to incorporate as much traditional content in their course.[7] It is true, for example, that students enrolled in my service-learning focused Shakespeare course study fewer plays than in my colleagues' sections of the same course. Of three of us who regularly teach the same 300-level Shakespeare course at my university, one typically teaches seven plays, another six; I now typically teach five plays in a sixteen-week semester in order to allow for more time to be spent immersing ourselves in the play that we are teaching and producing in the elementary schools. However, I argue that the complex, collaborative, project-based learning approach that I employ leads to student learning that is as valuable—if not more valuable—than covering more plays in less depth. Deep immersion in a single play text, considered from multiple angles—as script for in-class performance, through traditional written analysis, in early modern historical context, as the site of critical analysis in published scholarship, as content to be taught to others through collaborative performance—enables undergraduates to feel that they have significant understanding of that text and a kind of key with which to unlock and understand other plays by Shakespeare and his contemporaries.

I have argued elsewhere that Shakespeare's privileged position in English-speaking world culture makes the work of undergraduates teaching Shakespeare to socially and economically diverse elementary students an important act of social justice. But if Shakespeare were not as culturally significant or if the content being taught were not as immediately and widely recognized for its supposed value and significance, the complex work of asking undergraduates to take on the mantle of teacher and expert nevertheless has significant pedagogical payoffs and most certainly is an innovative and hands-on way of exploring the interconnectedness of the premodern and the postmodern worlds. Other literature (especially dramatic literature) could easily go in for similar treatment: undergraduates might edit and coach performances of Morality and Mystery Plays, the works of Shakespeare's English and continental contemporaries, or other forms of literature adapted for performance. Undergraduates and younger learners might collaboratively explore literature through other forms of creative expression (illustration for example, allowing for an exploration of the links between pre- and postmodern visual culture). History and in particular those elements that constantly re-remind us of the cyclical nature of life and the tendency for lessons to reiterate themselves in different times and places could likewise be adapted.

[7] Amy Strage, "Long-Term Academic Benefits of Service-Learning: When and Where Do They Manifest Themselves," *College Student Journal* 38, no. 2 (2004): 257–62.

When we ask students to teach aspects of the content they are learning in our courses, we help them to understand that content in profoundly practical ways. Indeed, what I am proposing here is an appropriation of the basic structure of medical and other practical forms of education, in which the learner is guided to increasing levels of skill mastery because they "see one, do one, teach one." In medical terms this may mean that one sees a procedure (say drawing blood, for example), then does the procedure under supervision, and then later teaches someone else how to do the procedure. This basic framework, I believe, can be a useful foundation for applying a service-learning approach to a wide variety of fields. It has an immediate ability to get our own interest in the rich and strange features of premodern history and literature out of the sometimes further bewildering domain of academic discourse of scholarship and university classrooms and out into the world beyond our campuses. It asks our students to learn the academic content we seek to share with them in such a way that their mastery of it emerges not only as a student and a learner, but as a teacher as well.

Shakespeare and the Experimental Classroom

Jonathan P. Lamb, University of Kansas

In 2012, I began a more or less carefully controlled experiment in my ENGL 332: Shakespeare course at the University of Kansas (KU). The experiment involves offering students the option of a creative assignment, among others, to replace the standard end-of-term paper, and asking them to design the means and standards by which their projects will be assessed. After two semesters (Fall 2012 and Fall 2013), the assignment has produced surprising and illuminating results.[1] Overall, the experiment aims to understand and to improve student engagement with the writings of William Shakespeare, which remain at once normative and exceptional among the majority of students enrolled in my sections of 332 (as I will now call the course). Such students, as instructors of similar courses can attest, enter an introductory Shakespeare course deeply aware of Shakespeare's cultural capital.[2] Just as often, however, these students possess little working knowledge of Shakespeare's plays and poems, to the extent that Shakespeare appears as an exception, ever familiar and yet just out of reach.

I integrated this experiment for three reasons. First, the standard, academic term papers I previously assigned (and which students still exercise the option to write) failed to account for the seething mass of creativity among students. A huge proportion—about half—of KU's English majors focus on creative writing. Although these students arguably should learn to write a six- to eight-page academic essay about Shakespeare, that essay does not put their creative faculties into contact with Shakespeare's writings. Second, students in past 332 sections found the term paper redundant rather than climactic. Throughout their course with me, students practice the activities conventionally associated with the term paper: entering a "scholarly conversation," thesis-driven close-reading, integrating primary or archival materials, and bringing theoretical principles to bear on literary texts. I offered a creative option not to set aside those foundational

[1] Not approved for human subjects testing.

[2] See John Guillory, *Cultural Capital: The Problem of Literary Canon Formation* (Chicago: University of Chicago Press, 1993), and Jonathan Bate, *The Genius of Shakespeare* (New York: Oxford University Press, 1998).

activities but to energize them and ask students to forge connections between the academic content of the course and their creative responses to it. Third and perhaps most controversial, the conventional term paper too narrowly met the aims of the course. Table 1 outlines those aims:[3]

Students in ENGL 332 will learn:

- basic knowledge of William Shakespeare's writings and their significance
- what constitutes a scholarly, critical conversation about Shakespeare, and why it matters
- to read, study, and discuss critically a Shakespeare play or poem
- to write thesis-driven interpretive arguments that draw on appropriate evidence and reasoning
- to forge connections between past/other cultures and students' own cultures, and to respond in a thoughtful and sustained manner to those connections

Table 1: ENGL 332 Aims for Learning

By "too narrowly," I mean that the conventional term paper does help meet those aims, but that it is not the only integrative assignment to do so, and certainly not for students with a variety of backgrounds, interests, and aspirations. Based on my conviction that a bachelor of arts degree in English—and, as a subset, an introductory Shakespeare course—educates the imagination, I introduced the creative option.

Name	ENGL 332: Shakespeare
Enrollment	Usually between 18 and 35 students, ranging from freshmen to graduating seniors waiting until the last possible moment to take Shakespeare
Makeup	Most KU English majors must take 332; the course also draws secondary education students and students from neighboring disciplines
Level	KU courses range through the 600 level; a 300-level course is considered "upper-level" and is appropriate for sophomores and juniors
Reading	Seven plays, usually including two comedies, two histories, two tragedies, and a late play

[3] I am intentionally avoiding the term "outcomes" because it is fundamentally distinct from "aims" or "goals," which connote distinctly less instrumentalization of pedagogical practice.

Papers/Exams	Five short papers, often in the form of two-page close-readings and digital medium projects; one long final project; midterm and final exams
Format	Most often, directed discussion; some lecture/preaching; some performance/group reading; occasional jokes

Table 2: ENGL 332 Snapshot

The Assignment

The creative assignment experiment proceeds as follows: five to six weeks in advance of the project deadline, I lay out the final project options. They include the creative project option, a standard academic paper, a film adaptation, and more. Students have about a week to make their choice and narrow down their topic of interest, and they consult with me throughout the process (or they should). While students who choose other options have just one final deadline, those who choose the creative project must follow a series of deadlines. They choose their project and then define its parameters and the ways in which they will consider its creative merits. Once they have finished and submitted the project, they assess their own work according to the scheme they themselves had composed. Finally, they write a report about the whole process from beginning to end. Their final grade, assigned by me, is based on the sum of their labors. Thus, a student who marked her project very low could still earn a high grade. Or, alternatively, a student who marked her project high could fail utterly. Below is the assignment prompt from Fall 2012:

> **Final Project, Option 3**
>
> Creative Project
>
> Due: December 9, 2012 (but see below for other deadlines)
>
> For this final project option, you will make a creative project dealing with Shakespeare. You may use performance, film, props, costumes, food—really, anything you want to use to do something creative with Shakespeare's writings (pending instructor approval, of course). By **November 15th,** you must tell your instructor 1) that you are choosing this option and 2) what you intend to do. **The catch** here is that you are responsible not just for the project, but for deciding how it will be assessed.
>
> **Form and format:** Because of this assignment's creative component, the form and format are deliberately vague. You are free to "range within the zodiac of your own wit," in Sir Philip Sidney's words. Some examples of what's possible include: an in-class performance of a scene or scenes; a film production or adaptation of a scene; a musical version of something

from Shakespeare; some kind of mashup or parody; a piece of artwork that draws on Shakespeare's works somehow; *Othello* with zombies; a Shakespeare book like you'd find at Urban Outfitters. **Don't feel restricted to this list, however.** The sky is the limit here—pending instructor approval, of course. If your project involves using class time (e.g., for film screening), we will agree on a time during the last two weeks of class.

Goal: The goal of this assignment is for your creative work to meditate on, respond to, think about, make new, adapt, or simply perform the works of Shakespeare, in creative ways that *tell us something new about Shakespeare*. Interpret this last part broadly, since "something new" could include a surprising amount of stuff. For instance, an in-class performance could lead us to ask new questions about a scene that we think we have a grasp on. A film adaptation could bring new perspectives to old texts in such a way that we learn something about Shakespeare and ourselves. And so on, as long as you are thinking rigorously about Shakespeare in and through your project.

Group work: For this assignment, you are free to work with a group of classmates. This will make possible a wider range of creative options, and presumably it will make your creative project better. But choose wisely: you need to make sure that you share a group with people you trust to complete their part of the work. Like the project itself, you must receive instructor approval to form your group officially. You may not change groups after the November 8th deadline.

Assessment plan: As part of the project, you must create the standards by which your project will be assessed and report on your work after its completion. First, *before the project is completed*, you must create a set of goals or learning outcomes, some kind of rubric for assessing how well you met the goals, and a brief explanation of why you chose the project you did. Be sure to ask yourself what components of the project need assessing. (For example, an in-class performance might include such specifics as line memorization and larger elements such as dramatic conceptualization.) This document must be sent to your instructor via email by **November 26th**. If you're working as a group, you only need to submit one such document, but it needs to account for all of the group's contributions (that is, it needs to specify how different members of the group will be assessed for their contributions, even if each member will be assessed the same way).

Final report: *After the project is completed on or before December 16*, you must assess your own performance based on the assessment model you designed. (Hence, when you create the assessment document you should design it with your own use in mind.) *You must also write a two-page, double-spaced report* on the project as a whole. The report should include:

1.) Reflection on the project's conceptualization, especially the way it constitutes a creative use of or response to Shakespeare's writings.
2.) Reflection on the completed project (be it performance, artwork, or otherwise).

3.) Reflection on the assessment process, specifically why you chose the assessment criteria you did and why you assessed yourself the way you did.
4.) Explanation of any group-work, including a detailed statement of your own contributions to the group.

You must send both documents (assessment and report) as separate files to your instructor via email by **December 16, 2012.** Note that all members of a group must submit both documents individually—failure to do so will result in an F on the assignment, even if you did a Picasso-caliber painting of Desdemona.

Grade: The grade for this assignment is based on several criteria, all of which ensure the grade's fairness. Of course, each of the project components will be assessed individually: your self-assessment parameters must be thoughtful and rigorous in how they judge your creative project. The project itself must follow those parameters well. Your own self-assessment must be realistic and honest. And your final report must provide a thoughtful meta-commentary on the project as a whole. Overall, therefore, the main criterion for the grade is the degree to which your self-assessment parameters, the project itself, your self-assessment, and your final report work in harmonious rigor.

For the written sections of the project, a very successful paper will:

- be properly formatted
- be free of grammatical errors and stylistic unclarity
- address the central questions of the assignment clearly and cogently
- be thoughtfully organized into a paragraph structure
- have paragraphs that contain discernible topics, transitions, and a cogent structure
- marshal appropriate evidence and analysis to advance the thesis
- cite all sources appropriately

Do not hesitate to contact me with questions or problems—especially in the early stages of writing, when you are choosing and researching a topic. Past students have described paper consultations with me as "soul-searching," "I wept with pure gratitude all winter break," and "he's a nice guy."

The "catch," as the prompt calls it, is the central component to this assignment. It comprises what we might call the independent variable, the key difference between the creative option and the other four. The assignment asks students to make the doubly counterintuitive commitment to consider how their creative work might be assessed alongside standard academic writing and then to perform such an assessment. The central question at stake in the assignment concerns the level of critical engagement with the course material. My working supposition is that students working on the creative assignment will learn at least as much as the students who write a standard essay.[4]

The two sections of 332 selected for this experiment included forty-nine enrolled students, forty-six of whom submitted a final project and three of whom dropped the course mid-semester. Given the number of creative writing students in the KU English department, it comes as little surprise that seventeen students (or roughly 37 percent) chose the creative option. Most other students spread relatively evenly over three other options: eleven (24 percent) chose the film option, ten (22 percent) the standard paper, and seven (15 percent) the anthology introduction. Among the fifteen creative projects (including two groups of two), ten focused on a tragedy (*Hamlet*, *Othello*, or *Lear*), one on the histories (*Henry IV, Part I,* and *Henry V*), and four on multiple plays. The fact that I give the final project assignment while we are studying the tragedies probably explains this pattern. Nonetheless, despite the heavy emphasis on tragedy, the projects feature a surprising variety of creative media. Table 3 lists the projects.

Iago's diary, "discovered" after the action of *Othello*, in which he divulges all his secrets and contemplates his manipulation of the super-subtle Venetians.

A Shakespeare Restaurant menu, offering dishes inspired by (and calculated to mimic the feelings produced by) Shakespeare's plays. Includes photos of popular items.

A Microsoft PowerPoint presentation "as presented by a ninth grader who only skimmed the text of *Hamlet*."

A murder mystery rewrite of *Hamlet*.

A "sorting" of Shakespeare's characters into their proper Hogwarts houses.[5]

A cupcake representation of Shakespeare's *Othello*.

A book of comics, adapted from Gary Larson's comic strip "The Far Side," which follows the plot of *Henry IV, Part I,* and *Henry V*.

A long, free-verse poem inspired by Shakespeare's plays, performed in class.

An adaptation of Othello's speeches (and only his speeches amid the whole cast of *Othello*) in the form of "bro" or "fraternity star" idioms.

---

[4] See Joanna Williams, *Consuming Higher Education: Why Learning Can't Be Bought* (London: Bloomsbury Academic, 2013).

[5] Hogwarts is the boarding school in J. K. Rowling's bestselling Harry Pot*ter series.*

A King Lear board game.

A movie trailer for an *Othello* prequel.

A musical playlist of songs to follow Othello's emotional progress through the play.

Cupcakes created to represent Shakespeare's most memorable characters.

A *Lear* family Tumblr page, containing entries by Goneril, Regan, and Cordelia and including posts that cover not just the action of the play but a time before that action begins.

A cookie representation of King Lear's late-life crisis.

Table 3: Creative Project Topics

Even the most fanciful, off-the-beaten-path projects tend to originate during class discussion. The *Hamlet* PowerPoint, for instance, began with a running in-class joke about making uninformed, overly hasty claims, while I suspect the dessert-themed projects take some inspiration from our (read: my) frequent in-class references to dessert. The results of the assignment divide into the phases of the project: design and parameters of assessment,[6] the projects themselves, and student reflections on their projects.

Project Design and Parameters of Assessment

The assessment plans varied widely in their scope, length, complexity, and rigor. Some students, following the cue of the term "rubric" in the assignment prompt, created detailed charts for measuring creative value. Others simply listed what they sought to accomplish, in some cases using broad terms. For instance, one student simply stated (here quoting this student's assessment plan):

- Have I devoted consideration and time to the project? Was this a concept that appears fleshed out to its fullest extent?
- Did I take the source material (*Hamlet*) and expand upon it in a way that shows a particular understanding of the text?
- Is the intention of the project clear, and was that intention fulfilled?

[6] Or "rubric." See, among many other manuals and guides of varying usefulness, Mary J. Goggins Selke, *Rubric Assessment Goes to College: Objective, Comprehensive Evaluation of Student Work* (Lanham, MD: Rowman & Littlefield Education, 2013).

These goals could serve as aims for most projects about Shakespeare's *Hamlet*. They are not nearly as specific as the goals and parameters listed in other plans. The vagueness of the plan, however, does not correlate with a poor quality creative project. Indeed, the student who wrote this plan submitted what I quite unscientifically consider one of the most creative and skillful projects in the entire testing group, a project that showed a thoughtful and critical understanding of *Hamlet*. At the same time, other students who set equally broad project goals and assessments produced comparatively less engaged work. For example, one plan simply enumerated the aspects of the project rather than dimensions of evaluation.

In most cases, students showed thoughtful, critical engagement with the question of how to (and whether to) evaluate creative work. The student who created the *King Lear* board game, for instance, recognized the problem with such an endeavor—that board games are supposedly fair to all participants—and incorporated it into his assessment plan:

> 4. Does the playability of the game match the (un)fairness of *King Lear*? I.e., the *King Lear* universe is uncaring about its residents; is this essential element of *King Lear* captured within the game?

From the outset, he confronted the play's insistence upon the unfairness of human existence. To be sure, this problem first inspired his idea for a board game, where rules are uniform and universal and where the prize goes to the most skillful player whose luck is identical to that of other players. In the end, he created a game that was fundamentally unfair, especially for players who chose the game pieces of Lear, Cordelia, Kent, Gloucester, Goneril, Regan, Edgar, Edmund, Cornwall, Albany, and the Fool.

The two cupcakes projects, meanwhile, confronted not simply the question of how confection can sustain a critical response to Shakespeare's plays but also that of how such a response might be measured. One project, with cupcakes representing Othello, Desdemona, and Iago, allotted thirty percent of the overall assessment to Taste:

> What might appear to be the most enjoyable part of the cupcake will in fact be broken down into particular signifiers and become the most interesting technique of manifesting the most crucial qualities of these three characters. Each cupcake's texture and integrated flavors should be enjoyable principally as a dessert, but the flavors should additionally represent the ideas that I am trying to convey about each character. It is here that I must define what I want to convey and this must correlate to the cupcake's flavor.

Plenty of nuance here. The student has thought about the relationship between taste ("should be enjoyable principally as a dessert") and what that taste signifies ("manifesting the most crucial qualities of these three characters"). The taste qualities of the cupcakes have a clear conceptual link with the rest of the project, and with *Othello*. Elsewhere, the plan stipulated that:

> Each cupcake must furthermore have a strong relationship to the major elements [of] the particular [character] it describes and my cookbook should explain how and why I choose to embody the features that I do in the cupcakes. Even more, this could be considered the cupcakes "decorum," which should appropriately symbolize the character it represents.

Here the student applies the course content (the rhetorical principle of decorum, which we discussed while studying *Othello*) to situate the flavors and makeup of the cupcake with respect to the three characters the cupcakes represent.

The other cupcake project presents an illuminating contrast.

Cupcake Assessment Plan

> For the project I will be baking four different types of cupcake, each based on one of the plays we read in class. Here are the categories I will be assessing myself on:
>
> For each cupcake:
> Written description of how it relates to the play: 35% of grade
> How well the cupcake relates to the play (why each flavor is chosen etc.): 35%
> Creativity/Originality: (not just using dark chocolate because Othello is black, etc.): 20%.
> Taste: 10%

Here taste makes up only a tenth of the overall assessment, while the relationship to the play and the description of that relationship make up seventy percent. In one sense, this distribution is ridiculous, because the cupcakes could taste like a Norton Anthology and, according to this measure, still be considered ninety percent successful. Considering that the main criterion for the grade is "the degree to which your self-assessment parameters, the project itself, your self-assessment, and your final report work in harmonious rigor," however, the approach makes much more sense. This student wants to emphasize as much as possible the reflective aspect of her project, rather than the project itself.

In sum, the assessment plans from the first phase of the assignment feature a wide variety of evaluative possibilities. Some plans demonstrate greater sophistication and reflection than others, but a quality plan cannot predict the quality of the subsequent creative project. Across the whole range, probably due to the constraints of the assignment, students proved willing to reflect thoughtfully on what counts as a valuable, skillful, compelling creative response to Shakespeare's writings.

The Projects

These creative projects blew my mind. The range of topics came as a real surprise, as did the fact that no one put on a performance in class, which seemed to me the natural course. The variable in question in this experiment, however, concerns the level of engagement with Shakespeare's plays. In this regard, perhaps unsurprisingly, those students who spent serious effort and thought and who consulted with me at least once produced the most technically proficient, detailed, and careful work. Those students, however, did not necessarily put forward the most "creative use[s] of or response[s] to Shakespeare's writings" (in the words of the assignment prompt). That is, the technical proficiency of the project did not correlate with the level of engagement with Shakespeare's plays, though often it did.

How, then, did these projects constitute "creative use of or response to Shakespeare's writings"? Some did so through the lens of **character**. The *Othello* cupcakes project, for instance, took character as its basic unit. Here are the cupcakes, photographed immediately before I ate them: taste was, after all, thirty percent of the score. (Color Plate 6).

Likewise, the "Iago's diary" project took up one of Shakespeare's most puzzling (and indeed, impenetrable) characters. The diary, which the student actually constructed and for which he handwrote entries using Iago's voice, explored the longstanding question of Iago's motives. The entries revealed Iago's response to Cassio's promotion, unpacked Iago's suspicion that Othello had sex with Emilia, and then followed the narrative of the play to its conclusion. In a nice touch, the student hollowed out the back half of the book to create a hiding place for Desdemona's handkerchief. Similarly, the Sorting Hat project took character as its basic unit of organization.

Other projects took **narrative** as the focus of their response. The murder mystery *Hamlet*, for instance, reconceived of the revenge play as a kind of detective novel. Instead of a ghost, Hamlet finds a note from his father in a book:

> Hello son,
>
> I won't waste a lot of time here, but suffice it to say: I've been murdered. By now your uncle will have poisoned me and married your mother. Hah! I bet you were hoping for something like that, right, son? Either way I have a business trip scheduled at the same time as your next visit, so I hope this little note will make up for my absence. Goodbye, Hamlet, you know what you have to do for me now.

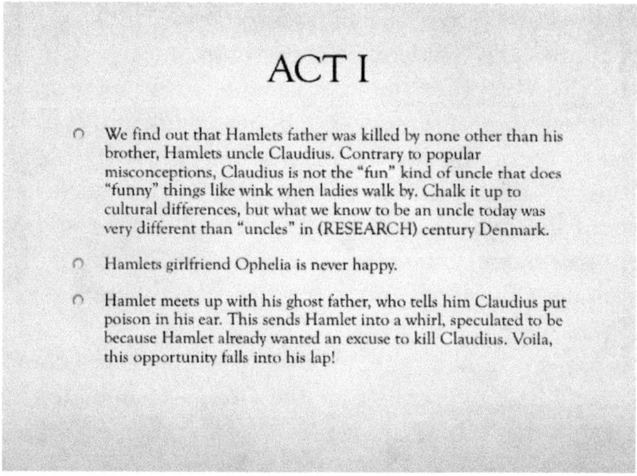

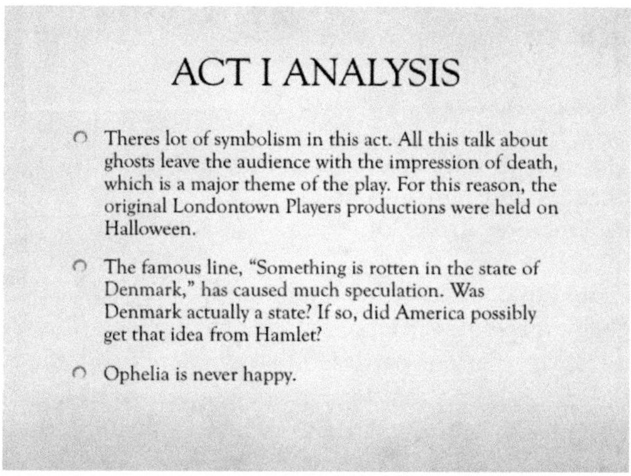

Figures 7, 8: PowerPoint Presentation about *Hamlet*, act 1.
Class of Jonathan Lamb.

The final line of the story reads, "'Tell this story, Horatio,' Hamlet said as the screams and sirens filled the air." Shorter than Shakespeare's *Hamlet*, "Hamlet Take Two" focuses on the issue of proof raised by the play and made visible when the basic plot is imported into a genre (detective fiction) often concerned with proof. In a slightly different way, the faux-PowerPoint presentation of *Hamlet* followed the play's narrative trajectory. Figures 7 and 8 show the slides about act 1.

The style of these slides captures the ethos of a confused, over-hasty reader of *Hamlet*: the invention of "the Londontown Players" as Shakespeare's acting company, the naïve, America-centric view of "state," and the misreading of Hamlet's "my prophetic soul!" as a statement of desire to kill Claudius. Yet ironically—and by intention—the slides also make contact with Shakespeare's writings and culture. The "student" is not wrong to notice that Ophelia is never happy, and the slides capture the way Ophelia's unhappiness punctuates the play's action. Although there were no Londontown Players, the notion of *Hamlet* as a play suited to particular holidays is perfectly reasonable and even insightful. Further, the notion of Claudius as a lecherous, "fun" uncle captures the way Hamlet imagines him.[7] Still more subtly, throughout the slides the "student" spells Shakespeare's name "Shakespear," a nice reference to the variable orthography of early modern England, and to the fact that Shakespeare spelled his own name several ways.

Still other projects took up **theme** or **topic** as the central component of their creative response. The movie trailer for the *Othello* prequel, for instance, promises to show viewers the "adventurous youth" of the eloquent warrior: "Before he was ever conned by the un-loyal Iago, the two were dutiful allies in their adventures" (this in movie voiceover). For this idea, the students took inspiration from the moment in Shakespeare's play when Othello says "farewell" to his glorious martial life:

> Oh, now, forever
> Farewell the tranquil mind! Farewell content!
> Farewell the plumed troops and the big wars
> That makes ambition virtue! Oh, farewell! (3.3.363–66)

The students noted that when Othello talks about his past as a warrior he rarely refers to Iago being present, yet Iago, as Othello's ancient, must have taken part in at least some of the glorious battles. They wondered how the two men's relationship formed, speculating that Iago at some point saved Othello's life, earning Othello's deep trust. In the end, they produced a thrilling trailer (now pulled from YouTube because the music they used violated copyright!).

Post-Project Reflection

This aspect of the assignment, like the others, varied widely from project to project. Some students wrote lengthy treatises reflecting on and even defending their work. Others narrated the trajectory of the project from concept to fin-

[7] Hamlet takes notice that Claudius "drains his drafts of Rhenish down," causing those of other nations to "clepe us [the Danish] drunkards." See William Shakespeare, *The Complete Works of Shakespeare*, ed. David M. Bevington, 7th ed. (New York: Longman, 2013), 1.4.10, 19. This and all following references are to act, scene, and line in that edition.

ished product. Amid this variation, several trends emerged from these reflection essays.

First, students assessed their work realistically and rigorously, even if they gave themselves good "grades" on their assessment plans. One wrote, "My assessment plan was direly anemic. . .. My assessment standards are generic and ultimately don't seem to seek much reflection out of the assignment." All the same, he gave his project nearly full credit. Another student noted that his "idea was good, but actually putting it together was the difficult part," and he ultimately concluded that "I gave myself great grades on the Assessment because I really do feel that I did A work." One of the cupcake-makers wrote that "overall I think the symbolism and representation element of [the cupcakes were] dead on when it came to understanding the central characteristics to each character being represented." The maker of the *Lear* board game described how "by the end of working out the details, I just couldn't think of ways to transform a few of [the play's] events into events in the board game, and so this aspect of the project deserves a B." Nevertheless, he gave the overall project an "A," perhaps knowing that he had created a rather detailed game, even if it omitted some events from the play. The maker of Othello's playlist declared that "the most difficult part [of the project was] not writing the analysis, but finding songs whose lyrical message could make sensible connections to the dialogue." Whatever the results of the selection process, the student felt she "met the criteria" she had set out in advance.

Second, students willingly put the course content into conversation with their projects and creative media. That is, with a high level of sophistication, students integrated into their creative process what we read, discussed, and debated about Shakespeare's writings during the course. For example, the student who created the cookie representation of Lear's late-life crisis explained that she chose the project "because I liked the idea. . .about Lear, his sense of place and the Verge." Here the student refers to the class period in which we discussed Lear's retinue of knights, and how his loss of the knights corresponds to his marginalization and placelessness in his former kingdom.[8] Another student explained that in the process of making her project, "I was required to think about the various components that are conveyed by the lines of each individual character, thus better understanding the significance of how and why Shakespeare uses particular words to symbolize significant themes." The course's focus on close reading led this student to forge strong conceptual links between the verbal texture of the plays and the texture of cupcakes. The translator of Othello's eloquent speech into slang, meanwhile, described a rather different inspiration:

[8] See Doug Eskew, "'Soldiers, Prisoners, Patrimony': *King Lear* and The Place of the Sovereign," *Cahiers Élisabéthains* 78 (September 1, 2010): 29–38.

> My creative project. . .was inspired by the way I and other students of Shakespeare tend to paraphrase the complex content of the plays, when prompted to do so. Most often, I've noticed, students tend to go beyond simply explaining the metaphors and tricks of language Shakespeare employs; instead, they reduce long speeches to as brief a statement as possible, often relying on modern slang to do so. This, in itself, often produces very humorous results, whether or not intentional. I realized, however, that the greatest humor of these "translations" lies in the dramatic juxtaposition of style between the newly translated lines and the original text.

This student observed the habit, surely familiar to instructors of early modern texts, of students taking "paraphrase" literally: they often phrase *alongside* Shakespeare using familiar or slang language. This inspiration led him to rephrase Othello's "Let him do his spite. / My services which I have done the seigniory / Shall out-tongue his complaints" into "Let him come at me: / I'm a god damn *legend* around here."

Third, with few exceptions, students intimated that the creative project helped them comprehend Shakespeare's writings clearly and critically. Although the maker of the *Hamlet* PowerPoint presentation self-deprecatingly asserted that "I can honestly say that my project did not in any way inform a greater understanding of the text," he actually demonstrated a rather splendid understanding of Shakespeare's play. The author of "Hamlet Take Two," the murder mystery, began the final report with the claim that "by writing the story I definitely gained a new appreciation for the intricacies of Shakespeare's plot." Likewise, another student wrote that "this creative project allowed me to first and foremost better understand the intricacy and depth of [Shakespeare's] characters individually, as well as the significance of each to the plot of the play." The creator of Iago's diary, working upon "the understanding that Shakespeare's characters aren't real people, rather they are characters that function within the context of the play and seem extremely real," concluded that "Shakespeare created characters that are far more alive than even he could have expected." The writer whose free verse poem rewrote the ending to *The Merchant of Venice* described how:

> Understanding the basic premise of the characters and making sure that they seem human and actually help us relate to their dilemmas is something that I had to do in order to write this poem. If the story never touched me and made me actually think of what could have happened then I would not be able to relate with Shylock on a higher level and actually make a new ending for *The Merchant of Venice*.

Finally, for the student who designed an Othello playlist, only by understanding "Othello's descent from a good natured and virtuous man to an insanely jealous lover" could "the playlist on *Dangerous Conceits* [the title of the collection] reflect this progression." Although these statements may seem rather straightforward and even a bit coerced as a result of the assignment prompt, the consistency of these responses demands some explanation.

Case Study: The Lear Family Tumblr

I want to offer a more extensive look at one creative project. This case study involves a social-media take on *King Lear*, in the form of a Lear family Tumblr feed. The student behind this project created houseoflear.tumblr.com, along with three users: "ReganCornwall," "GonerilAlbany," and "CordeliaFrance." She then created posts for these users that followed the action of *King Lear*, including some pre-play events (e.g., Cordelia posting cat pictures and self-motivation for talking to her father). The feed envisioned a world in which Lear's daughters interact with one another via social media even as they are separated and estranged. The assessment plan belongs among the simplest of all the projects (see Table 4, below).

	1	2	3	4	5
Characterization			×		
Quantity of material					×
Diversity of material					×
Timeline structure					×

Table 4: Assessment Plan for Lear Family Tumblr

The student scored herself lowest on the aspect of the project that involved complex evaluation. "Characterization" does not yield to easy codification or quantification. This fact bears itself out in the Tumblr posts, many of which take the form of free-verse poetry.

The feed incorporated aspects of Tumblr's distinctive style (e.g., memes, idiom) along with verbal and thematic aspects of *Lear* (e.g., a post from Regan, whose husband gouges out the Earl of Gloucester's eyes, about how she's attracted to a man's eyes). In her final report, the student worked hard to negotiate the relationship between assessment and creativity:

> In coming up with assessment criteria for this project, I chose aspects which I thought would best emphasize an understanding of the Lear family. I wanted to ensure that the characters on my blogs sounded like, and thus were accurate reflections of, the three daughters. I also included quantity of posts & types of posts. It is very difficult to give a good representation with only a small amount of material; not much can be said in so little a space. . .. Incidents in the play and their results were crucial to the development of the characters, and having a clear depiction of the chain of events helps one to understand what is happening to the Lear daughters and their motivations.

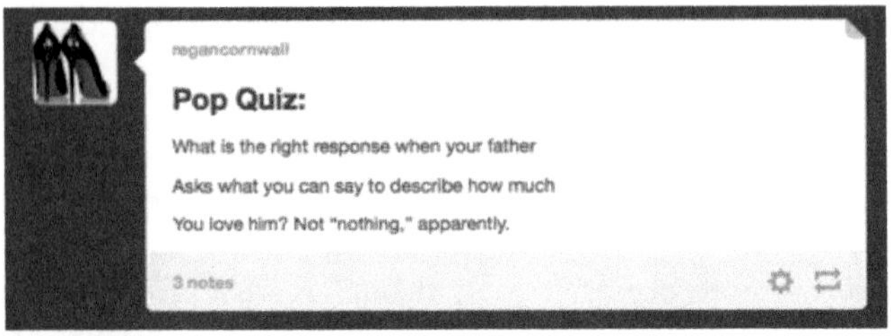

Figure 9: Sample of Lear Family Tumblr.
Class of Jonathan Lamb.

Figure 10: Sample of Lear Family Tumblr.
Class of Jonathan Lamb.

Concluding Thoughts

Having surveyed the results of the assignment, we return to its basic supposition: if students working on a creative project have creative freedom but must also decide how they will be assessed and graded, then they will produce work equally as rigorous and, on the whole, measurably more engaged with the course content than students who choose other options. The central question concerns whether the reflective parts of the assignment (i.e., the assessment plan, the assessment, and the final report), along with the projects themselves, provide evidence of equal rigor and a higher level of engagement with Shakespeare's writings than do other, more conventional projects? The answer, based on the experience of two semesters, is a qualified yes (which in Science usually means "No").[9] The process of planning, making, and assessing a creative project enhanced measurable student engagement beyond the process of writing one of the other essays. We must, however, consider the qualification: the main reason for the visibly higher level of engagement among creative projects is the mandated process of reflection.

The question of how to evaluate creative work, which the assignment asks students to consider, frequently goes hand-in-hand with thoughtful engagement with Shakespeare's writings. This is one of the most fascinating results of the experiment. In asking how they will evaluate their own artistic activity, students almost invariably confront the question of Shakespeare's artistic activity. For instance, the *Lear* family blogger reported that "in coming up with assessment criteria for this project, I chose aspects which I thought would best emphasize an understanding of the Lear family." This choice created a new problem: "it is very difficult to give a good representation [of a character] with only a small amount of material." When she described the project in class, she reflected that such compression is one of the great qualities of Shakespeare's plays, the ability to convey a great deal about characters using very few words. This trend provides a key insight: to assess one's own creative response to Shakespeare's writings necessarily involves contemplating those writings themselves. This experiment has made that connection clearly visible.

These results do not, however, give the creative project unqualified, universal preference. I will not mandate a creative project. The main reason for this is that the assignment revealed no reliable correlation between, on one hand, sophistication of engagement with Shakespeare and, on the other, the choice of the creative project over others. Although the creative project encourages, incentivizes, and systematizes that engagement, it does not ensure it. All the same, the results produced in both iterations of this experiment suggest that the integration of course content into a process of artistic production sets the creative projects apart from others. The assignment generates connections between, on one hand, Shakespeare's writings and our class's intensive study of them and, on the other, students' own interests, values, and imaginative faculties. As one of the Hogwarts sorters wrote in the final report, "I loved this project because it took something as challenging as Shakespeare, and applied it to something I am really passionate about." In this regard, the creative assignment achieves one of the main aims of 332, "to forge connections between past/other cultures and students' own cultures, and to respond in a thoughtful and sustained manner to those connections."

Creative projects that involve robust self-evaluation help students think critically about and engage thoughtfully with Shakespeare's writings. They also encourage students to think carefully about the artistic process—their own, and

[9] See Karl Popper, *The Logic of Scientific Discovery* (London: Routledge, 2002).

those of others. Furthermore, these projects allow students to explore questions of "What if?" that traditional assignments do not. In this sense, the creative project outlined here is rather more scientific than other, more traditional paper options, because it is by definition experimental, hypothesis-driven, and yet controlled by a refined method. It allows for—and indeed encourages—failed experiments, a feature that nicely supplements the positivist impulses of expository writing at the undergraduate level.

Applicability in Chaucer's *Miller's Tale* and Virgil's *Aeneid*

Craig E. Bertolet, Auburn University

One of the challenges of teaching texts written in the Middle Ages or earlier to undergraduates is in convincing them of the relevance of these texts. [1] When they respond to an early text, students often comment on how "relatable" a writer or any one of his or her characters may be to them. By "relatable," they could mean either "believable" or "applicable." Both responses are limited in understanding the text in its own culture and, the older the text, the more difficult it is to bridge the gap between contemporary readers and the possible readers of the time of the text's composition. However, of the two responses, believability keeps the conversation only on the level of verisimilitude or "realism," two concepts that are not aspects of cultural aesthetics before the nineteenth century and from which little significant literary analysis can be generated beyond the level of a review.

By contrast, applicability is a useful means of beginning a serious literary conversation about early texts because applicability allows the readers to discover how that text can delight and instruct them. J. R. R. Tolkien famously defined "applicability" in opposition to "allegory" (which he "cordially detested") by writing that applicability "resides in the freedom of the reader, and [allegory] in the purposed domination of the author."[2] In our context, applicability in a text does not just mean how the written work of an early author can help us understand our lives better. Instead, I use applicability as a way to show my university students how the elements of the text can tell us something about the text and the culture of its author. In other words, I turn applicability from an enquiry into how an early text speaks to a twenty-first-century reader to how we can apply the things that twenty-first-century readers know about understanding literature and our world to analyze and interpret the early text. This practice brings, then, a freedom for the student-reader to find meaning in early texts by using the

---

[1] The many useful posts in the online blog, *In the Middle*, provide different approaches to making primarily medieval texts accessible to contemporary students (http://www.inthemedievalmiddle.com).

[2] J. R. R. Tolkien, "Forward," in *The Fellowship of the Ring* (New York: Ballantine, 1965), 10.

student's experiences in our twenty-first-century culture as a means of access to those texts.

Pierre Bourdieu's explanation of the *habitus* provides a useful methodological framework for talking about applicability through behavioral practices. Bourdieu writes that the *habitus* "is the universalizing mediation which causes an individual agent's practices, without either explicit reason or signifying intent, to be none the less 'sensible' and 'reasonable.'"[3] In other words, individuals act in a way consistent with their society without thinking about it and are able to recognize those practices that they would consider deviant. The *habitus* is what governs acceptable versus unacceptable rules of behavior. These rules are learned, though not necessarily written down. Following them brings social acceptance in this world, breaking them brings some form of separation from the society, either physically through exile or socially through shunning.

My classes work to discover what texts seem to construct of a *habitus* for the characters that provides formulas for inclusion and exclusion. I then want to provide applicable frameworks from our contemporary society in a way to help students interrogate the *habitus* of a text. In other words, I want them to use a twenty-first-century cultural construct to read an earlier text. In this essay, I want to show how I help students make twenty-first-century cultural experiences and literary interpretations applicable to two texts written before 1400: Virgil's *Aeneid* and Chaucer's *Miller's Tale*. The two texts are disparate in both their periods of construction and subject matter. However, they are useful to show how applicability through Bourdieu's *habitus* works in any period. Also, these two texts indicate how social acceptance and rules of inclusion/exclusion appear in a small social group (a medieval town trying to keep the peace) and a large social group (ancient-world nations at war).

Applicability in the *Miller's Tale*

I will take Chaucer's *Miller's Tale* first since this is a work I have taught at different levels of undergraduate studies. I teach this text in its original Middle English so that we can see what the author actually wrote rather than what a translator decided he wrote. I want the students to be able to do three things: 1) study how Chaucer constructs his characters through acceptable and unacceptable behavioral practices of his time, 2) learn how texts represent and reflect culture, and 3) construct an interpretive argument about the text using good reasons to prove their points. The creative format for this lesson is to analyze the *Miller's Tale* as a problem in public relations. Public relations is a useful device because it

[3] Pierre Bourdieu, *Outline of a Theory of Practice*, trans. Richard Nice (Cambridge: Cambridge University Press, 2005), 79.

has as its motivating purpose to ensure a client's inclusion in society, regardless of whether that inclusion is valid or not.

At the end of his tale, the Miller sums up the outcomes of his four principal characters: John the Carpenter is cuckolded for all his jealousy, John's wife Alisoun commits adultery, Absolon the parish clerk kisses Alisoun's bum in his quest to sleep with Alisoun, and Nicholas (who has just committed adultery with Alisoun) gets his bum branded by Absolon. The judgments against the men appear to be punishments for something they have done against the acceptable behavioral practices of late medieval English society. Alisoun's adultery would also be against the acceptable behavioral practices of this society, but the Miller may not have considered her adultery something for which she should be punished. In fact, many scholars examining this summary question the fairness or justness of the Miller's judgments. I want the students to answer this question from the character's perspective to explore how and why the characters behave as they do and what assumptions would the Miller and Chaucer's readers have for allowing these characters to remain as completely acceptable members of their society.

To prepare them for answering this question, we would have been discussing behavioral practices of Chaucer's time, especially involving late medieval urban life since many of Chaucer's pilgrims originate in towns rather than in courts or cloisters. I have provided background material concerning life in medieval London, particularly. Applying Bourdieu's theory of the *habitus* to the tale, we see that each character seeks to behave in ways that may bring what they want while being mindful of how the other inhabitants of the town, in this case Oxford, expect them to behave. John is a successful carpenter and, as the Miller describes him, "a riche gnof" (1.3188).[4] His marriage to the eighteen-year-old Alisoun, many years his junior, is not exactly against the *habitus*. It does, though, cause him anxiety because he fears that she may cuckold him. As a result, he restricts her freedom. He keeps her "narwe in cage" (3224). Both Nicholas and Absolon go against the *habitus* by trying to have adulterous sex with John's wife. Moreover, as clerks, they should be celibate.

But the one person who is clearly the most aware of what is acceptable behavior is Alisoun who, after giving in to Nicholas's entreaties for sex rather quickly, encourages him to be secret or "I nam but deed" (3296). Alisoun's concern is not that she will be killed should she be found committing adultery with Nicholas. Women in late medieval England were not executed for adultery. Instead, she expresses the concern that the public acknowledgement of her adultery would give her a social death through shunning or worse. She understands, as John does too, that the neighbors would not be surprised to find a young wife cheating on

[4] Geoffrey Chaucer, "The Miller's Tale," *Canterbury Tales*, fragment 1, line 3188. All citations from Chaucer follow this format and are from *The Riverside Chaucer*, gen. ed. Larry D. Benson, 3rd ed. (Boston: Houghton Mifflin, 1987).

her older husband and her more perverse or bored neighbors would possibly be anxiously awaiting such news. Also, the presence of so many young men close by at the university can only add to that likelihood. Alisoun's encouragement to Nicholas to be secret or "deerne" is her plea that what they do will be condemned unless no one knows it. Therefore, everything that Nicholas and Alisoun plan and execute is done with the knowledge that they can be ostracized if they were found out. The Miller has already described Nicholas as a clever or "hende" clerk. His character would be best able to meet such a challenge because he seems most qualified in keeping this social transgression secret.

Absolon, by contrast, is the parish clerk and is described as a very public personality. He appears less interested in the *habitus* and more in how to get into Alisoun's bed. Later, he concerns himself with how to punish Alisoun for tricking him into kissing her bum. None of these motivations are consistent with what would be expected from a late-medieval parish clerk who was faithfully fulfilling his calling. When Alisoun offers her bum for Absolon to kiss and when Nicholas does the same thing to him, they respond to an aspect of the *habitus* whereby bum-kissing is considered the worst insult to someone. Alisoun had been trying to fend off Absolon's unwanted attentions and the bum-kissing trick appears to have cured him of his love. Was such a trick necessary? As a consequence, Absolon intends to punish Alisoun for her insult with a white-hot coulter. James H. Morey argues that the coulter is the device used on an adulteress in a trial by ordeal.[5] Therefore, Absolon could be said to be enforcing the *habitus* by his action. That Absolon burns Nicholas instead does not invalidate Absolon's intention. But does it validate his action as just?

Nicholas repeats Alisoun's trick against Absolon when Absolon returns with the coulter, farting for good measure. Why does Nicholas believe he should punish Absolon? Nicholas receives the coulter and cries for "Water," causing the slumbering John to awaken with the thought that a second "Nowells flood" was upon him. John had been duped into hiding in a tub hung by a rope under the eaves of the roof to anticipate the flood. Thinking the call of "Water" was the signal for the flood, he cut the rope holding the tub in place ostensibly to free it to float away on the floodwaters. With no actual flood present, John falls to the street. To explain to the neighbors the reason for the noise and why John is in the street, Nicholas and Alisoun have convinced their neighbors that John is mad. Alisoun's concern for her position in society relative to the *habitus* seems secure when everyone focuses on John rather than on her. That explanation satisfies the neighbors as to the reason for the disturbance and saves her from their judgment as they condemn John's behavior by laughing at him.

Disturbing the peace at night normally would go against the *habitus*. For instance, the 1285 Statutes for London forbade anyone to go about after curfew

[5] James H. Morey, "The 'Cultour' in the *Miller's Tale*: Alison as Iseult," *Chaucer Review* 29 (1995): 373–81.

with arms and weapons to do mischief "or whereof evil suspicion might arise"; anyone found after curfew and judged to be a "nightwalker" was punished.[6] Their laughter may also be a psychological response to a release of anxiety since the cry for "Water" at night could mean that a house was on fire. In the days of wooden houses closely packed together, one house on fire could shortly mean all houses on fire. Finding no fire and only an old lunatic thinking a flood was upon him could have caused the neighbors to laugh in relief as well as in derision. But is this response, especially with John's broken arm, just?

The Miller asks the Canterbury pilgrims tacitly for their agreement on how each of the four characters were treated in the tale when he says that John is punished for "al his kepyng and his jalousye," Nicholas is punished by being "scalded in the towte" or branded on the bum, Absolon is punished with kissing Alisoun's bum or "hir nether ye," and Alisoun is "swyved" (3850–53). By these conclusions the Miller appears to be saying that each character has received a judgment fitting his or her offense. But, as my questions in the previous three paragraphs have asked, is this really the case? By asking the students to analyze the behaviors of the characters as the Miller invites all his readers to do, the students can see how Chaucer has depicted the *habitus* of his urban society while articulating how that society worked. I ask the question at the beginning of the class: Are the punishments fair?

To answer this question, I put the students into four groups and ask them to imagine themselves as public relations firms hired to rehabilitate the character of their client: John, Alisoun, Nicholas, or Absolon. The reason for making each group a public relations firm is that the function of these firms is to create arguments in order to explain or even validate their client's behavior. For the firm to be successful, the members of the firm must know the *habitus*, as it is the measure of social acceptance. A successful public relations campaign can rehabilitate a client's image; an unsuccessful one will cause the client to be separated from society in one form or another. By this explanation, I know that I am oversimplifying what public relations is and does. For the purpose of the class assignment, the figure of the public relations firm works by allowing the students to see applicability of a twenty-first-century cultural paradigm to a medieval text. At the same time, I can get them to see the applicability of the concept of the *habitus* to the reading of a literary text.

Each group is given as a client John, Alisoun, Absolon, or Nicholas. Each group may come up with a name for its "public relations firm," if the members wish. Each group must show how its client does not deserve the judgment he

[6] *Statutes of the Realm*, 11 vols. (1810–1828), 1:102. As many critics have noted, a cook named Roger of Ware (perhaps Chaucer's model for his own Cook) was convicted in 1373 of being a "nightwalker." See *Calendar of Plea and Memoranda Rolls of the City of London Preserved Among the Archives of the City of London at the Guildhall, 1364–1381*, ed. A. H. Thomas, Vol. 2 (Cambridge: Cambridge University Press, 1929), 156.

or she gets at the end of the tale. To make their cases, the "firms" can refer to anything in the text of the tale as evidence. They may also vilify any of the other characters. The groups have ten minutes to make their case, providing a list of reasons from the text to support their arguments.

When the arguments are prepared, all four "firms" have five minutes apiece to present their findings to the class in the forum of a press conference. Each "firm" has a spokesperson to present the case, but any other member of the group can provide corroborating evidence as well. Textual examples need to be quoted in Middle English rather than translated. Most speakers will cite only a few lines in these presentations. During these presentations, no member from any other group may interject or interrupt.

When the fourth "firm" has presented its case, each "firm" is allowed to respond to the arguments presented by the others. Normally, responses follow no particular order. Students can respond when they wish. They often attack the evidence of the others by showing different interpretations of the situations presented in the text, or additional evidence that contradicts the claims of another "firm." The exercise helps the students create their own arguments while also cultivating skills of critical listening so that they are able to rebut the arguments raised by others against their "client."

My role in this forum is to correct any potential misreading of the text (since we read the text in Middle English, errors in translating sometimes occur), answer any culturally based questions, and keep the peace during the ensuing discussion. During the ten minutes that the "firms" are preparing their cases, I circulate around the room in order to answer questions or help clarify passages that may be confusing. This would be the time also when I can offer help in understanding aspects of the *habitus* should that help be needed. Mostly, I listen to how the students are constructing their arguments and how they get energized from closely reading a text that really has not one wasted word in it.

There is no declared "winner" in this "press conference." The outcome of the exercise is that we have examined the tale from the point of view of the four principal characters. As such, I have achieved my objective of studying how Chaucer constructs his characters through acceptable and unacceptable behavioral practices of his time by having the students articulate a defense of those behaviors based on an understanding of the *habitus* of late fourteenth-century urban areas, such as London or Oxford. The students have achieved the objective of learning how texts represent and reflect culture by grounding their understanding of the *habitus* in their interpretation of the text in order to achieve the third objective of constructing an interpretive argument about the text using good reasons to prove their points.

Certainly, things in the text get left out of discussion because of our focus on the characters. For instance, we do not spend any time talking about how the tale is fitting for the Miller to tell. But much of the action in the tale is undertaken by these four characters, and the *Miller's Tale* is one of a very few Canterbury tales that has all the action of the tale concentrated in so many strong characters, each with his or her own motivations. Certainly, some students find themselves uncomfortable justifying Alisoun's adultery. Some also have difficulty validating Nicholas's and Alisoun's lie that John is crazy and making light of his broken arm. The students need to justify the Miller's read on how adultery and foolishness fit in with his society's *habitus*. It is not a question of "believability," but of "applicability."

As a public relations firm may need to defend unsavory characters or actions, so a literary critic must do so as well in order to best understand how that character or action works in the text. For these particular challenges, the *Miller's Tale* is ideal. Chaucer describes the Miller as one of the five churls among the pilgrims. The Miller confesses to being drunk when he tells his story. Chaucer also warns the reader that his tale is going to be problematic, encouraging any reader to turn "over the leef and chese another tale" (3177). Thus, he creates a morally ambiguous tale that justifies adultery, champions the clever over the stupid, and permits laughter at the expense of bodily harm. It is also one of the most intricately constructed tales that Chaucer wrote. Consequently, asking students to justify the behaviors of flawed characters not only helps them to understand better how Chaucer imagined his society, but it also gives them the applicability of the students' own contemporary familiarities to an older text in a difficult language. As such, they also find the text relatable.

Applicability in Virgil's *Aeneid*

Although Virgil's *Aeneid* is much larger in scope than the *Miller's Tale*, having all of the northeastern and central Mediterranean as its stage rather than a mid-sized medieval town, I can still help my students work through the vastness of this text by focusing on *habitus*. I teach the *Aeneid* in translation in a sophomore literature course on World Literature written before 1600. I do gloss important Latin terms from the poem that do not translate easily. Students tend to engage fairly well with the first four books of the *Aeneid*, which describe Aeneas's arrival in Carthage (Book 1), the account of the Fall of Troy (Book 2), Aeneas's travels from Illium to North Africa (Book 3), and Aeneas's affair with Dido (Book 4). Even the descent to the Underworld (Book 6) can garner useful conversations about Virgil's construction of the Land of the Dead and what Aeneas learns there. However, once we move to Books 7 to 12, the so-called Battle Books, conversation grinds to a halt. Lots of characters are introduced, only to have a brief reference later. The principal antagonist, Turnus, is crazy. Aeneas himself is a difficult character to understand. The challenge with this text is to discover how these six books work together and how students can see Ancient Roman culture in this text.

By this point in our conversation about *The Aeneid*, we have discussed how Virgil had made this poem about the Roman virtue of *pietas*, a term that is rendered unhelpfully into English translations as "piety." Piety is only a small part of Roman *pietas*. Essentially, the term means honoring the father, providing for the son, and serving the state. It is a concept that places the group above the individual. It is the principal aspect of *habitus* that is consistent throughout the poem. Our exploration in the first six books is in creating Virgil's sense of Trojan *habitus* and how *pietas* forms a large part of it.

We discuss how the Roman army's success in creating the Roman Empire was due to every soldier fighting as part of a unit rather than as an individual. It is the opposite idea that the Classical Greeks demonstrate in the *Iliad* or *Odyssey*. Achilles's responsibility in the Trojan War is to Achilles and not to Agamemnon or the "Greek cause"; otherwise, he would not have been sulking in his tent for much of the early action of the poem. Odysseus is only interested in Odysseus; otherwise, he would not have feigned madness to avoid joining the war and he also would have been more protective of his crewmen on his homeward journey. By contrast, Aeneas's personal desires mean nothing compared with the requirements of his destiny. Aeneas must find the prophesied land of Italy in order to found a race that would from there conquer the world. He is to do this so that he can provide a kingdom for his son Ascanius (or Iulus) and the other children that he will have in Italy by another wife. He also tries to keep as many of his people together, rather than needlessly sacrificing them as Odysseus does his men. Consequently, whenever he thinks that he can stop to enjoy himself (such as in Carthage with Dido), a god appears to remind him of his duty to his son and to his nation. Aeneas always appears to obey without an argument.

The nation or people are the focus of the *Aeneid* and Aeneas's significance is always relative to his role as father (not just leader) of his people. As the father shows *pietas* by abandoning his own desire for the sake of his son, so Aeneas forgoes his desires in favor of Ascanius's destiny. The focus of the Battle Books is building the nation that will one day become Rome by demonstrating how the Trojan (and Roman) *habitus* is the most successful. According to Virgil at the end of Book 12, the Romans existed before the City of Rome was built, an anachronistic point that fulfills the design Virgil has for the poem. The race that became the Romans began with various threads of different nations that had to come together to make Rome. The Battle Books are really the story of the making of Romans as compared with the first six books that describe how Aeneas gets to Italy and how he learned what his destiny must be. These last six books show how the races that form the Roman people share the same *habitus* and those nations (or individuals) who do not are co-opted or destroyed.

For twenty-first-century American students who have been trained to see individualism as a virtue and communities as groups of individuals electing to come together for a corporate goal, Virgil's Battle Books are difficult to approach. The characters and nations fighting in these wars often seem to have no choice in doing so, being told in dreams or prophecies, being compelled by kings, or being driven mad. Also, since every reader of the *Aeneid* knows how the story is going to end from the very first pages of Book 1, the modern aesthetic literary virtue of suspense is gone. We know that Aeneas will win. But the question remains and what I want the students to get out of this portion of the *Aeneid* is how do we get Romans out of all this? How is their *habitus* constructed and imposed on others?

To make these last six books applicable, I use the paradigm of the embedded reporter in a troop of soldiers popularized during the early years of the wars in Afghanistan and Iraq. The point of the embedded reporter was to provide a perspective on the military action from the level of the soldier. The reporter in this position also tended to do two things in reporting what he (or in rare cases, she) was observing: how what was being done was successful or not and how the practices of our troops compared with those of our allies or enemies. From that perspective, it was impossible to see the entire picture of the campaign and many reporters were needed to provide a comprehensive understanding of the conduct of the war. The reporters found it necessary to focus their attention on individual soldiers in order to give the conflict a human face and also a distinctly American face. But these individual profiles were always within the overall argument that the soldier was doing whatever noteworthy activity to further the war effort. Therefore, the reporter's job was to explain how the actions of the soldiers he or she was covering were praiseworthy and devoted to the collective goal. Praiseworthiness fulfilled the collective goal of the military enterprise. It is also similar to Virgil's *pietas* and his Trojan/Roman *habitus*.

The class exercise of the embedded reporter is to provide an applicable paradigm for students to see how Virgil constructs *pietas* as the successful *habitus* in the second half of his poem. To do so, I form the class into groups that will constitute a reporter pool. Each group or pool will be randomly assigned one of four nations dominant in Books 7–12: the Trojans, the Arcadians, the Latins, or the Rutulians. Each student chooses a slip of colored paper that has the name of the nation to which he or she has been assigned and two or three names of characters. These names are the prominent representatives of the particular nation. For the Trojans, the principals are Aeneas, Ascanius, Nisus, and Euryalus; for the Arcadians, the principals are Evander and Pallas; for the Latins, the principals are Latinus, Amata, and Drances; and for the Rutulians, the principals are Turnus, Camilla, and Mezentius. I give out these slips of paper on the day we discuss Book 7, since this book introduces the conflict that will cover the rest of the *Aeneid*. For class meetings concerning Books 8–12, the students begin each class in their reporting pools to create a five-minute "news report" for presentation later in the class. They spend the first ten minutes of class compiling their "news report."

In preparation for class, the students must read the entire book under discussion for the day, but pay particular attention to what their assigned nation and principals do. My role during the first ten minutes of class on these days is to circulate among the groups to answer questions or provide clarifications. After the reports are prepared, each pool presents its report. I function now as the anchor who directs each group to speak. Each book gives prominence to a different nation, while the reporters for other nations may not have much to say. For instance, the reporters "embedded with" the Latins have a great deal to report in Book 11 but not so much in Book 8. This balance allows the conversation to be on different nations for each class period, so that each group does have an opportunity to be the center of class discussion for at least one day.

Once every group has given its report, we turn to questions on why the actions of the different nations were significant and how they contribute to create the Romans by establishing their *habitus* as being successful. In these conversations, we ask what practices seem to be praised and what condemned. For instance, in Book 9, Ascanius mourns Nisus and Euryalus, two men who betrayed a promise to bring help from Aeneas to the besieged Trojans by plundering the Rutulian camp while the enemy slept. In Book 10, Aeneas kills Magus who begs for mercy. In the final book, Turnus is killed while also begging for mercy. We discuss how these instances should be read relative to the *habitus* Virgil has created, especially since these characters are motivated by personal, rather than collective, good and they all fail. We also discuss with the last book how all the nations that come together to form the Romans adopt the *habitus* of Aeneas.

My pedagogical objectives here are the same as those for teaching Chaucer's *Miller's Tale*. We have been able to study how Virgil constructs his characters through acceptable and unacceptable behavioral practices of his time by understanding how *pietas* is used or complicated. The students have also been able to learn how texts represent and reflect culture by focusing on how each of Virgil's nations are constructed. We discuss what virtues from the different nations are shared or coopted and which are discouraged. Lastly, by having the students focus on how Virgil creates one nation, they are able to construct an interpretive argument about the text using good reasons to prove their points. This approach makes the huge numbers of characters and individual battles in these books manageable by removing the distraction of looking at everyone and everything. It also helps students see how they have been constructing a national identity for their groups over the course of the five class days that address Books 8–12. Finally, the pool of reporters has shown them a collective model applicable to understanding Virgil's Romans.

For both of these texts, Bourdieu's concept of the *habitus* provides a tool to make these early works applicable to them. They are aware of their own rules of social inclusion and exclusion. Giving them the vocabulary to find these same rules in other texts allows them to read these texts as describing cultures that follow similar paradigms as their own. The *Miller's Tale* asks them to see how the individual motivations of a particular character can be justified in that character's own context. The last six books of the *Aeneid* show how collective good in military cultures tends to be more successful than individual heroism. In each case, there are important exceptions and the students discover how the exceptions work (such as justifying Alisoun's adultery in the *Miller's Tale* or the individual combat between Aeneas and Turnus that concludes the *Aeneid*). The students also learn that those exceptions show how each text is a complex exploration of human communities and how the students' own experiences as twenty-first-century readers can make these early texts applicable to them.

Hare We Go!: Deploying Films as Historical Texts in the Freshman Classroom

Charles Beem, University of North Carolina at Pembroke

There is a tired old cliché that says, "you can lead a horse to water, but you can't make him drink." College freshmen can also be highly resistant to what their professors want them to do; you can lead students to knowledge, but you cannot make them think. For those of us who teach for colleges and universities welcoming students of all academic comprehension levels, getting incoming students to apply their critical skills in a history classroom is often a search for a holy grail that remains beyond our grasp. When that transcendent moment does occur, it recalls the climactic moment of the 1962 historical film, *The Miracle Worker,* in which the blind and deaf Helen Keller makes the connection between the sensation of feeling water, and the abstract expression of the word water, which her teacher, Annie Sullivan, has been inscribing onto her hand for much of the picture.

Film possesses an ability beyond the scope of the written word to create visual representations of such historical breakthroughs. As a technological form, film inhabits a variety of contexts: as science and art, as a purveyor of popular mass culture, and also as a means to construct historical narratives. In freshman history survey courses such as my World Civilizations class, whose chronological framework is a runaway train covering the entire premodern world, historical films can be an effective enticement for getting students to think about history and apply their innate critical skills to its study. In this class, students' term papers use scholarly analysis to assess the value of a historical film as historical text. By historical films I mean specifically feature films made for a mass audience, like *The Miracle Worker,* that feature a dramatized, visual representation of a historical narrative. Over the past ten years, I have refined my list of films that lend themselves easily to this form of analysis, and allow students to choose whatever film they want; invariably, I have read countless reviews of *300*, *The Ten Commandments*, *Braveheart*, and *The Other Boleyn Girl.*

What students seem to realize, right away, is that commercially produced feature films, regardless of their level of historical quality, are perceived in our wider culture as historical texts.[1] As film historian Robert Rosenstone has noted, the majority of Americans obtain what they consider to be historical information from visual media such as television and movies.[2] In what has been termed an increasingly postliterate society, the debate has moved from whether to use historical films in the classroom to how best to incorporate them into a meaningful intellectual process.[3]

Before they actually begin to perform such tasks, students warmly embrace the *idea* of watching a Hollywood blockbuster and analyzing its historical qualities.[4] One aspect of my course curricula consists of a series of classroom discussions and exercises that conceptually prepare students for their term paper concerning the relationship between film and history. Initial classroom discussions concerning the value of filmed history tend to agree that feature films are a type of historical artifact possessing enormous popular appeal, which renders them a powerful medium for the shaping of historical perceptions in popular culture.[5] At the end such discussions, students have begun to conceptualize the notion that the construction of historical narratives, both written and visual, is a highly subjective process that wields a hegemonic influence upon how we as a culture view and understand history.

This is not to suggest that studying films is the only way to understand how and why historical narratives are constructed. Manuscripts and printed texts of all kinds are also important historical artifacts possessing many of the subjective complexities of film. However, the more traditional path for enticing critical thinking in the study of history, such as the study of primary texts, or the discussion of historiographical trends, frequently encounters resistance from students fresh out of high school who basically think that the primary task of the historian is the objective search for a collection of "facts." But as soon as they cross the college campus threshold, it is the history instructor's responsibility to convey to students a more nuanced understanding of the discipline—that history remains primarily identified as a body of texts, written or visual, that are interpreted and constructed by a wide range of subjective motivations evolving through time and space. I lecture as lucidly as possible on these ideas, semester after semester,

---

[1] Pierre Sorlin, "How to Look at an 'Historical' Film," in *The Historical Film: History and Memory in Media,* ed. Marcia Landy (New Brunswick, NJ: Rutgers University Press, 2001), 25–27.

[2] Robert Rosenstone, *Visions of the Past* (Cambridge, MA: Harvard University Press, 1995), 22.

[3] Rosenstone, *Visions*, 46.

[4] Robert Brent Toplin, "The Filmmaker as Historian," *American Historical Review* 93, no. 5 (Dec 1988): 1210–27.

[5] See Ray B. Browne, "Foreword," in *Hollywood as Historian: American Film in a Cultural Context,* ed. Peter C. Rollins (Lexington: University Press of Kentucky, 1983), ix–x.

in the introductory phase of the course. Unfortunately, at this still bewildering stage of the semester, not all freshmen are sufficiently oriented academically to comprehend that studying history involves making critical judgments upon contradictory interpretations of historical texts.

For students to engage in such a process, they need to use their critical skills, and all college students possess finely honed critical skills. However, the ones usually recognized and labeled as such are those that are applied to scholastic achievement, and it should be recognized that students who initially lack scholarly critical skills, still bring other forms into the classroom with them. For instance, in this age of social networking and instantaneous forms of communication, nearly all students are trenchant observers and critics of contemporary culture and society, and have had a lot of practice absorbing a plethora of information and making critical judgments upon the world in which they interact, in particular, to the quality of the feature films that they have spent their entire lives viewing and critiquing.[6] Since they come into the class fully equipped with these critical abilities, it represents the closest point at which an explanation of the nature of history meets the intellectual interest and critical savvy of the incoming freshman.

While written texts remain paramount in the classroom, classroom discussions of film narratives can open the door to conceptualizing broad and interconnected categories of historical deconstruction, allowing students to visually identify political structures, economic systems, and the social constructs of race, class, and gender that subdivide all human societies. In this broad context, nearly all feature films are historical, occurring in some recognizable place and time. On one occasion in a classroom discussion the only film the entire class could agree that they had all seen, besides *The Wizard of Oz* (1939), was *E.T. the Extra Terrestrial* (1982). While the class identified the film as fiction, the discussion located the historical context within which the story took place, concluding that E.T. chose Ronald Reagan's first term of office to come to earth to visit a white, middle-class, Southern California suburban landscape, including a single mom who initially had no clue who the children were playing with. As a group, the class did a fine job of historically deconstructing *E.T.*, producing multiple and conflicting interpretations for the motives and agency of the film's characters, a clear display of engaged, intellectual discussion. At this point, the students are ready to tackle a more recognizably historical film.

The next discussion follows the classroom viewing of key scenes from the very first historical blockbuster, D. W. Griffiths' *Birth of a Nation* (1915). [7] To the contemporary student, *Birth of a Nation* is shocking, as its prosegregation-

[6] See Brian Goldfarb, *Visual Pedagogy: Media Cultures in and Beyond the Classroom* (Durham, NC: Duke University Press, 2002), 1–6.

[7] See Tony Barta, "Introduction," *Screening the Past: Film and the Representation of History*, ed. Tony Barta (Westport, CT: Praeger, 1988), 7.

ist, Ku Klux Klan endorsing narrative unfolds. In one of these discussions, one student reached the startling conclusion that historical films contain two interlocking historical narratives that unfold simultaneously. The first is centered in the historical context that the film is attempting to convey, a sense of time, location, and character that the viewer can identify as taking place in the past. The second, more subtle narrative was the film's reflection of the *mores of* the society and culture in which the film was produced and for which it was marketed, as students absorbed the realities of race relations from a century ago through the medium of film.[8] What usually becomes clear to the class is that *Birth of a Nation* functions as a historical text, when a usually, appalled group of students firmly grasps the film's hegemonic message. Such observations revealed that historical films provide an obvious means to understand the concept of subjectivity and its relationship to the construction of historical texts.[9]

Written historical texts also have their own subjective influences—political biases, selective or inadequate research, or, that ultimate of sins, pandering to a popular audience. Films, however, visually amplify the discernible motivations behind historical subjectivity, making a critical analysis of film itself a historical process that possesses obvious corollaries to understanding our current capitalist driven, globally hegemonic, celebrity saturated, popular culture-oriented society, whose features are at least somewhat identifiable to the incoming freshman. In fact, students tend to recognize the different categories of subjectivity present in film much more easily than they do in written texts, as they come to realize that the 300 Spartans who gave their lives at Thermopylae probably did not run around wearing leather jockstraps, or that the pivotal battle scene in the 1995 film *Braveheart* actually occurred upon a bridge.

At this point, students are ready to apply their awareness of subjective influences to a classroom deconstruction of a historical film. While it is not possible for a fifty-minute class to watch an average length feature film in one classroom session, a shorter film can allow the class to both view and deconstruct it within that time frame. To accomplish this task, I use a seven-minute, 1951 Warner Brothers cartoon entitled *Hare We Go!,* which features representations of Christopher Columbus, Ferdinand and Isabella of Spain, and the biggest star on the Warner Brother's lot, Bugs Bunny.[10] In this film, Bugs Bunny displays his unique ability to defy time and space to find Christopher Columbus after he has been tossed out of the palace after losing a debate with King Ferdinand concerning whether the earth is round or flat. After Bugs helps Columbus convince

[8] Michele Faith Wallace, "The Good Lynching and 'The Birth of a Nation': Discourses and Aesthetics of Jim Crow," *Cinema Journal* 43, no. 1 (Autumn 2003): 85–104.

[9] William Hughes, "The Evaluation of Film as Evidence," in *The Historian and Film,* ed. Paul Smith (Cambridge: Cambridge University Press, 1976), 55.

[10] *Hare We Go!,* directed by I. "Fritz" Freleng. See Will Friedwald and Jerry Beck, *The Warner Brothers Cartoons* (Metuchen, NJ: Scarecrow Press, 1981), 158.

Queen Isabella that the world is round (through the deft use of a baseball), he and Columbus set sail for the New World. The crew, however, considers Bugs to be a jinx, and blames him as the weeks pass by with no land in sight. Through the use of trickery, his usual stock in trade, Bugs outwits the crew, who abandon the voyage, while the film concludes with Columbus taking sole credit for the discovery of America, thanks to Bugs Bunny's magnanimity.

It is meant to be funny, and usually catches the class off guard, but the first question posed to them is whether any aspects of this film can be considered to be historical. All class discussions have agreed that the answer is, of course, yes. Most of my students have tended to agree that, if we discount the presence of Bugs Bunny as a highly subjective, extrahistorical addition to our historical narrative (as is Maximus in *Gladiator*), the rest of the cartoon conveys the essence of Columbus's first voyage, and conforms to our collective recognition of this momentous event in world history.

Once the film's historical basis was established, the class explored the unhistorical aspects of the film in wide ranging detail. Returning to the question of subjective motivations, nearly all class discussions concluded that the film was designed as a vehicle for Bugs Bunny, rather than a means to film the story of Christopher Columbus. Further discussion revealed that this situation was not an isolated incident; historical films, from *Marie Antoinette* with Norma Shearer (1938), to *Lady Sings the Blues* with Diana Ross (1972), were conceived as historical vehicles primarily to showcase the performing talents of their stars, rather than a desire to create an accurate historical narrative. As the historical characters Marie Antoinette and Billy Holiday suffered serious distortions for the sake of Hollywood glamour, it was the same for Queen Isabella, in this cartoon depicted as a bleach blonde caricature of Lana Turner who talked like Mae West, hardly an accurate portrayal of a pious, hard-working, but dour fifteenth-century female monarch whose actual hair color was auburn.

The manner in which the rest of the film's characters talked, also allowed the discussion to uncover the cultural norms of 1951 America. Legendary voice artist Mel Blanc, who supplied all the voices in the film, was famous for his ability to recreate a kaleidoscope of stereotypical inflections: Italian, Hispanic, southern, as well as Bugs Bunny's famous Brooklyn accent. So, King Ferdinand speaks in a Mexican accent reminiscent of cartoon character Speedy Gonzales, another one of Blanc's creations, while Columbus speaks in a caricature of the Italian stereotype, as do the sailors on the Santa Maria; when Bugs fooled one sailor into thinking the ship had landed, by placing a postcard in front of a periscope of the Manhattan skyline, circa 1951 (as seen from the Jersey side) the sailor screamed "she's a land!" Are these accents acceptable in our present-day society? Most class discussions indicate no, agreeing that contemporary historical films no longer contain such outdated stereotypes of ethnic speech patterns, and concluding that this film could not be made today without substantial rewrites of the ethnic stereotypes that audiences found so funny in 1951. When they thought about it, students also realized that new forms of archetypal stereotypes such as gang members or gays and lesbians are continuously created and deployed in historical films, displaying their collective recognition of the dynamic means by which societies reflect themselves in their art forms as they move through time and space.

In the final phase of the discussion, I try to steer the class to an even deeper deconstruction of the film, to see whether the film conveys a hegemonic message. In this part of the discussion, I attempt to negotiate deftly the line between suggesting lines of inquiry while allowing the discussion to go down whatever productive avenue it follows. Our discussion of *Birth of a Nation* has already enlightened students to the notion that even in capitalist and democratic countries historical films are capable of conveying hegemonic messages designed to further "condition" the movie-going populace, who then give their consent to the social, economic, and political objectives of the dominant ruling classes.[11]

The question the class needs to consider is whether *Hare We Go!* fits within this model. Students have noted that Columbus's voyages have long symbolized the process of European colonization of the Americas, and have been invariably presented in a positive light in American history. Most of my classes have agreed that the cartoon presents this basic historical message, and reinforces the legitimacy of neo-European hegemony over North America. Increasingly, Native and African American students have challenged the view of Columbus as a positive historical figure, seeing him instead as the iconic representation of a historical process that inflicted untold suffering on the ancestors of both of these racial groups. These viewpoints emerged from classroom discussions, as students displayed their ingenuity in deconstructing the cartoon's possible ideological motivations.

Following this series of classroom discussions concerning the relationship between film and the construction of historical narratives, the class is now prepared to tackle their final semester written project, a scholarly review of a historical film of their choice. The assignment's structure includes making the distinction between fiction and nonfiction, deducing the film's accuracy in recreating a historical setting, and drawing a conclusion concerning the film's value as a historical text. Students tackle the different components of their review in stages throughout the semester and are required to revise graded drafts for their final product. Since the project requires evidence of scholarly research, students go off in search of historical evidence, increasingly on the Internet, which abounds with

[11] See Marcia Landy, "Introduction," in *The Historical Film: History and Memory in Media* (New Brunswick, NJ: Rutgers University Press, 2001), 1–8. Landy draws the correlation between the making of historical films and the concept of "cultural hegemony," originated by Italian Marxist theorist Antonio Gramsci. See also Antonio Gramsci, *Selections from the Prison Notebooks,* ed. and trans. Quintin Hoare and Geoffrey Nowell Smith (New York: International Publishers, 1978), 323–33, 419–25.

historical information of widely varying quality. Students are warned of this and encouraged to cross the threshold of the university library, and use the search engines available to them in order to arrive at a critical judgment of their chosen film's value as a historical text. Even those students who fail to engage in any meaningful historical analysis often write lively and well-constructed narratives describing the film that in many cases exceed the quality of their essay examinations. But the best ones reveal an application of critical skills applied to the scholarly analysis of historical texts, and meet the instructor's overall goal of conveying to students an understanding of the nature of historical study and analysis.

Putting Sir Gawain on Trial

Kimberly Jack, Athens State University

In my five years as an instructor at Auburn University, I taught a total of twenty sections of World Literature I. Each year I faced the challenge of introducing premodern texts and their historical, religious, and cultural contexts to students who, as non-majors, often began the class dreading the subject matter and the reading load. Most terms, course evaluations included at least one variation on the statement that the subject matter was not "relevant to anything [the student] intend to pursue with a career." This response reflects a student perception that their "eventual contribution. . .to the economic well-being of society is the key criterion of effective schooling,"[1] and that general education requirements that do not clearly relate to job placement are superfluous. To that end, students focus on concrete, easily measurable markers such as the memorization of terminology and processes related to specific jobs. Rather than vocationalizing higher education, I advocate efforts like those of Henry A. Giroux that focus on "providing students with the skills, knowledge, and authority they need to inquire and act" in society, "[cultivating] the capacity for critical judgment."[2] As an educator, I endeavor to encourage in my students the desire to learn, the ability to assess individual circumstances and make critical decisions, and the self-confidence to assert authority and make informed decisions in their lives within and outside of academia.

Putting these beliefs into practice challenges me to craft creative and engaging approaches to premodern texts, tailored to a multi-disciplinary student body. For one of my most successful assignments, my students are tasked to put Sir Gawain, the hero of the fourteenth-century Middle English poem *Sir Gawain and the Green Knight*, on trial. My experience running this exercise has been that it inspires self-motivated learning and critical assessment, creative play, improvisation, and the forging of connections across disciplines.

---

[1] Michael P. Breen, "Teaching Language in the Postmodern Classroom," *Barcelona English Language and Literature Studies* 10 (1999): 49.

[2] Henry A. Giroux, "Critical Pedagogy and the Postmodern/Modern Divide: Towards a Pedagogy of Democratization," *Teacher Education Quarterly* (Winter 2004): 39, 40.

The mock trial is a flexible format that can be adapted to multiple disciplines and class contexts. The use of mock trials for education purposes has been documented in "several disciplines, including law, psychology, business, and nursing."[3] The mock trial provides an interactive framework that may be tailored to each instructor's discipline and goals. Future lawyers and family therapists train in the protocols and ethical considerations regarding expert testimony.[4] Nursing students learn the merits of evidence-based practice in examining the medical ethics of family-witnessed resuscitation.[5] Freshmen in a literature-based composition course debate, collaborate, and write closing arguments for the trial of the title character in *Tess of the D'Urbervilles*, a scene not included in Hardy's novel.[6] Whatever the subject matter, the mock trial encourages students to "employ critical thinking skills in an active learning environment."[7] In my own mock trial exercise, I challenge students from a variety of disciplines and backgrounds not only to assess the actions of the fictional characters of *Sir Gawain and the Green Knight*, but also the premodern and postmodern contexts through which we determine the meaning of and ethics behind the four crimes with which Gawain is charged.

In the poem around which my mock trial activity revolves, a mysterious, green-skinned, green-garbed knight enters Camelot during a Christmas feast and proposes an exchange of strokes, which is accepted by King Arthur's nephew Gawain. Gawain beheads the Green Knight, at which point the headless knight stands, picks up his head, and tells Gawain to seek him in a year and a day at the Green Chapel. After a fruitless search, Gawain accepts the hospitality of Lord Bertilak, master of Castle Hautdesert, over Christmas. Lord Bertilak offers a

[3] Andrea M. Centrella-Nigro and Donna Flynn, "Teaching Evidence-Based Practice Using a Mock Trial," *The Journal of Continuing Education in Nursing* 43, no. 12 (2012): 566. See also Judith Ettinger, "Using a mock trial activity for interdisciplinary learning," *Developments in Business Simulation and Experiential Learning* 28 (2001): 49–56; A. L. Marsh, et al., "The mock trial: A collaborative interdisciplinary approach to understanding legal and ethical issues," *Nurse Educator* 36, no. 2 (2011): 66–69; and B. Staffileno and C. McKinney, "Utilizing a mock trial to demonstrate evidence-based nursing practice: A staff developmental process," *Journal for Nurses in Staff Development* 26, no. 2 (2010): 73–76.

[4] John K. Miller, Deanna Linville, Jeff Todahl, and Joe Metcalfe, "Using Mock Trials to Teach Students Forensic Core Competencies in Marriage and Family Therapy," *Journal of Marital and Family Therapy* 35, no. 4 (2009): 456–64.

[5] Centrella-Nigro and Flynn, "Teaching Evidence-Based Practice," 566–70.

[6] Michael W. Young, "The Classroom Trial of 'Tess of the D'Urbervilles': A Way to See, Speak, Hear, and Live a Persuasive Essay" (paper presented at the Annual Meeting of the Conference on College Composition and Communication, Cincinnati, OH, March 19–21, 1992).

[7] Norma J. Shepelak, "Employing a Mock Trial in a Criminology Course: An Applied Learning Experience," *Teaching Sociology* 24 (2006): 395.

Guide to lead Gawain to the Green Chapel, and proposes an entertainment for the interim. Bertilak will lead hunts over three successive days while Gawain sleeps late and spends his days with the ladies of the court, including an old woman and Bertilak's wife. At the end of each day, they will exchange their winnings. While Bertilak hunts deer, a boar, and a fox, Lady Bertilak enters Gawain's chamber each morning while he's still abed, engaging him in suggestive conversation leading to an increasing series of kisses. On the third morning, she offers him a green girdle or sash, promising that it will protect him from bodily harm. Gawain dutifully remits the kisses to Lord Bertilak each evening, but he conceals the girdle. During the ride to the Green Chapel, the Guide suggests that Gawain not face the Green Knight, and promises to lie to protect Gawain's reputation. Instead, Gawain continues to the Green Chapel, flinches from the Green Knight's first stroke, and on the first stroke receives a non-fatal cut to his neck. The Green Knight reveals that he is Lord Bertilak, his wife acted on his orders, and the plan was devised by the old woman, who is actually Gawain's aunt and King Arthur's enemy, Morgan LeFay. Gawain initially reacts by blaming women and then his own flaws, and returns to Camelot wearing the green girdle as a sign of his own failings.

The Trial of Sir Gawain, which I facilitate for seventy-minute sections (Tuesday/Thursday) or ninety-minute sections (Summer term) of World Literature I, involves staging a mock trial of Sir Gawain on each of four charges: adultery, avarice, cowardice, and oath-breaking. Students are assigned to study groups of four to eight students (depending on class size) at the beginning of the term, and each of these groups is assigned a role in the trial. Two groups function as prosecution and defense teams. Other groups take responsibility for pairs of witnesses—one major and one minor—such as Gawain and Arthur, Lord Bertilak and the Guide, or Lady Bertilak and Morgan. They are directed to look for evidence and witness statements in the official "deposition" of the events, the Tolkien translation of *Sir Gawain and the Green Knight* available in the *Longman Anthology of World Literature*. Groups are also encouraged to look up definitions and contexts for the specific charges. As the instructor, I serve as judge, and I invite faculty members and graduate students to sit in as a jury. Rather than break up the mock trial over two days for fifty-minute sections of this course, groups instead present legal briefs for each of these roles, followed by in-class debate over the charges.

The mock trial activity engages students in a performance of the legal dramas and crime procedurals that have been ubiquitous on American television for decades. My students at Auburn rarely have experience of real courtroom dynamics or knowledge of legal precedent, but most are familiar with the basic jargon and procedure of theatrical courtrooms from television dramas ranging from *Matlock*, *Perry Mason,* and *JAG* to *Boston Legal*, *Ally McBeal*, or *Drop Dead Diva*. Situating discussion of a medieval narrative poem within the familiar framework of legal drama gives students the confidence to assert their own authority and expertise. The context allows students to "[play] out the new, but familiar roles. . .[giving] the students the invigoration to think critically on their own."[8] Instead of reading for basic plot details, expecting the instructor to highlight thematic connections in lecture or writing prompts, students take ownership of the poem. They assume the mantle of witness, prosecution, or defense, creatively and critically exploring textual evidence for the characters' motivations and actions. Although students are sometimes intimidated by the language, structure, or cultural context of the Middle English poem, they feel that they can enter and interact within the world of the imaginative courtroom as long as—in the words of one student—they "brush up on their *Law & Order*."

Because of the ubiquity of legal procedurals in American popular culture, students often respond to the activity with creativity, imagination, and a spirit of playfulness.[9] In one memorable section, the prosecution team scored a hit to the defense's morale when they filed into the room for an 8:00 a.m. session attired in suits and carrying briefcases. Despite the effort the defense had put into preparing arguments, their opponents' attire placed them off-balance, causing the team-member responsible for delivering opening statements to lose his place in the notes and falter in his delivery. The tension in the room during "jury deliberations" was later alleviated when the one male member of the prosecution complained bitterly about having to wear closed-toe shoes, a protestation met with glares from his group-mates wearing heels. Students from this section of the class gained a practical awareness of our enculturated responses to sartorial display, knowledge unrelated to the official course content but invaluable in future business and social situations.

In another class, a carefully-prepared line of questioning was derailed when the student taking the stand as Lady Bertilak left everyone in giggles over her tearful protestations that she was "simply a good, dutiful wife" who flirted with Gawain against her wishes because, as she declared: "my husband made me do it!" This one student's improvised response effectively countered the defense's main argument, which was that Gawain was innocent of adultery because Lady Bertilak, the "whore" and seductress, had entrapped him. The defense was unable to adapt their strategy to the alternative characterization of Lady Bertilak as obedient but maligned wife, worthy of sympathy rather than condemnation. The performance dynamic of the mock trial allowed for improvisation and reinterpretation of the text by one creative student, producing unexpected and memorable results.

Because students are not equally comfortable with the performance dynamic inherent in the exercise, assigning the roles to groups rather than individuals provides students with the authority to negotiate their own division of

[8] Young, "The Classroom Trial."

[9] Breen promotes such "discoursal play" in the classroom as participating in some of "the key features of *child-like* learning," in "Teaching Language," 54, 59.

responsibilities.[10] Those students within each group most comfortable with public speaking take the stand as the "voice" of a given witness, present opening and closing arguments for their legal team, or question the witness on a specific charge. Students who are acutely uncomfortable with public speaking or performance adopt the roles of researcher, speechwriter, or notetaker, providing necessary support for the speaking members of their group. In practice, this division of labor takes various forms determined by the group themselves. During mock trial performances, some groups take the stand together, allowing the support members to identify relevant textual passages and feed them to the appointed speaker on the spot. In one instance, this tactic backfired when two members of the group representing Sir Gawain answered a yes or no question simultaneously with opposite answers. The prosecutor then declared that he would like to direct further questions to the "part of Gawain's brain" that had answered as he wished. Other groups keep their speaker and researchers physically separated, requiring a runner to ferry notes between them. In some instances, groups assign different members to research and present on each of the four charges—adultery, avarice, cowardice, and oath-breaking. Other groups assign a small portion of their members to the lesser witness role (such as the Guide), reserving the larger number to focus on the major witness (Bertilak). Each group must negotiate internally to determine the division of responsibilities and how they will present themselves during the mock trial, mirroring the real-world dynamic of group work practiced in many job fields, including the legal profession.

In addition to navigating group dynamics, successful participation in the mock trial requires self-motivated, independent research and discovery. Group assignments are given before students begin reading the poem. The assignment prompt includes the suggestion that they read carefully, taking notes on evidence pertaining to their assigned role as they read. One or two class periods are devoted to discussion of the first three sections of the poem before the date of the mock trial, during which I model the identification and interpretation of textual evidence relevant to each of the four charges. For example, I often question the ramifications for the charge of adultery of the precise terms of Lord Bertilak's proposed exchange, highlighting Bertilak's expectation that Gawain spend his waking hours comforting himself with Lady Bertilak's company (1100), or the assumption from Bertilak's court that they will learn the art of "love-speech" from the knight (925–27).[11] Likewise, we examine the ring and ornamented sash

---

[10] Breen advocates a postmodern classroom in which "learners are immediately confronted with key decisions to be made." In the case of my own mock trial exercise, the group structure permits students to negotiate their own "preferences in the focus and procedures of the work to be done" ("Teaching Language," 57)

[11] Anonymous, "Sir Gawain and the Green Knight." vol. B, 2nd edition. Trans.: J. R. R. Tolkien. Ed.: David L. Pike, Sabry Hafez, Haruo Shirane, and Pauline Yu. New York: Pearson, 2009. Citations are to line numbers.

that Lady Bertilak offers to Gawain on the third morning, discussing potential interpretations of this scene for the charges of avarice, cowardice, and oath-breaking. I clearly indicate that in-class discussion does not include all potential textual evidence, and that groups are responsible for identifying additional textual references from these parts, as well as for combing part four for passages that represent the depositions of witnesses.

When a witness takes the stand during the mock trial, they further practice critical-reading techniques when they read and interpret passages from the poem as the basis for their testimony. The attorneys often request that the witness read or respond to specific passages to support a line of questioning, or use one passage to counter the apparent meaning of another passage during cross-examination. For example, the statement that Gawain "wore not for worth nor for wealth this girdle" (2038) is often cited as defense against the charge of avarice. Savvy prosecution members may then reference Gawain's self-accusation of "Coveting" in line 2381. The support members of each group sit with books open before them, thumbing through and noting relevant lines to feed to the groups' speakers in an ongoing battle of references. This activity, more than any other I have tried with my World Literature classes, excites the students to engage in close reading, and fixes the intricate details of the poem in their memories. Students have told me, years afterward, that they still recall both the in-class activity and the specific passages upon which key arguments in the trial hinged. This result is noted by others who utilize mock trial activities in the classroom. For example, Shepelak states that "such an applied approach not only helps [students] acquire and retain the substantive material, but also increases their motivation and enjoyment in the class."[12] While the mock trial frame is more directly applicable to the subject matter of Shepelak's criminology course, analysis of this fourteenth-century poem's details within the formal constraints of witness testimony, cross-examination, et cetera. enhances student retention, focus, and enjoyment.

While all groups must cite primary textual evidence, the most successful groups often expand their research into secondary sources to establish context, both pre- and postmodern, for their arguments. The assignment prompt recommends researching definitions of the precise terms of the charges, since I intentionally do not provide definitions of "adultery," "cowardice," "oath-breaking," and "avarice." The English language has undergone significant shifts since the fourteenth century, a development that students can best understand by confronting specific examples. Rather than expounding on linguistic changes in lecture, I encourage students to research definitions and argue meanings to gain advantage in the trial. Students generally assume that they know what "adultery" and "cowardice" mean because they have encountered the terms in current cultural contexts. However, they are sometimes taken aback by interrogation of and

[12] Shepelak, "Employing a Mock Trial," 397.

clever framing of these definitions. For example, one defense team successfully argued that Gawain should be found innocent of the charge of adultery because his actions involved no more than an exchange of kisses, and by those standards both Lady and Lord Bertilak were as guilty as the knight. Since the prosecution had introduced Lord Bertilak as the victim of Gawain and Lady Bertilak's adultery, the implication that their client was equally guilty caught them off guard. Students are less comfortable relying on assumed definitions of "avarice" and "oath-breaking." My choice of "oath-breaking" rather than "perjury," and "avarice" rather than "greed" in the assignment are deliberate attempts to prompt students to research for clarification. These archaic variants imply historical and religious contexts, leading students to question the appropriate signification. In most cases, students seek clarification of these concepts through Internet searches. Prosecution and defense attorneys regularly quote postmodern popular speakers and writers to illustrate the distinctions between feeling fear or lust, and acting on those feelings. In many cases, they also turn to scriptural evidence for definitions of the four charges as sin, and for analogous stories demonstrating sin or the possibility of forgiveness. In one memorable instance, the prosecution confidently opened with a single scriptural condemnation of adultery, only to be overwhelmed by a series of scripturally based counters from a witness who also happened to be a religion major.[13] In order to provide historical and cultural context for definitions of "oath-breaking" and "cowardice," students often choose to read up on medieval concepts of chivalry. Although the sources these groups cite for definitions of chivalry are usually general rather than scholarly, the material they quote is readily identifiable as paraphrases from medieval sources, most commonly Caxton's translation of Ramon Lull's *Libre del orde de Cauayleria*, or Geoffroi de Charny's *Livre de chevalerie*. This level of scholarship is not mandatory for the completion of the assignment, but the spirit of competitiveness regularly inspires students to engage in independent research.

The deliberate lack of definitions for the four charges in the assignment prompt regularly triggers a linguistic battle over the meaning of these terms. I encourage the interplay of competing definitions to raise the students' awareness that a given word may function within a multiplicity of contexts. Students quickly recognize the slippery relationship between signifier and signified (without knowing the formal terminology) as they attempt to assert their group's preferred definition of a key term. I have observed prosecution and defense teams quoting various online dictionaries, theological treatises, legal precedents, psychology textbooks, and occasionally premodern sources. The response of the students to these competing definitions is intriguing, although the students them-

[13] Breen encourages a classroom dynamic in which "the pluralism of the learners'. . . identities become resources to be *explicitly* valued and mined," just as my student "valued and mined" the cross-disciplinary knowledge of his own major ("Teaching Language," 53).

selves may not be aware of their reactions. When confronted with one group that assumes a shared cultural understanding and another group that quotes a definition from an outside source, students generally respond by reiterating the phrasing of the quoted source. When faced with competing definitions drawn from current dictionaries (print or web) or specialized sources (i.e., theology, psychology, et cetera), students privilege the specialized sources over general dictionaries, regardless of potential anachronism. This was particularly evident to me, as an observer, when a member of the defense openly read a twentieth-century definition of cowardice from their psychology textbook, after which both witness and prosecution representatives attempted to echo and work around key phrases from this definition. However, when a definition is presented—correctly or incorrectly—as pertaining to the same cultural milieu as *Sir Gawain and the Green Knight*, students privilege the premodern definition over postmodern sources. Although these observations reflect a small sample of students from a single institution and a relatively short period of time, they raise interesting questions regarding students' automatic hierarchizing of sources. Students appear to privilege specialized jargon over general definitions, and do not always analyze the appropriateness of applying a late-twentieth-century theoretical understanding to premodern texts. When presented with a definition supposedly contemporary to the poem's composition, however, they prioritize this phrasing over modern or postmodern constructions.

I initially created the Trial of Sir Gawain assignment in an effort to engage the interest of undergraduate non-majors who viewed this poem as intimidating and irrelevant to their career goals. In practice, the activity became one of my most entertaining and challenging group projects. Students were energized by the alternative use of class time, the competitive dynamic of the trial setting, and the threat of looking unprepared before an outside audience invited in as jury. They responded with a depth of preparation few students applied to other texts, and with creative and often surprising arguments reflecting the application of independent research and knowledge from their disparate fields. The result was not only entertaining, but extraordinarily diverse. For each section of the class, the jury was instructed to deliver separate verdicts on the four charges. These verdicts were never precisely the same between any two sections. The quality and ingenuity of students' performances, their research, and their ability to adapt to new tactics on the spot inevitably resulted in surprising conclusions to the exercise. Where one class proved Gawain guilty of adultery based on predominantly scriptural arguments, another class would achieve an innocent verdict because he did not, according to current legal definitions, have sex with and therefore commit adultery with Lady Bertilak. While most juries ruled Sir Gawain guilty of oath-breaking, the most clear-cut of the four charges, others found him innocent due to entrapment, or declared that he was guilty, but had "served his time" in the form of the scar upon his neck. Students regularly left class engaged in friendly bickering over the various verdicts, reiterating key textual evidence, or laughing at particularly clever ploys.

The Trial of Sir Gawain is an active learning exercise[14] designed to allow students to engage a fourteenth-century Middle English poem through a postmodern, pop culture context. The ubiquity of theatrical legal proceeding provides students with a comfortable framework in which to assume authority over their readings of the poem and presentation of the details before a larger audience. The competitive dynamic of the trial regularly inspires students to independently research the premodern context in which it was composed, or alternative definitions of key terminology. In an undergraduate literature survey course for non-majors, students indicate that they are overwhelmed or intimidated by lectures intended to establish the premodern context of each of the compositions they read. In contrast, the Trial of Sir Gawain is a playful, challenging, and memorable exploration of a premodern text, as well as an exercise in negotiating meaning between premodern and postmodern cultural perspectives, beliefs, and laws. The activity encourages students to assume authority in determining workload within their groups, to draw on knowledge from their own disciplines to enhance their arguments, and to utilize critical thinking skills in an improvisational performance. The positive response I have received from both students and the colleagues invited to serve as jury members during these exercises suggests that this exercise strikes that delicate balance Sir Philip Sidney claimed for poetry, the ability "to teach and to delight."[15]

---

[14] Shepelak describes the mock trial as a "simulation that encourages higher-order learning" in "an active learning environment" ("Employing a Mock Trial," 395).

[15] Sir Philip Sidney, "An Apology for Poetry," in *Critical Theory Since Plato*, ed. Hazard Adams (Fort Worth, TX: Harcourt Brace Jovanovich, 1992), 143–92.

Talking with the Dead: Teaching Early Modern History with Social Media

Renee Bricker, University of North Georgia

What if Martin Luther had had a Twitter account when he purportedly posted his ninety-five theses? What Tweets would express the challenges of the sixteenth-century religious reformations? Instead, with nail and mallet, Luther hammered his set of propositions to a cathedral door. In doing this he invited the debate and discussion that eventually exploded into the Protestant Reformations.[1] Argument, discussion, and conversation—all are important components to the exchange among people that can lead to intellectual and personal growth. In a history class, events like Luther's posting centuries ago are remote and seemingly inaccessible. Fortunately, social media offers tools to help our students navigate the distance between them and "back then." Here historiographical concerns arise organically because these activities situate students at the border between consumer and producer of history. What follows is a rationale and discussion with examples of these digital tools put to work in my own early modern undergraduate history courses.

In the twenty-first-century classroom, various social media and interview assignments can be used to create student projects that tap into the impulse to make the past less foreign and distant. Along with readings and lectures, each of the activities described below addresses outcomes essential to learning in ways students find engaging, familiar, and challenging to varying degrees.[2] Social media are wholly about interactions between people. The following projects include using a course blog, Twitter, and social bookmarking. Each assignment described below is adaptable to course goals and styles. Moreover, assignments already used in class can often be refashioned to be a digital enterprise. The blog is one such example.

---

[1] See Tom Standage, "How Luther Went Viral," *The Economist* December 29, 2011. http://www.economist.com/node/21541719

[2] See American Association of Colleges & Universities http://www.aacu.org/leap/essential-learning-outcomes.

Social Media: Blogging

A course blog, or web-log, is a social networking platform that can be a simple online diary or a complex information conduit with many authors, as with students collaborating in a course. The blog assignment described here combines features of both. It is also an adaptation of another of my traditional pen and paper assignments for which students create commonplace books, then write responses to quotations from their readings and to each other's work. Students choose a historical persona to assume in order to compose a series of blog posts from that perspective, which also becomes a device to compose responses to the others in the class.

The answers students construct are drawn from their synthesis and analysis of research done on their topic. Assessment is based on the substantive quality of the initial post and the quantity and substance of their responses to others. Further, the blog assignment scaffolds the tasks of research and crafting an essay required later in the course. It is also the basis for a final class presentation. The presentation asks for an informal report on students' topics with their bifocal reflection of the blog itself as it relates both to what they learned about their topic and about digital literacy. The first step is simply to get the project ready to launch.

For the instructor this means creating a site; for the students this means choosing a historical figure from a list I provide of people, events, or objects. One method I have used asks them to make three ranked choices from which I make the final assignment. The other is more random and asks them to pick pieces of paper from a hat, with a brief opportunity to trade. In both cases, the idea is to avoid duplication, though this would make an interesting exercise as well because of the opportunity to consider different interpretations of the same person or event. They also have the option to propose something. With their topic chosen, next they research it to prepare a biopoem, discussed further below, and to compose a series of posts to other participants.[3]

Through their blog compositions, students mediate concerns of the past using that persona. As Charles Beem observed elsewhere in this volume, students can be stumped by the realization that historical interpretation is just that, interpretations drawn from sometimes competing sources. Wrestling with the concerns of the past from a historical figure's perspective creates conditions for students to achieve deep learning and practice skills of inquiry and critical analysis, along with communication. Because I emphasize relationships of authority and social organization, I pose questions for them to undertake that challenge them to ponder and address a situation not as they would wish but according to

[3] The biopoem is an activity I did not develop but came across years ago and adapted for the blog.

the constraints of their figure, to consider what was at stake for the people of the past. What means were available for resolving disputes? What might influence one or another choice made in the end?

Inviting students to see and engage these questions through the eyes of their historical figure complicates the past for students in tangible ways. Students shift from individual work to networks of communication as they engage the subject matter and one another in volleyed posts. As they interact in the guise of their respective historical personae, the class blog becomes a virtual environment populated with late medieval and early modern artifacts. To achieve any of this requires creating that chosen persona. That is where the biographical profile assignment, called the biopoem, gets students started on research and prepares them to blog.

The biopoem is a list poem bracketed by a line each for the first and last names. Nine lines between them include a line naming four traits, followed by lines that describe the character as a relative of, lover of, feels, needs, fears, gives, would like to see, resides where, then the final line. Students use their own words with the reassurance that poetry-writing skills are not among the benchmarks for assessment. They also submit a references list. The example below is from a student who chose Johann Gutenberg's printing press for his biopoem persona. The bold face words in each line indicate the specific order of composition.

1. My **first name** is printing, indeed it is true.
2. **(Four traits that describe the character)** I'm made of metal, useful, heavy, and expensive too.[4]
3. **I was born (relative of)** from innovation, paper, and ink from Flanders
4. I **love (should list several things)** literature, top shelf ink, and Gutenberg the print master
5. Crafted from metal, I **feel (should list several things)** slick, metallic, and cold.
6. I **need (should list several things)** paper, ink, and skilled hands, truth be told.
7. I **fear (should list several things)** rust, censorship, and the Catholic Inquisition.

Any of these can ruin my book-making mission.

[4] This line unfortunately declares incorrectly that the fifteenth-century press was metal, not wood. The author knew the movable type was metal not the press; this became part of a larger classroom discussion about source evaluation and precision in communication.

8. **I give (should list several things)** knowledge, books, and power to the masses.
9. **I'd like to see (should list several things)** higher literacy rates, more patrons, and school reading classes.[5]
10. **(Resident of)** I became popular in **Europe** and her various colonies.
11. I suppose my **last name** would have to be press.[6]

A bold choice, this student provides a good illustration showing that not all selections need be confined to people.

Once the biopoem is complete, students upload it together with an appropriate image to create their blog presence. Often a good source for copyright-free images is Wikipedia, though at first this information is withheld from them. I want them to try to locate material on their own without help from me. This is another opportunity to cultivate and hone Internet research skills using databases and multiple search engines to locate textual and visual sources. It is also an important opportunity to discuss what it means to plagiarize or violate copyright, and to help them understand fair use.

Taking the example above, with the biopoem and image posted, students then react to the printing press from the perspective of their historical figure. Thus, Luther, Queen Elizabeth I, Erasmus, Peasant Woman, and Catholic Church each post something that also relates to their respective historical conditions. In this way, students apply the research done for their character to consider the situation of another. Finally, students respond to reactions both to their biopoem figure in three to five sentences, and to a minimum of five different personae. These parameters are arbitrary, predicated on my hope that simplicity ensures quality. Inevitably, some biopoems garner more attention than others. To offset this, so that everyone has a reaction to which they must respond, students are directed to look first for post sites with no reaction entries.

Students enjoy the opportunity to be creative with the biopoem while the less adventurous among them happily choose predictable topics other than the Pope's Elephant or the Tower of London. Responses they formulate are often thoughtful, even meditative, sometimes asking questions, sometimes expressing a flared temper, as did the student who chose to personify Gustavus Adolphus hearing news of the Sack of Magdeburg. Students are given creative latitude in character development, if they so wish; but, all of these require historical research. A student interested in Ireland chose "peasant woman." This complicated the discussions of religious reformation with the addition of an amalgam composed

[5] Originally, this line in the biopoem began, "**I want,**" which the student-author interpreted as, "**I'd like to see.**"

[6] Christopher Patterson, blog post, HIST3220 Renaissance-Reformation, University of North Georgia, April 2007.

of Ireland, gender, and non-elite experiences. Students who chose the Russian Ambassador, Suleiman the Magnificent, or commercial enterprises such as the East India or Muscovy Companies brought the global into the early modern European experience. In evaluations, interaction with course material unfettered by classroom dynamics is one factor students observe. They also report that subsequent class discussions are enriched as blog reactions provoke lively exchanges.

A course Facebook page could easily accomplish the same things. It may also be easier to create than a blog. Technological preferences or limitations, including particular campus Internet server constraints, will influence the decision. Depending on the bells and whistles of a learning management system (LMS), a discussion board may have a capacity similar to that of blogs or Facebook for embedding music, images, or video rather than merely creating hyperlinks. In such a case there is no significant difference. Yet, blogs or Facebook pages have the advantages of aesthetic appeal and are often more familiar to students. Wiki projects like those described elsewhere in this collection by Elena Woodacre can also be a platform for the biopoem activity amplifying collaboration with wiki technology that makes editing each other's contributions easy. Such projects also have the advantage of interactive capacities to link with other social media tools easily incorporating communication with platforms for social bookmarking or Twitter, for example. Of these other tools, it might seem that Twitter is the most superficial; so, what can Twitter do for you and your students?

Social Media: Twitter

Twitter assignments are useful to gauge in a concise way what students absorb.[7] They are also vehicles for me to learn reactions to what they catch or miss during lectures. Three assignments allow me to accomplish these goals: the first asks students to comment on lectures in real time with the additional task to note connections they observe between course materials. The second assignment is a question and answer format modified for application to several uses throughout the semester, such as discussion sessions in the survey course, and test review. A third assignment enhances their involvement and allows me to assess their understanding quickly. Like the blog assignment described above, this microblog assignment requires students to write posts appropriate to their chosen historical figure. The key difference is brevity: Tweets cannot exceed 140 characters.

If they do not already have one, students create a Twitter account. I have learned not to assume that all of my students have Twitter accounts—many do not, or need my help or that of a classmate to get started. Fortunately, they are easy to create. Students who are regular and adept users have been excited to

[7] See Twitter.com for information on getting started and creating hashtags.

have an expertise of their own to share with classmates and me. About twenty minutes of one class session is allocated to opening a Twitter account. Often it is easier, even when they already have one, to create a new Twitter account for the course. This may mean creating a special email address that will only be used for this purpose because Twitter restricts accounts to one for each email address. It is critical that everyone (instructors, too) have one Twitter account for the course and a different one for personal use; otherwise, everyone in the class sees every post everyone makes including those that should not be for the professor's eyes. We do this together with the main Twitter page projected on a screen in class so we can walk through it. While they are setting up their own accounts, I create a list for the course that they then follow. Though the list may be public, I prefer a private one, but this means students need to be added to the list. This is easily done because they are already following the class and so appear on a specific list of followers that can be added

The next step is to get started with the assignments by creating hashtags, then composing Tweets relevant to what, or whom, we are studying.[8] When I have assigned this with the blog assignment, the Twitter feature, available on most blogs, is activated so the two assignments can complement each other. A Tweet or hashtag question makes a good test question, too, for example asking what a Tweet exchange between Philip Melanchthon and Martin Bucer would say.

The Twitter convention of following and having followers is a convenient structure for student responses between historical personae and hashtags. For me, observing whom students choose to have their persona follow tells me what they know about that history. To give an example, a female student picked John Knox, followed John Calvin, and retweeted what the student who was Calvin said. Students had the choice to block followers as happened with Calvin and Knox. Another short project from my early modern England course asks students to imagine the intelligence network Sir Francis Walsingham would develop from following tweets.

The brevity of Twitter comments makes it useful for quick in-class polling to ascertain what students understand. It is also a convenient forum for them to pose thoughtful questions of their own and a way to have fun with the material. In a course on the French Revolution, students comment from the crowd scene in Paris during Louis XVI's execution as if they were reporting: "king's head roll-

[8] Hashtag is a Twitter convention that uses the pound symbol with a word to mark keywords in a Tweet so that all the messages associated with that keyword can be located. For example, in a private list for one of my courses, we used '#Luther,' '#ERI'; so with these keywords in a Tweet, a reply included that tag and keyword. The course Tweet list name was bricker3220, not very imaginative I know, and replies to it were preceded by the '@' symbol.

ing LOL." Tweets about the Haitian Revolution, with the same class, were more substantive with remarks about its successes and failures.

Like the blog exercises, Twitter can be a useful way to encourage participation from the entire group, including the shyer ones among them, between both individual students and other sections of the same course. I exploit this to interesting effect. Even in the same course, there are different levels of participation and enthusiasm. Another attraction of Twitter is that the immediacy of the technology lends itself to impromptu interactions between my class and me. It also provides a small window through which students offer feedback during times of typically low student-instructor interaction, such as in lectures. Our university classrooms and lecture halls have wireless Internet connections and projectors connected to the instructor's computer. This makes is easy to toggle between screens with the Twitter feed and other media such as PowerPoint or film. In these settings, the projection screen displays the Twitter feed live so that students can see what their peers are saying and respond.[9]

A number of resources exist for tracking participation and responses.[10] This allows for a live stream of communication similar to direct messaging. To keep the discourse civil and relevant to the historical topics at hand, ground rules are set at the outset. In class discussion, students contribute ideas about what is or is not acceptable. Some examples of rules include common sense things like not posting personal information, avoiding personal attacks, and requiring that opinions be supported by source evidence. Anonymous posting is not allowed either. Though not encouraged, some students want to get "into it" by attempting archaic language and syntax.

One caution. Twitter has failed miserably in my smaller classes with no more than twenty students, particularly in upper level seminars. Students observed that it served no beneficial function; indeed, was more of an irritation. Their impression was that there was no need for something electronic given the immediate human interaction in the close setting of a seminar. However, Twitter has been quite useful in larger lecture contexts where groups of students numbered around forty.

[9] I used Tweetdeck, a Twitter companion available free at http://tweetdeck.com/. Students received points for participation without assessing the quality of posts for this exercise.

[10] Twitterfall.com is one that I have used in lectures, but care should be taken lest it distract rather than facilitate learning. Others include Tweetchat; aggregating programs, like Tweetbot and Tweetdeck, are freely available online.

Social Media: Internet Bookmarking

This assignment uses social bookmarking to conduct web-based collaborative research. Social bookmarking is a tool that allows users to bookmark, tag, and share web content with classmates. In an upper level undergraduate seminar, my students used Diigo, one of many widely available programs. I use it in two different ways: as an adjunct to an essay assignment that also uses physical sources and as an independent project that functions as a web research endeavor. In the latter case, students produce a written justification of the sources they choose and how they might be used.

The class begins with discussion of what tags would be helpful to use so that bookmarks can be found readily when searching the group site. In the early modern England course, for example, tags include monarchy, ritual, gender, and Reformation among others. They are broad enough to encompass a number of artifacts, but not so broad as to be useless. Creating appropriate tags is an exercise itself in making decisions about including the wide and narrow such as one might observe in a library catalog listing. Developing tags has proven kinetic over a project's life as new material demands a label not yet on the list. Therefore, students amend tags, even existing ones as they work together. There are classroom opportunities to talk about progress on the project among each other and with guidance from me.

With a working list of tags—the initial twelve grew to thirty with some redundancy—students locate sources to bookmark, annotate, attach sticky notes, and highlight specific text. Materials include web databases of images and sites for primary source holdings, such as A2A at the British National Archives. Other sources include film, museum exhibits and material objects, music, or architecture. They are also asked to locate cartographic sources. Though connected to an essay, this exercise is graded separately according to criteria that include the range of sources, and annotations.

Conclusion

Why bother with a blog, Twitter, or any other social media tool? There are several reasons. They are vehicles to develop tasks that help to achieve information and Internet literacies while facilitating communication and collaboration. One aspect of using social media is that these are tools that require all of us—teacher and students alike—to participate with one another and to learn together. This makes scholarship collegial and reinforces the notion that it is a community of ongoing conversation and debate. Yet, there are limitations and that of facility with the technology is one of them.

When students are tech savvy, they are patient guides for me, perhaps because of the appeal of teaching the teacher something. They are also good to mine for helping less tech adept classmates. Contrarily, it is surprising to discover how much of this is foreign to many students. This revelation challenges my expectation that because they are younger, they will all be familiar with social media and know how to use the Internet beyond the Google search bar. The solution for this is in changing my assumptions so that I begin at the beginning with the basics and adjust according to the group. Integrating web tools in the classroom where possible serves another teaching goal besides that of delivering our particular content goals. It is one more way our courses can help our students prepare for their professional lives.

While every tool discussed here can be used appropriately in any course, often the early modern classroom is overlooked as a forum for social media as we trade in a field of time that was excited about moveable type. Yet using social media suggests many opportunities for not only engaging with the past but also making scholarship less solitary in the learning environment. Further, its use invites students to create a community of scholarship of their own in the classroom.

Student responses have been positive, focused on the opportunities to engage with one another and to study the past in ways that are stimulating personally and intellectually. From their evaluations, that has significant appeal for them as they have reported to me that they simply try harder on assignments for me that they know their peers will also see. Students who tend to be reticent in discussions shine in the blog forum and they all reported to me that they are more concerned with their performance when peer review is involved than when only I am their audience.[11] Even when these social media projects stumble, and sometimes they do, students still respond positively to the effort to do something new and exciting and, in the case of failure, to provide useful critiques as I have asked of them. By assuming a historical persona, as in some of the activities described here, students are talking through the dead to use their imaginations to try to breathe life into the past, into content that is mired in the debates, anxieties, hopes, and fears of the past.

[11] In their written assessments of the projects student comments were blunt about their trying harder to impress peers because they assumed their peers to be harsher critics and less fair.

Experimenting with the Use of Wiki Projects in the Postmodern Classroom

Elena Woodacre, University of Winchester (UK)

The use of wikis in educational practice has accelerated rapidly in the last decade and now features in many educational venues from elementary schools to the echelons of higher education.[1] Indeed wikis are only one of a whole arsenal of technological tools that can be employed in the postmodern classroom, including blogs, podcasts, social media content, RSS feeds, and apps for smartphones and tablets.[2] For educators, integrating the use of technology into pedagogical practice can result in a significant learning curve in order to understand how these technological tools work and how they can best be implemented in the classroom, particularly as the technology itself is constantly changing. Yet, despite these challenges, there are significant rewards to be gained from embedding technological tools in the postmodern classroom. Mark Sandle argues that using technological tools to teach history has the ability to alter fundamentally a student's experience of the past; turning them from a passive "tourist" to an active "explorer" by engaging them with the interactive nature of electronic media.[3] Wikis in particular, due to their very nature, require students to take an active role in learning and allow positive collaboration with other students through

---

[1] The entire concept of a wiki was created in 1995 and is now an easily recognized feature of the Internet experience, particularly due to the incredibly popular and somewhat infamous *Wikipedia* site. For a useful overview of the history of wikis, both in and beyond education, see R. Cummings, "What is a Wiki and Why do I Care?," in *Wiki Writing: Collaborative Learning in the College Classroom*, ed. Robert E. Cummings and Matt Barton (Ann Arbor: University of Michigan Press, 2008), 1–18. Wiki projects in elementary schools in New York City were profiled in Rhea R. Borja, "Educators Experiment with Student-Written 'Wikis,'" *Education Week* 25, no. 30 (2006): 10.

[2] See Will Richardson, *Blogs, Wikis, Podcasts and Other Powerful Web Tools for Classrooms* (Thousand Oaks, CA: Corwin, 2010) and Ben Woodcock, Andrew Middleton, and Anne Nortcliffe, "Considering the Smartphone Learner: An Investigation into Student Interest in the Use of Personal Technology to Enhance Their Learning," *Student Engagement and Experience Journal* 1, no. 1 (2012): 1–15.

[3] Mark Sandle, "Studying the Past in the Digital Age: From Tourist to Explorer," in *History in the Digital Age*, ed. Toni Weller (London: Routledge, 2013), 129–48.

building a community resource of information.[4] In this environment, students are interacting not only with the premodern world but with each other, employing and enhancing their technological as well as historical skills. This combination of factors makes wikis a powerful tool in the postmodern classroom, with benefits for students and educators alike.

This paper is a reflective survey of six academic years of experimentation with the use of wiki projects in a number of different settings, in different courses (known in the British university system as modules, and referred to as such for the rest of the essay), with divergent subject areas, with both first- and second-year undergraduate students, at different institutions, and on different Virtual Learning Environment (VLE) platforms. The aim is to take the reader through the highs and lows of my experience with wiki projects, using a compilation of observations and reflective practice, pedagogic research in this area, and feedback from students on their experience, both formal and informal. It is hoped that this paper can not only document the results of this experimentation but provide guidance to others working in the premodern classroom on how wikis can be employed effectively by demonstrating both what has worked well and particular combinations that were less successful in achieving the desired results, as well as suggestions for additional ways of implementing wiki-based activities in the postmodern classroom.

Chronicling the highs and lows of my experimental journey with wiki projects

My initial foray into the use of wiki projects resulted from a combination of inspiration and a response to a particular pedagogic need. The inspiration came from a workshop on developing new undergraduate modules that featured methods of implementing new technology into both module development and general teaching practice, using a wiki-based project as one example. At that time, I was wrestling with the task of adapting a module on early modern Europe, which had previously run as a semester long module, into a year-long course. The introduction of an element of art history was a key part of the reinvention and expansion of the module. A wiki project appeared to be the ideal place to introduce art history as well as an excellent opportunity to embed information technology (IT) skills into the module that could potentially enhance the students' employability. Lloyd-Jones and Lewis note the importance of integrating IT into the history curriculum, although they acknowledge that one of the barriers to this is a ten-

[4] For an excellent delineation of various types of wiki projects with illustrated examples, see Mark Phillipson, "Wikis in the Classroom: A Taxonomy," in *Wiki Writing: Collaborative Learning in the College Classroom*, ed. Robert E. Cummings and Matt Barton (Ann Arbor: University of Michigan Press, 2008), 19–43.

sion "between the accumulation of transferable skills as against subject-specific knowledge."[5] However, instead of taking them away from the core content of the module, the wiki project had the potential to develop both students' IT skills and their historical knowledge.

In the British system there are formative assignments that help students with improving their leaning but count for little, or more likely not at all, in the final grade. This is opposed to the summative assignments, which are a significant part of the final grade. These are also referred to as "assessed work." The wiki project was a formative assignment, and offered an opportunity for independent, student-controlled learning and had potential to move the content of the module beyond the "print model," which as Ferris and Wilder have noted, has dominated education, particularly in the humanities sector.[6] The creative, visual element of this formative task was a positive contrast to the summative assessment for the module; a traditional essay and a documentary exercise. While both the summative assessments and the formative wiki reinforced research skills as research-oriented tasks, the wiki project gave the students a greater degree of creativity and freedom in how they structured their findings than the rigid formats of the essay and documentary exercise.[7]

The wiki was set up as a "Presentation Wiki," a closed site with access only for the students on our module, focused on a specific topic—in this case the artists and artistic output of the period.[8] After an introductory lecture on the artistic style and innovation of the period, each student was assigned a particular artist to investigate. They were asked to research the artist's life and work and produce a wiki page that gave a biographical summary and highlighted the key works and their distinctive features. I cautioned the students not to simply cut and paste from Internet sources (particularly *Wikipedia*) but to summarize their artist's work in their own words and give their own perspective and interpretation. In-depth instructions were given in seminar and were also available on the front page of the wiki. They were informed that the entire class would be examining the results in seminar on the week that their contribution to the wiki project was due.

---

[5] Roger Lloyd-Jones and M. J. Lewis, "Integrating Information Technology into the History Curriculum," in *The Practice of University History Teaching*, ed. Alan Booth and Paul Hyland (Manchester, UK: Manchester University Press, 2000), 72.

[6] See S. Pixy Ferris and Hilary Wilder, "Uses and Potentials of Wikis in the Classroom," *Innovate: Journal of Online Education* 2, no. 5 (2006), http://www.learntechlib.org/d/104294.

[7] For more discussion of developing research skills see Mick Healey and Alan Jenkins, "Developing Students as Researchers," in *Linking Research and Teaching in Higher Education: Proceedings of the Newport NEXUS Conference*, ed. Simon K. Haslett and Heflin Rowlands (Newport: University of Wales, 2009), 7–11.

[8] This term comes from Phillipson, "Wikis in the Classroom," 23–24.

Overall, the students embraced the project with enthusiasm and produced excellent results. The novelty factor, both in terms of working on a wiki and on art history, an area that most of the students had not had the opportunity to explore previously, was a key factor for the strong uptake. Although the work was formative, the notion that it would be available to their peers and scrutinized in class reinforced the need to complete the assignment in a timely and thorough fashion. While the scrutiny of the wiki contributions was carried out in an informal manner, this allowed an element of peer assessment, which allows students to learn from other students' successes and weaknesses.[9] The visual element worked extremely well in the wiki format, allowing the students to include examples of the artists' key works, even though a few students did run into technical difficulties regarding the insertion of pictures into their wiki page.

Buoyed with the success of the initial project and the students' positive reaction, I decided to add a second wiki project into the module, this time on ruling women, connected to the topic of early modern queenship and the "Monstrous Regiment." Although the second project ran fairly smoothly, there was a noticeable difference in the level of uptake and the students' enthusiasm for the project. This was due both to the loss of the novelty factor and because the subject for the second wiki project was not necessarily visual. This assignment could have easily been transferred to a written assignment or a mini presentation on their assigned female ruler; there was no "added value" to using the wiki as a tool for this formative assessment.

The following academic year I decided to implement a similar project in a first year survey medieval and Renaissance history course, on the art and artists connected with the period. However, due to the much larger number of students on the course, it was necessary to extend the focus to include architecture. The new wiki project was designed and implemented in a similar fashion to the art-based wiki that I had previously run in the second year early modern history course, however this time the outcome was not as positive. The uptake for the project was around fifty percent and the enthusiasm was decidedly mixed. As the assessment was formative in both courses, there was no difference in the incentive level. However, there were a few key differences that were crucial to the running of the project. One obvious difference was that the medieval group consisted of first year students, yet no particular skill set or previous knowledge was needed to complete the task, which might have necessitated the implementation of the wiki with only a second year group. Another key difference was timing: the projects in the early modern course both ran in the first half of the academic year, when enthusiasm is generally higher and fatigue is less of an issue. In the medieval and Renaissance course, the project ran over the Easter break. The students were introduced to the project in the week before the break and given

[9] For more on the use of peer assessment, see Phil Race, *The Lecturer's Toolkit*, 3rd ed. (London: Routledge, 2006), 86.

the whole of the Easter holidays to complete their wiki page. Many of the students were not inclined to work on a formative assessment over the Easter break, either due to the distractions of holiday or due to pressure from other summative assignments due in for the end of the academic year. In addition, the Easter holidays took place later than usual that year with the consequence that most of the summative assessment for the module had already been completed. Many students felt they had effectively completed the course, giving them very little incentive to participate in the wiki project.

Another key difference was the lack of a dedicated lecture on the topic to engage them with the subject. Although the wiki project was introduced and explained in class, art and architecture was not the focus of study for that week due to scheduling constraints. In order to help them prepare for the wiki task, the students were assigned background reading and given links to several useful resources to help them acquire the necessary knowledge to inform their investigations. However, many students had little interest in doing independent research on a topic they knew little about and would not be "tested" on. This correlates directly with the MacFarlane report for HEFCE and a study by Higgins et al. that noted that students "tend to ignore activities which do not directly contribute to grades and degree class".[10] A final factor was the large number of students on the course meant that that some of the students were assigned minor artists, architects or lesser-known buildings that were more difficult to research. Some students abandoned their wiki page as they felt they could not find enough information on the topic that they had been assigned.

All of these factors were taken into consideration when the medieval and Renaissance course ran again the following academic year. I decided to continue with the wiki project, making key changes in order to improve the student engagement with the activity. The wiki project was placed earlier in the year, over the February reading week. This gave the students a chance to work on the project, but as the break was much shorter it prevented some of the distraction issues of the long Easter holidays. A full, interactive lecture was scheduled for the week before the February break which gave key background knowledge that the students could use to help them understand, access, and interpret the art and architecture that they were assigned to investigate. A recent news story on the discovery of a "new" Mona Lisa was embedded into the lecture, which made the topic more immediately relevant and helped to engage students with the subject.

---

[10] A. MacFarlane, "Teaching and Learning in an Expanded Higher Education Section (The MacFarlane Report)" (Bristol, UK: HEFCE [Higher Education Funding Council for England], 1992); Marilyn Higgins et al., "Effective and Efficient Methods of Formative Assessment: CEBE Innovative Project in Learning and Teaching" (Edinburgh, UK: Heriot-Watt University, 2010), 6, http://www.cebe.heacademy.ac.uk/projects/funding/pdf/Formative%20assessment%20final%20report.pdf.

The individual assignments were revised to ensure that all of the artists, architects and buildings were easy to investigate, in order to eliminate the excuse that there was not enough information on a particular figure or building.

Consequently the exercise was considerably more effective in 2011–2012, with a noticeably higher uptake. Students were asked for feedback via email on the wiki project and seven voluntarily responded with comments. The feedback from students was very positive on the whole, however this sample was purely derived from students who volunteered which can result in only those students with the most positive or negative experience, or those who are generally very willing to participate in class activities, taking the time to reply. In the feedback, students repeatedly noted how much they had enjoyed the activity and appreciated the change from traditional assignments, commenting that it was "a lot simpler than a paper or presentation" and "it was less intense, all in all it was nice to do something different." While several students commented about the frustration they experienced when working with unfamiliar wiki software, they also noted that it helped them learn new skills in addition to increasing their knowledge of Renaissance art as "You had to think about it maybe more than an assignment as you had to consider different aspects, like the appearance and lay out, what details are important, what images to use, etc." This feedback also supports the concept of constructivism; one of the key facets of this approach is that learning should be "Active and manipulative, engaging students in interactions and explorations with learning materials and provid[ing] opportunities for them to observe the results of their manipulations."[11]

After such positive feedback, I was keen to implement a wiki project again when I began work at a new institution the following academic year. The new institution used Moodle instead of the Blackboard VLE platform; this presented an immediate learning curve for using the wiki project feature on the Moodle software. The wiki interface was much less intuitive and "user friendly" than it had been on Blackboard and necessitated some training in order to be able to set up a wiki on the new VLE. The wiki interface was also very stripped down, allowing both the students and myself little ability to be creative and personalize the wiki space. Text and pictures could be added fairly simply but there was little ability to customize the wiki, giving it minimal visual appeal.

Despite the limitations of the Moodle wiki tool, I rolled out a wiki project on a second year, semester-long module on the Golden Age of Spain with approximately thirty-five students. Building on what had worked well the previous academic year, the wiki project was designed to tap into the rich cultural heritage of the Golden Age, giving the students a chance to investigate artists, architects, buildings, musicians and composers, poets, novelists, playwrights, and spiritual figures. A week of the module was specifically dedicated to the

[11] Kevin R. Parker and Joseph T. Chao, "Wiki as a Teaching Tool," *Interdisciplinary Journal of Knowledge and Learning Objects* 3 (2007): 59.

wiki project and the cultural heritage of the Golden Age; this occurred midway through the module in an attempt to avoid conflict with assessment deadlines. As the warm-up lecture had been a factor in the success of the previous wiki project, a lecture was inserted into the first hour of the customary three-hour session, leaving the remaining two hours for the students to independently research their given topic and begin their wiki entry.

In spite of careful planning to replicate what had worked well before, there was minimal participation in the wiki project, and those who did participate generally did a cursory amount. One student wrote one single sentence only as their contribution. Attendance at the lecture was also lower than usual. In order to understand why this version of the wiki project had such poor take up and participation I tried to pinpoint the differences between the 2011–12 year, when it had been so successful and the 2012–13 year when the results were, frankly, disappointing. Many factors were different: second-year students instead of first-year students, a different institution, and a different VLE platform. The second-year students were perhaps somewhat more cynical and less enthusiastic than first-year students, but they were generally a good group who participated well in seminar sessions. In addition, my very first wiki project had been successful with a second-year group so this was unlikely to be the root of the difficulty. The change in institution made little difference, but the VLE was a potential issue. The wiki tool on Moodle was clearly not as easy to work with nor did it allow creativity to customize the page in the same way that the Blackboard tool had. As I had found it hard to work with and limited, the students may have either given up at the first sign of difficulty or been uninspired by the lack of creative potential that it offered.

To get the students' perspective on the wiki project, I ran a small focus group of seven students. These students did not volunteer but were asked to participate in the focus group. While they may have felt less willing to be critical in an intimate focus group run by their tutor than if they had been allowed to make anonymous written comments, the focus group gave much more balanced and detailed commentary than did the email feedback I had previously received.[12] On the positive side, the students enjoyed the fact that they had to be proactive and research their figures. They felt it was a great opportunity to learn more about the cultural aspect of the Golden Age; one student commented that many history modules did not give them the ability to investigate this facet of the periods and civilizations they studied. However, the students admitted to some difficulty using the Moodle wiki tool, particularly with uploading pictures and text they had written on word processing software; they generally felt that it was straightforward, though inelegant. Although much has been made of the

[12] For further discussion of the use of focus groups to collect student feedback, see John Brennan and Ruth Williams, *Collecting and Using Student Feedback: A Guide to Good Practice* (York, UK: Higher Education Academy, 2004), 46–48.

technical ability of this generation of "digital natives," they agreed simplicity was paramount. One student argued that the wiki interface "needs to be easy enough for a five-year-old to use." The students said they were disappointed at the lack of participation by their peers, noting that this severely undermined the collaborative nature of the wiki. When asked for ways to improve participation, they said it was important to avoid clashing with deadlines in other modules as students would always prioritize assessed work over formative assignments. They agreed that it was better for the wiki to be formative work but suggested that more students would participate if they felt that their work on the wiki would feed into their essay or another piece of assessed work. The students claimed that they were more motivated to participate in formative work when they could see a benefit or reward for their effort and research.

Once again, I went back to the proverbial drawing board and used this feedback to rework the wiki project for the following academic year. One of the key issues had been participation; students either failed to show up for the lecture and take part in any form, or attended the lecture but failed to actually complete their entry on the wiki. In order to counter this, I booked an IT suite with enough computers for all of the students to use. We had a three-hour block in this computer room, the first hour contained a lecture on the art, architecture, and cultural achievements of the Golden Age, and during the remaining two hours the students were expected to produce their entry in class. They had Internet resources to work with as well as a selection of books and materials that I had brought in to help them research. I was on hand throughout to answer questions, check on progress, and help with technical problems. Purely by coincidence, one of my doctoral students, who is a Spaniard and well-versed in Golden Age history, happened to be in observing the class as a requirement for a teaching module that she was enrolled in. She also helped students where necessary, and they enjoyed engaging with her and benefitted greatly from her knowledge. I also tried to create a relaxed environment, playing music from the period in the background in order to increase their exposure to the cultural output of the period and hopefully make working on the wiki as enjoyable as possible.

The combination of these factors: the novelty of the IT suite, which broke up our normal lecture and seminar patterns; having all the materials to hand and dedicated time to complete the assignment; and having help from myself and my graduate student readily available, helped make this version of the wiki project much more successful than previous outings. Even though their essay was due the following week, nearly every student on the module attended the session and all of them completed their entry within the allotted two hours. The quality of the entries was also very high and the students were engaged and enthusiastic throughout. Given this positive result, I ran the wiki project for the Golden Age module again the following academic year in an identical fashion with similar results. However, I noted that a few students struggled to finish their wiki assignment in the two hours after the lecture and felt that I was rushing to complete the lecture element in an hour. For next year's wiki project, I plan to podcast the lecture element in order to give students a full three hours in class to work on their assignment and to ensure that there is adequate time to cover the cultural achievements of Spain's Golden Age in the lecture. A short "pop quiz" at the beginning of the wiki session will hopefully ensure that students watch the podcast lecture before they start work on their wiki entry.

Learning from success and failure: suggestions for future experimentation

As my experience has demonstrated, there are many factors that feed into the relative success of a wiki project, and their mixed reception by students over the course of these experimental outings has not dampened my enthusiasm for using wikis in the postmodern classroom. Each and every time they have been implemented in the classroom, I have learned from the experience. It has taught me that while there is no one recipe for success, there are factors which appear to encourage greater participation and a better response from and experience for the students. The following are my recommendations to any educators who are considering running a wiki project in their modules or courses:

- Choose a topic that is relatively easy to research and ideally has a high degree of visual interest
- Use a wiki tool that is easy to use, interactive, and customizable
- Give a "warm-up" lecture before they start the project (live or prerecorded)
- Only use one wiki project per module
- Include some form of peer assessment (in-class or comment boxes on the wiki)
- Time the project carefully so as not to conflict with breaks or assessments
- Consider supervised research and a dedicated session in a suitably equipped facility such as a computer room or IT suite

In this chapter, I have shared my experiences with "Presentation" style wikis, and, while I have found these to be incredibly useful, it is important to consider alternative project styles and ways to extend the use of wiki projects in different contexts. There are several ideas that could be implemented in connection with a similar "Presentation" type of wiki project in order to expand its potential. Ideally, the wiki project should be a truly interactive resource that the students can continue to use, rather than being simply a one-off contribution. This could be achieved through the introduction of a follow up assessment or in-class exercise that would require students to return to the wiki; for example, asking students to use the wiki to find five different artists who have painted a given subject or created a particular type of work, such as an altarpiece, and asking them to compare the style and approach of the different artists. Another, more simple assessment or exercise would be to develop a quiz or questionnaire that would require students to use the wiki to find the answers.

A further for expanding use of the wiki is to deploy it as a group project to enhance the collaborative nature of the activity. Parker and Chao have argued that "cooperative teams achieve higher levels of thought and retain information longer than students who do their work individually."[13] Implementing the wiki project as a small group activity instead of an individual exercise would be an interesting test for this theory on the power of collaborative work. One possible method of turning the wiki into a group project would be to have small groups working together to create a page that is a subsection of the overall class wiki; For example, working together to create a page on music in the Spanish Golden Age as part of a wider wiki project on Golden Age culture. Another option is to give each small group an entirely separate mini wiki of their own to create that can be viewed and used by the rest of the cohort.

A wiki project could also run over the entire length of a course by adding periodic assignments. This would be very similar to student blogs or reflective journals that can run for the duration of a module. For example, in addition to cultural aspects, there could be assignments on particular figures, places, or political events. These formative assessments could either be preparatory work or follow on from the seminar. These could also be group projects instead of individual endeavors. An alternative option is to construct a "resource wiki," working on the premise that each successive cohort taking the module adds something to the wiki, which can be used by all the students who take that module in years to come or can even be used by the general public. Mark Phillipson argues that this type of wiki "can give students the sense of contributing to a large and unfolding project," giving them a sense of reward and achievement for formative work.[14]

In conclusion, the experience of running the wiki project has been extremely beneficial to my pedagogical development. Although it has been challenging and the results have been mixed, each time the project has run, I have developed a greater understanding of what makes a successful interactive project. I intend to continue to integrate wiki projects into the modules that I teach, refining and updating the concept to continually improve the end result and make the greatest possible use of technological advances to engage the students and deepen their knowledge of the topic in question. Wikis are an incredibly valuable tool for the postmodern classroom, offering the potential to be adapted to different disci-

[13] Parker and Chao, "Wiki as a Teaching Tool," 58.

[14] Phillipson, "Wikis in the Classroom," 22.

plines and subject areas and can be employed in a variety of settings with groups of different sizes and at various levels of academic progression. They could also be integrated into blended or distance learning as a means of collaborative activity to engage remote students. I believe that wiki projects are a particularly powerful resource to help students engage deeply with the premodern world, by allowing them to have a more interactive experience with the distant past. The projects discussed here have demonstrated that wikis can be a helpful way to introduce the artistic and cultural output of the premodern world to students through the use of visual and auditory media. It is hoped that the key factors for success highlighted by this study can serve as a guidepost for other educators to use in the design of their own wiki projects. Wiki projects demonstrate that cutting-edge technology can be an incredibly helpful tool for educators who want to bring the premodern world into the postmodern classroom.

Reshaping, Refilling, Reimagining: Teaching Shakespeare through Intertextuality

Anna Riehl Bertolet, Auburn University

In May 2010, the board of *Shakespeare at Kalamazoo* (an organization that hosts annual panels and special events at the International Congress on Medieval Studies at Western Michigan University) made a decision to launch a series of explorations titled "Pre-texts, Texts, and After-texts," focusing on one play annually. The series commenced in 2011 with *Hamlet* as a focal point and has become a *Shakespeare at Kalamazoo* staple, including, to date, panels held in 2012 (*Macbeth*), 2013 (*Merchant of Venice*), and 2014 (*Richard III*). As a member of the board, I have witnessed a wonderful array of presentations inspired by the series and an even larger panoply of proposals submitted for consideration. Not only did the scope of this series reveal the ongoing interest in the study of Shakespeare's sources and adaptations, it also resulted in a concentrated discourse whereby the presenters and the audience explored how Shakespeare's text opens up in both retrospective and prospective ways in the presence of its predecessors and successors.

Around the time the series was born at Kalamazoo, I taught a course called Shakespeare Spin-offs and Retellings, twice: once as a six-week study abroad summer course at Regent's College (now Regent's University) in London, and once as a full-semester course at Auburn University. The success of the Pre-texts, Texts, and After-texts series moved me to reinvent my course to include Shakespeare's sources and thereby create triads of texts in which Shakespeare would occupy an intermediary position rather than that of an original.[1] Such positioning not only facilitates the destabilization of Shakespeare's text for students, it also leads to a greater awareness of what T. S. Eliot called the "main current" of literature whose movement is never-ending and whose ultimate sources are unknown.[2] In their creative projects in this course, too, the students benefit

[1] I found additional inspiration in Susan Gushee O'Malley's essay, "Cultural Appropriations of Shakespeare in the Classroom," in *Shakespeare Matters: History, Teaching, Performance*, ed. Lloyd Davis (Newark: University of Delaware Press, 2003), 138–50.

[2] T. S. Eliot, "Tradition and the Individual Talent."

from this trilevel textuality as they realize that it is but an elementary unit of a vast, multidimensional cultural enterprise in which their writing has a legitimate place just as much as Shakespeare's seemingly privileged voice. As the course progresses, these privileges are qualified rather than stripped, and as the Bard's texts are divested of their supposed sanctity, the students are able to engage with them not only in scholarly, but also in playful and even intimate ways.[3]

In my teaching methodology, I am a firm believer in complementarity of research and creative work. For this reason, my upper division undergraduate courses include a creative project that precedes and somewhat overlaps the work involved in crafting a research essay. The creative projects I assign in my classes are usually open-ended, with only a few guiding parameters. In my Renaissance Women Writers course, for instance, my students were asked to recreate a literary work in a new genre, and the students were quick to reveal their talents in song-writing, poetry, creative fiction, painting, sculpting, drawing (Color Plate 10), and even needlework (Color Plate 9). In my course on Milton, I let the students choose one book of Milton's most famous epic and simply asked them to bring *Paradise Lost* into the twenty-first century with creativity and flair. And the students followed suit, creating a cake featuring the elaborate landscape of Eden, complete with three scenes involving gummy Adam, Eve, Satan, and Uriel (Color Plate 7); a narrative quilt (Color Plate 8); Milton's Twitter feed; a repurposed book of impressionistic drawings; a musical piece dramatizing the falls of Eve and Adam; paintings of the War in Heaven, Eve's Fall, and a diptych starring Sin and Death. In this essay, I will address the creative project assigned in my Shakespeare: Pre-texts, Texts, and After-texts course in Fall 2013. I will move from explaining the structure of the course, to my ways of dealing with the problems of terminology, and finally to the description of the creative project and its relationship to the fundamental goals of this course.

The Structure of the Course

In the course of the semester, we examine four Shakespeare plays by following the triad approach. We begin with the story of Pyramus and Thisbe from Ovid's *Metamorphoses* whose manageable length allows it to be read in class and serve as

[3] The fundamental concepts that comprise the framework of this course (demystification of authorship, uncovering the instability of the text, and recognition of literary texts as cultural capital) are recurring concerns in theoretical discussions of appropriations. See, for instance, Christy Desmet's introduction to *Shakespeare and Appropriation*, ed. Christy Desmet and Robert Sawyer (London: Routledge, 1999), 4–6. See also Daniel Fischlin and Mark Fortier's general introduction to *Adaptations of Shakespeare: A Critical Anthology of Plays from the Seventeenth Century to the Present* (London: Routledge, 2000), 1–5.

a warm-up before embarking on *A Midsummer Night's Dream*. The students easily recognize Pyramus and Thisbe as archetypal precursors of Romeo and Juliet, but I position this text in the *Midsummer Night's Dream* triad to encourage more subtle analysis of the relationship between Ovid and Shakespeare. As we revisit the pre-text, we move beyond the plot confirming that the "course of true love never did run smooth" as the students recognize Shakespeare's inspiration for Cupid's flower whose change in color from white to purple mirrors the metamorphosis of the mulberry berries in Ovid's story. As they explore the symbolic meaning behind these changes, the persistent associations between love and violence in Shakespeare's play are elucidated.

We conclude the triad with a feminist play by a New Zealand writer Jean Betts, *Revenge of the Amazons* (1983), and a film about gay empowerment, *Were the World Mine* (dir. Tom Gustafson, 2008). The students find these after-texts equally delightful as an unapologetically overt ideological agenda is foregrounded in each of these appropriations of Shakespeare's play. Betts' play has an added comedic element while Gustafson's film combines the pleasures of the musical with the deeply gratifying effects of a comic revenge on homophobia, a revenge accomplished by a musically talented gay youth with the help of his English teacher and a little Shakespearean magic. In addition to the opportunity to engage with the strategies of reading Shakespeare through the lenses of feminist and queer studies, these two works of art allow the students to see that an effective after-text, whatever media it engages, itself functions as an interpretation of the preceding text. In that sense, these after-texts are rhetorical exercises similar to the essays the students write in their English courses, complete with a clearly conveyed thesis and a body of evidence shaped to prove the main point. However, these after-texts are creative rather than scholarly, and therefore the shaping of the evidence has fewer restrictions than expected in proper academic writing.

At this point of the semester, the students write short essays analyzing two items from a *Midsummer Night's Dream* triad of their choice. I explain the assignment as follows:

> In this essay, your task is to consider *A Midsummer Night's Dream* from one of the following points of view:
>
> 1) as a text that functions as an after-text in relation to Ovid's rendition of the story of Pyramus and Thisbe;
>
> 2) as a text that itself functions as a pre-text to one of the retellings considered in class (either Betts' play *Revenge of the Amazons* or Tom Gustafson's film *Were the World Mine*).
>
> As you construct your argument, choose your own focus. Some of the questions you may wish to address may include the reasons for revisions of the earlier text and consequent effect of such revisions; specific and concep-

> tual changes, such as reshaping of characters or circumstances; why some aspects of the earlier text are left intact; and why other aspects are gone without a trace. Consider attending to specific literary issues such as portrayal of gender; difference in genre; issues related to performance and theater.

The Twelfth Night triad is our next string of texts. We begin with Barnabe Rich's *Apolonius and Silla* and conclude with a film *She's the Man* (dir. Andy Fickman, 2006). *Romeo and Juliet* is the center of the next group, preceded by Arthur Brooke, *The Tragicall Historye of Romeus and Iuliet,* and concluded in a class period dedicated to discussion of spin-offs featuring star-crossed lovers. Prior to that class meeting, the students are assigned to explore the website hosted by Open Air Shakespeare Theater in the New River Valley, featuring or describing a dozen or so spin-offs accompanied by analyses.[4] I ask the students to bring Internet-capable devices to class and work in pairs. They have an option either to analyze a spin-off found on the assigned page or search the web for another after-text of *Romeo and Juliet* (I suggest they try a few keywords such as *retelling, spin-off, version, adaptation, appropriation*). The assignment asks the students to perform the following tasks:

> Consider one after-text of *Romeo and Juliet* (choose from the two options below). If it is a song or a visual image, you will have access to the entire "text," but if it is a book or a film, you will have to rely on the synopsis or review (for example, you may rely on a movie database or a site such as Amazon.com or Barnesandnoble.com).
>
> **Your task**: Figure out the strategy (or strategies) employed by this after-text.
>
> 1. Describe the way the strategy is used.
>
> 2. Define it (feel free to draw on the terminology established in class).
>
> 3. Address the effect produced in this after-text. Consider questions such as:
> - what does it add to or subtract from Shakespeare's text?
> - what does it change about the meaning?
> - what does it change about the audience's experience?
> - WHY?

The pairs present their findings to the class, and thus collectively we create an ample database of the after-texts that follow *Romeo and Juliet*. By this time in the

[4] Open Air Shakespeare NRV, "Romeo and Juliet Spin Offs," https://openairshakespearenrv.wordpress.com/2012/09/08/romeo-and-juliet-spin-offs/.

semester, the students have been working for about three weeks on their creative project. This last exercise before they finalize their projects and present them in class serves as a touchstone to ensure their awareness of their own strategy of (re)interpretation of Shakespeare through creation of an after-text and provides them with some additional tools for realizing this strategy in the project and articulating it in the reflective portion of the assignment. I will return to the discussion of the creative project proper after I finish describing the course and its conceptual underpinnings.

The last quarter of the course is dedicated to *Hamlet.* These strings begin with Saxo Grammaticus' *Life of Hamlet* and conclude with Mary Cowden Clarke's Victorian story "Ophelia: The Rose of Elsinore," Jean Betts's play *Ophelia Thinks Harder*, Thomas Stoppard's absurdist play *Rosencrantz and Guildenstern Are Dead,* and Salman Rushdie's short story "Yorick." While we have begun the process of contextualization with the after-texts of *A Midsummer Night's Dream*, these diverse appropriations of *Hamlet* are especially useful in highlighting the ways in which the plays' main concerns—cultural, ideological, and stylistic—are informed by their historic context, a context that may either displace that of Shakespeare's sources and his own texts, or enter a dialogue with the preceding aesthetic, political, and social values.

The last week of the course is dedicated to *Kill Shakespeare,* a two-volume graphic novel by Conor McCreery, Anthony Del Col, and Andy Belanger. While this work brings together major and minor characters from Shakespeare's oeuvre, its superhero/romantic leads, Juliet and Hamlet, enrich the course by offering an after-text of an entirely different nature than those discussed thus far. Just when my students thought they could not take any more versions of Hamlet (to be fair, in every after-text we have read, Hamlet has been stripped of his melancholic-intellectual-tragic appeal while his less attractive qualities are generously amplified), they welcomed a more heroic and less arrogant Hamlet and a superhero Juliet who has already became a favorite strong character in many creative projects. We have ended the semester not only as somewhat accomplished scholars, with a review of terminology and a conversation about Shakespeare as the cultural capital, but also as satisfied readers, relieved that liking Hamlet as a character is still appropriate and gratified by McCreery, Del Col, and Belanger's recognition of Juliet's often overlooked assertiveness and bravery in Shakespeare's play.

To be sure, my choices of pre-texts and after-texts to Shakespeare are highly selective and motivated by considerations of accessibility as well as manageability in terms of their length. For example, scholars tend to agree that Shakespeare likely read the French retelling of Saxo's *Life of Hamlet*—François de Belleforest's *Histoires tragiques* (1570)—rather than the Latin text of *Vita Amlethi* itself (first printed in Paris, 1514). Belleforest's work is now available in *The Norse Hamlet,* published by Hythloday Press once my course was already underway.[5] Numerous after-texts did not make it to my syllabus because they were out of print, lengthy, or uninspiring. In the end, my selections were meant to represent different types of engagements with Shakespeare that highlighted multiple facets of his plays while foregrounding, for my students, the oblique and otherwise obscure ways in which these texts are connected to and mirrored in our own culture.

Terminology

In a course with a somewhat vague title such as Shakespeare: Pre-texts, Texts, and After-texts, suggesting a generally sequential approach to Shakespeare-related texts, discussion of more precise terminology may be either important or inconsequential. As noted by Daniel Fischlin and Mark Fortier in the introduction to *Adaptations of Shakespeare*, the terminology of adaptation studies remains unstable: "there is no right name. There are only labels with more or less currency, connection to history, and connotations both helpful and misleading."[6] For this reason, instead of providing the students with a set of terms from the start, I invite them to think about the intertextual relationships analytically and conceptually as the class slowly accumulates examples of the cultivated links among the texts we discuss.

I use the available accounts detailing the history of variously proposed terms to compile a handout for my students, but I do not distribute it till the last week of classes.[7] Instead, we begin our first class by looking at two sets of images. One set features David Tennant (who played Hamlet in the Royal Shakespeare Company production in 2009 and is also famous for his role as the Tenth Doctor on the British Broadcasting Corporation (BBC) television show *Doctor Who* in 2005–2010). One image in this set is a mash-up of *Hamlet* and *Doctor Who*: Tennant is holding a head of a Cyberman (a monster from *Doctor Who*) while the caption makes a familiar reference to "poor Yorick." The second image extends the frame of reference to another BBC show, *Sherlock* (closely related to *Doctor Who* in that it shares the same writers): Tennant as Hamlet, wearing a crown askew on his head, is accompanied by the line from *Sherlock*'s delightful villain Jim Moriarty, in reference to his near-theft of the royal jewels: "Honey, you should see me

[5] François de Belleforest, "The Hystorie of Hamblet," in *The Norse Hamlet*, trans. and intr. Søren Filipski (Hythloday Press, 2013).

[6] Daniel Fischlin and Mark Fortier, eds., *Adaptations of Shakespeare: A Critical Anthology of Plays from the Seventeenth Century to the Present* (London: Routledge, 2000), 2–3.

[7] My main sources for this digest of terms are Fischlin and Fortier, see note 6; and Margaret Jane Kidnie, *Shakespeare and the Problem of Adaptation* (London: Routledge, 2009), 2–6.

in a crown."[8] As we look at these images of Tennant, the class is faced with the questions that will run through our conversations in the upcoming weeks: How much does the audience need to know to appreciate the intertextual reference? How does the new "text" retroactively transform its "pre-text"? What is gained by adding new layers to the frame of reference (following the chain of association in the second image: from Shakespeare's *Hamlet* to Tennant's acting as Hamlet, to the unusual choice of placing a crown on his head—albeit askew—and thus invoking the hidden frustration at the thwarted succession that Shakespeare's Hamlet never quite voices, to the implied link to Tennant's role in *Doctor Who* and then its writers Steven Moffat and Mark Gatiss doubling as the creators of *Sherlock*, finally to the iconic image Moriarty decked in the Crown Jewels and his subsequent line to Sherlock in the "The Reichenbach Fall"). These first images allow us to address the concept of cultural capital, a notion that we revisit more fully at the end of the term, and to establish the course as a space where the attitude toward Shakespeare's texts will do away with their supposed sanctity or originality and will place them instead in the line of creations in dialogue with each other. At the same time, I establish that, for the purposes of this course, the products of visual culture will be treated as texts, and therefore after-texts under discussion will include two films and a graphic novel with a proviso that the changes in genre and media will be admitted in the discourse about the work performed by such visual after-texts.

We then proceed to the second set of images that begin with two ubiquitous depictions of Shakespeare (the Folio image and the Flower portrait, itself a nineteenth-century adaptation of Martin Droeshout's engraving) and move to progressively imaginative iterations that involve substitutions of features with other faces accompanied by quotations that insure recognition of the source image, caricature renditions that supply the body, and appropriation of the image in an advertisement where, in mirror-like fashion, Shakespeare is perusing a theatre program with his own face on its cover. Once again, we talk about the changes that are brought about in transposition from one genre to another (from engraving to formal portrait to caricature) and changes caused by a shift in rhetorical purposes (from frontispiece to advertisement).

In this first class, following our discussion of the images whose shared links model many of the intertextual relationships that exist among the texts on our syllabus, I give my students a list of crucial terms such as transformation, abridgement, version, appropriation, adaptation, offshoot, and spin-off. We discuss some preliminary definitions of these terms and return to them from time to time throughout the semester. As explained below, at the midpoint of the semester we devote some time to compiling the list of strategies used in creation of after-texts. This list is in many ways related to the definitions of the afore-

[8] "The Reichenbach Fall," episode 3, season 2 of *Sherlock*, dir. Toby Haynes, wrt. Steve Thompson (Hartswood Films, BBC Wales, and Masterpiece Theatre, 2012).

mentioned terms though the terms themselves are muted: this exercise is about craft rather than theory. However, as the course draws to an end, it becomes clear to the students that the two inform each other and are, in fact, two sides of the same coin.

When, toward the end of the term, we revisit the theoretical approach to intertextuality, I distribute the handout that spans the suggested terminology from Ruby Cohn (1976)[9] to Margaret Jane Kidnie (2006), and the students see that some of the terms have received quite dissimilar definitions from various scholars and that the lines between the terms are blurred and penetrable. I introduce this array of scholarly definitions at the very end of the semester, both to de-emphasize their stability and to equip the students with the vocabulary and tools that they can use to evaluate the after-texts studied in the course of the semester. At this point, their textual database is sufficiently populated to allow an attempt at categorizing the after-texts in relation to their predecessors by using the terminology of adaptation studies. This approach culminates in one of the final exam essays where the students are asked to explore the relationship between two texts, using a term or two from their handout (or suggesting a new term) and explaining what the terms mean in their own essay. Giving the students authority to define their terms in their own way and then support their definition of the relationship between the texts drives home the point addressed in the writing of their research essays: literary criticism is a conversation where the interlocutors can engage with each other effectively only if their views are expressed precisely and clearly. In the end, the terms themselves may be flexible, but what matters is the students' ability to assign precise meaning to a chosen term and then supply analytical defense that explains the nature of the intertextual relationships according to that meaning.

The Creative Project

The creative project comes in the midst of this grappling with terms and definitions and allows augmenting the students' grasp of the process as well as aiding the rhetorical purpose of creating an after-text. After the students have completed analytical essays addressing the first triad of the course, we compile a list of strategies for creating after-texts. The students brainstorm their lists in groups, basing their suggestions on the textual evidence at the center of their papers. The list below was collaboratively compiled in my class. It is by no means exhaustive or definitive, but it provided the class with a common set of references that emerged from observations and concerns of that particular group of students and thereby bears the imprint of their intellectual curiosity.

[9] Ruby Cohn, *Modern Shakespeare Offshoots* (Princeton, NJ: Princeton University Press, 1976).

Pre-texts, Texts, After-Texts: Categories Useful for Analysis
melding multiple characters into one
making a minor character play a major role (from margins to center)
role reversal (gender, race, class, power)
new time period/culture (transplantation)
change the genre/medium
changing the themes/messages
retaining some original elements and sometimes making a direct reference to the source
creating a frame language (updating, retaining, imitating)
demonizing the undercurrents (as in an example offered by one student, "taking the idea that Pyramus and Thisbe never get to marry and using that to make the institution of marriage in *MND* an ominous prospect)

In the creative project described below, the students were asked to refer to this list of strategies in order to choose a combination of approaches that would allow them to make a persuasive point by means of creative repurposing of their chosen pre-text.

As a result of the triple engagement with each story, the students come to appreciate Shakespeare's intermediate place in the textual sequences. In addition, because the creative project is due about two weeks after the midterm, the students also have mastered three Shakespeare plays in some depth and are therefore able to tap into a cloud of Shakespearean drama in recognizing a developing set of concerns and devices common to these plays. This twofold contextualization of each play allows for an intertextual awareness that tends to inform many of the resulting projects in this class, both creative and scholarly.

As seen in the assignment sheet below, students have freedom of choice as to what type of after-text they create, even if they choose to extend their inquiry backward into real or imaginary prehistorical incarnations of their story. Understanding Shakespeare's intermediate positioning in a textual sequence is now put into practice when the students have to occupy a position in relation to their pre-text similar to that of Shakespeare or his successors. One of the students, Alyson Smith, summarized the experience in her post-production reflection: "I was able to successfully adapt a Shakespearean mindset and imagined what Shakespeare might have been thinking about as he was writing his plays."

Prequel, Spin-off or Retelling Project

The three final products of this assignment are going to be 1) **Creative Portion**; 2) **Written Portion** and 3) **Performance / Sharing Portion**. You will work on one of the following plays:

Romeo and Juliet *A Midsummer Night's Dream* *Twelfth Night*

> You may choose to work in a group or independently. Two weeks before the project is due, submit a proposal on Canvas, including a description of the option you have chosen, your reasons for making this choice, and (if you will be working in a group) the names of your group members.

Your options include, but are not limited to the following:

Creation	*Writing*	*Sharing*
Graphic prequel or adaptation	Justification report	Photocopies, PowerPoint or Document camera
Musical prequel or adaptation: compose a song expressing thoughts of a character or narrating events that precede the play	Justification report	Performance (in class or recorded) or Photocopies of music and lyrics
Write an additional scene (ex., revealing something about the plot / character)	Justification report	Performance or Photocopies or PDF
Rewrite the ending of a play	Justification report	Performance or Photocopies or PDF
Facebook	Justification report	Projector or Photocopies
Rewrite from a minor character's point of view: in prose, verse, or as a short play	Justification report	Photocopies or Recitation or Performance or PDF
Modernize a scene (or two)	Justification report	Performance or Photocopies or PDF
Film a scene (or two) as an adaptation (ex., set in a different time period)	Justification report	Projector
Analyze a film spinoff	Justification report	Presentation (with film clips)

> In your **justification report** (about 2 pages), explain your rationale for the choices made for various aspects of your creative portion. If you are working in a group, only one report needs to be submitted.

Once the creative projects were completed and shared, the students were asked to write two sets of reflections, explaining the most challenging and most rewarding aspects of the assignment. In the remaining part of this essay, I will charac-

Figure 11: Hippolita and Theseus.
Drawing by Shelby Hancock. Class of Anna Riehl Bertolet.

terize the types of after-texts produced in my most recent class, describe three of them in more detail (with permission of their authors), and share the reflections associated with these projects.

Because this assignment includes a possibility of imagining a "pre-text"—an image or story to which Shakespeare was responding, the students had a unique option to "serve" the Bard with food for inspiration. For example, one student painted an androgynous fairy in a crown, hovering over some purple flowers and offered Shakespeare's possible question about the reason for the fairy's interest in this flora as an impetus for writing *Midsummer Night's Dream*. Others chose to create a prequel and thus explain some murky point in the characters' prehistory: one student composed a graphic narrative of the encounter between Hippolita and Theseus that explained why Hippolita agreed to marry him despite her lack of affection (Figure 11); another student explained the forgotten reason behind the Capulet-Montague feud. Most of the class, however, created after-texts that redirected the play's romantic relationships. They endeavored to bring together Mercutio and Rosaline, on the one hand, or Antonio and Sebastian, on the other; many students reversed gender roles (see the Cover Image for this book), rewrote the characters' sexuality (Romeo and Juliet gave way to Julius and Ryan), and transposed the stories into modern setting ([Friar] Lawrence became a student councilor seeking to end the feud between the fraternity and sorority on his college campus). The projects included paintings, film editing, rewriting of song lyrics, and comic strips, but most of the students opted for creative writing in various genres. Interestingly enough, it is the creative writing majors who gravitated towards the graphic arts, grateful for a chance to engage with drawing and painting unavailable in other courses. On the other hand, literature majors seized the opportunity to author short stories, poems, and dramatic scenes. Many students commented on their delight with the open-endedness of this assignment that allowed for a variety of acceptable media.

The Process and the Product: Three Sample Assignments

Andrea Gonzalez composed and performed "Cupid's Lamentation," a monologue of (female) Cupid who had her wings clipped for missing Elizabeth I with her arrow. Andrea has a theatrical background so her delivery was dramatically enticing. The speech itself was inspired by two lines from *A Midsummer Night's Dream*: "Cupid is a knavish lad, / Thus to make poor females mad" (act 3, scene 2, lines 440–41). Taking a feminist stance by making a minor (and offstage) character her mouthpiece, Andrea set out to "vent her frustrations regarding Cupid's cruel manipulation of the female psyche. . .to highlight women's unique strength and respond to the disturbing aspects of female submission in *A Midsummer Night's Dream.*" The fifty-three-line speech unfolds the story as well as follows Cupid's "emotional progression" from frustration to triumphant assertiveness.

> I refuse to put another arrow through
> the heart of woman only to watch her wallow
> in piteous servitude and fatal sorrow
> only because the cruel masochist who gives our orders believes
> that a woman is too weak to lead.
> . . ..I am ashamed of my past injuries.
> I have driven strong women to their knees
> and made them plea at the feet of men
> for wicked abuse and a noose
> in the shape of a golden wedding ring.
> But now, I will make them see.
> I have changed the world by shooting an arrow at a tree.

In her justification report and reflection, Andrea analyzed the ways women such as Hippolita, Titania, and Helena either willingly submit to men or are forced to do so. Writing the monologue, Andrea explained, "was like working on a puzzle using pieces of *A Midsummer Night's Dream.* I wanted this monologue to be packed with obvious and subtle references to the primary work. It was also exciting to reference history in my description of Elizabeth I."

Alyson Smith likewise incorporated research in writing a mini-play, "Flower-Crossed: An *R&J* Retelling (Of Sorts)." Rather than looking into history, Alyson found herself exploring Shakespeare's bawdy language in order to fully understand the innuendo that tends to be missed by the contemporary audience. Alyson successfully imitated this innuendo to amplify the message she discerned in Shakespeare's play, "that measuring masculinity by sexual prowess can be an incomplete and poor way to judge men." Alyson's play centers on Mercutio and Tybalt who meet at the doors of heaven immediately after their demise. Their bickering is interrupted by God who orders them to figure out the reason for the Capulet-Montague feud in order to gain admission to heaven. Rather conveniently, Tybalt discovers that, because they "already reside in the stars," they now "possess all knowledge of history," and the two quickly proceed to work out the cause of the feud. The explanation, with a nod to cross-dressing on the Shakespearean stage and Shakespeare's own transvestite female characters, hinges on the hidden femaleness of a Capulet "male" child, some generations ago, who was later married off to a Montague "girl," a "victim of the same circumcision" (i.e., circumstance; Alyson made some use of malapropism she learned from Bottom). The feud started "after the Capulet true girl had borne the child, who was moreover a girl," and whose mother proclaimed: "Her name shall be Viola." In this delightful mini-drama, Alyson created a text alive with a multitude of references to Shakespeare's culture: cross-dressing; primogeniture; anxiety about powerful women, especially mothers; and homoeroticism. In phrasing of the dramatic naming of the child, Alyson additionally tied her play to the film that centers on cross-dressing, *Shakespeare in Love* (dir. John Madden, 1998).

Austin Spain's mini-play "Tea and Strumpets" is even more expressly layered in its use of pre-texts, texts, and after-texts. Throughout the semester, but especially in relation to the *Midsummer Night's Dream* and *Twelfth Night* triads, our discussions frequently turned to the meaning and representation of homoerotic and homosexual relationships as well as distinction between these terms. It is then unsurprising that many students pursued these themes in their creative projects, amplifying the possibilities they felt were not fully realized in Shakespeare's plays. Austin followed that route by bringing together Hippolytus from the eponymous tragedy by Euripides, Timothy from the film *Were the World Mine*, and Shakespeare himself for a katabasis. This dramatis personae effectively gathered stand-ins for the pre-text (with Hippolytus' implied relationship to Shakespeare's Hippolita, in Austin's view), Shakespearean text, and an inventive after-text that still maintained recognizable ties with the text and reached through it further down the sequence, to the times of Ancient Greece when homosexuality was socially unproblematic. Moreover, the dialogue itself "forms a commentary upon the nature of the adapted elements of the stories," with the characters venturing into critical analysis. For instance, Shakespeare berates Timothy for misunderstanding Shakespearean grammar and thus creating a foolish motto for himself that echoes throughout the film:

> **Timothy**. The language is just so uplifting: "Be as thou wast wont to be, / See as thou wast wont to see." Those lines made me think that I should live my life as I would, not as others would have me.
>
> **Bill**: I'm sorry; did you actually read the script? That's not what that means at all. Oberon, if I recall, utters those words as he is curing Titania of her magically coerced love of ass, having achieved his goal of cuckolding himself; in order to reassert his dominance in their relationship by lording his wife's sexual promiscuity over her; and all this so that he can make off with some boy that Titania had withheld from him.
>
> From that profoundly disturbing sequence of events, and the lines that you uttered, which in the modern vernacular actually mean "be as you used to be; see as you used to see," you got this "just be you" bullocks?
>
> **Timothy**: I suppose. . .well, really I think I just amalgamated themes that were already present in your work.

While this analysis is half-playful, it actually points to the problematic use of Shakespeare's language in the film; it also incorporates an argument from Gabriel Rieger's article we have read in class.[10] Austin's play, therefore, and many creative projects produced by his classmates amalgamate historical context, literary criticism, class discussions, and a multitude of texts and after-texts beyond the scope of merely one Shakespeare play that they chose as a main point of reference for this assignment.

The students' reflections about the challenging and enjoyable aspects of these projects reveal a common trend of appreciation of freedom to choose any approach and medium, but also to interact with the text in a playful and even intimate way. Many students noted that the project allowed them to "vent" or "celebrate" and shape the characters and their relationships to their satisfaction. As readers of literature, we cannot avoid an emotional engagement as well as an often visceral or strong moral response to the stories we consume. Creative projects allow—and welcome—the unconstrained and "unscholarly" responses that actively engage with the text. What comes out of these engagements is not a lack of reverence for Shakespeare, but greater, more careful and responsible knowledge of his work. Many students commented on their intense reading and rereading of the text in order to catch every meaning and every turn of the phrase so as to create an accurate after-text. Darcy Corbitt, who wrote a poignant short

[10] Gabriel Rieger, "'I Woo'd Thee with My Sword, / And Won Thy Love Doing Thee Injuries': The Erotic Economies of *A Midsummer Night's Dream*." *Upstart Crow: A Shakespeare Journal* 28 (2008–2009): 70–78.

story that follows the lives of Olivia, Viola, Sebastian, and Antonio after the end of *Twelfth Night*, noted that it took some effort to "overcome the notion that Shakespeare is 'untouchable'. . . What is an undergraduate student compared to arguably the best playwright to have ever lived?"

Darcy continues:

> what I found to be most enjoyable about this assignment was the intimacy it encouraged me to cultivate with Shakespeare and his text. What made this assignment so brilliant was the way in which it made me closely examine and respond to *Twelfth Night*. So often, we are required to examine texts and form a response to them. We can write response after response critiquing or exposing aspects of a text we dislike, but very rarely does the student have the opportunity to actually do something practical about his or her feeling for a text. I have never liked the ending of *Twelfth Night*. I did not like the hasty way in which Sebastian and Olivia get married. In past readings, I never picked up on the homosexual undertones of the relationship between Antonio and Sebastian because of how my teacher presented the play. When I finally did see this, I really wanted the two men to get together. This project gave me an outlet for expressing this desire and frustration with the ending in such a way that the two are forever immortalized in my story, if not Shakespeare's, and not just argued for in a short paper no one will ever see.

Throughout the semester, we treated after-texts as rhetorical statements strengthened by a set of purposefully employed strategies that conjured up evidence supporting their main point. Likewise, in their creative projects, the students had to have an organizing principle equivalent to a thesis, and they had to articulate their strategy of crafting the after-text in accordance with their purpose. While allowing for poetic license and inviting them to use it, this approach is otherwise similar to the research essays the students went on to write in this class when, instead of using a license to invent the evidence, they had to locate it in the primary and secondary texts. Interestingly enough, many students chose to find support for their creative theses in other texts, rather than inventing it outright. By doing so, they demonstrated their understanding of the rhetorical possibilities of a multidimensional intertextual engagement when a text, rather than standing alone like a self-sufficient pillar of canonized perfection, is always already a part of an interlaced network of texts.[11] I especially like Leah S. Marcus' reference to

[11] My objective and outcome here are in line with Thomas Leitch's idea of "active literacy" and his conviction that, "By treating every text as a text to be rewritten, [courses in adaptation studies] empower students with a sense of themselves as rewriters rather than consumers of texts," quoted in Sevgi Sahin and Laurence Raw, "Toward a Pedagogy for Adaptation Studies," in *Redefining Adaptation Studies*, ed. Dennis Cutchins, Laurence Raw, James M. Welsh (Lanham, MD: Scarecrow Press, 2010), 71.

early modern writing as "texts that won't stand still."[12] Throughout the course, the opportunities to desanctify and destabilize Shakespeare's texts in their own right are numerous. (One of my favorite exercises, likely shared by Shakespeare teachers across the world, is a comparative reading of a speech from *Hamlet* using its appearances in the Bad Quarto, the Good Quarto, and the Folio.) Achieving this awareness of intertextuality through the creative practice as well as scholarly inquiry was one of the fundamental objectives of this course, and the students' final comments indicate that their sense of Shakespeare's text as an absolute point of origin has given way to an empowering understanding that as they set out to create an after-text, they come to inhabit a position of rhetorical creativity much like the one occupied by Shakespeare himself.

[12] Leah S. Marcus, "Texts That Won't Stand Still," in *Approaches to Teaching English Renaissance Drama*, ed. Karen Bamford and Alexander Leggatt (New York: Modern Language Association of America, 2002), 29–34. Although Marcus begins by suggesting that, unlike the texts by his contemporaries, the texts of Shakespeare's plays are relatively stable, there is certainly plenty of instability in store for readers of *King Lear, Hamlet,* and *Othello*, to name the most difficult cases.

Teaching Global Shakespeares: All the World's His Stage

Jo Carney, The College of New Jersey

As part of the festivities surrounding the 2012 Olympics in London, a consortium of arts organizations created a World Shakespeare Festival, which featured nearly every play in the canon performed in some fifty different languages, including a *Coriolanus* in Japanese, a *Romeo and Juliet* set in Baghdad, and a Turkish version of *Antony and Cleopatra.* The premise of the festival—that Shakespeare's reach is global—is as indisputable as its execution was innovative and ambitious.[1]

Shakespeare's cross-cultural appeal is not a recent phenomenon: in the late 1700s Goethe and the German Romantics took up Shakespeare as one of their own, and in the nineteenth century Victor Hugo praised Shakespeare for representing the French spirit as vividly as any native writer. But an increasingly globalized age has resulted in an even greater awareness and appropriation of Shakespeare: his works are now widely translated and frequently adapted and performed in myriad locales, from Capetown to Mumbai to Budapest.

What is happening on pages and stages across the world can now become a part of our classroom experience. In the spring of 2013 I taught Global Shakespeares at the graduate level but the course could easily be adapted for undergraduates. This essay will describe the pedagogical and theoretical concerns of this course and its culminating creative project.

The course began by emphasizing how Shakespeare was himself a global citizen; though he most likely never left England, his attention to the larger world was reflected in the many foreign settings he employed, in his plays' attention to early modern England's engagement with exploration and trade, and in the many geographical allusions scattered throughout his work. In one play alone, *The Winter's Tale,* Shakespeare situates his plot—albeit with geographical imprecision—in both Bohemia and Sicily, describes Hermione's father as King of Russia, and gives Perdita a false identity as Princess of Libya. Other plays are filled with racialized Ethiopian references, sexual jokes at the expense

[1] For more information about the festival, including video footage and director and actor interviews, visit http://www.worldshakespearefestival.org.uk/.

of the French, and allusions to characters "turning Turk." A simple but effective way to illustrate Shakespeare's global curiosity at the beginning of the course is to show a brief excerpt from Michael Radford's 2004 film *The Merchant of Venice,* in which suitors from numerous countries travel to Belmont to woo Portia. As the Prince of Morocco proclaims, "All the world desires her / From the four corners of the earth they come" (act 2, scene 7, lines 38–39). To contextualize Shakespeare's attention to London's increasing cosmopolitanism and England's expansion and emerging notions of nationhood, we also read a variety of early modern political and historical works, from Montaigne's essay on cannibals and Richard Hakluyt's "Reasons for Colonization" to Leo Africanus' *A Geographical History of Africa.*

Keeping in mind Shakespeare's own outward—though to a contemporary sensibility problematic—gaze, we then turned to the primary focus of the course, recent and contemporary global Shakespeares. Most of the course was devoted to our examination of four major plays paired with adaptations in other languages and genres, works that have themselves achieved a certain canonical status:

- *King Lear* with Kozintsev's 1971 Russian film *Korol Lir* and Kurosawa's 1985 Japanese film *Ran*
- *Macbeth* and Kurosawa's 1957 Japanese film *Throne of Blood*
- *Othello* and Sudanese novelist Tayeb Salih's 1966 *Season of Migration to the North*
- *The Tempest* and Peter Greenaway's 1991 Australian film *Prospero's Books*[2]

Along with close analysis of the plays and the modern revisions, several theoretical issues informed our discussions and provoked departure points for the final projects. We began with anthropologist Laura Bohannan's well-known but dated essay from 1966, "Shakespeare in the Bush," an interesting if simplistic account of her experience sharing the plot of *Hamlet* with the Tiv in West Africa.

[2] There are multiple scholarly works on these Shakespearean adaptations. Among the most useful: Robert Hapgood, "Kurosawa's Shakespeare Films: *Throne of Blood, The Bad Sleep Well,* and *Ran,*" in *Shakespeare and the Moving Image,* ed. Anthony Davies and Stanley Wells (Cambridge: Cambridge University Press, 1994), 234–49; Alexander Leggatt, "Grigori Kozintsev," in *Shakespeare in Performance: King Lear* (Manchester, UK: Manchester University Press, 2004), 88–104; Edith Pearlman, "*Macbeth* on Film: Politics," in *Shakespeare and the Moving Image,* ed. Anthony Davies and Stanley Wells (Cambridge: Cambridge University Press, 1994), 250–60; and Richard Wilson, "Global Shakespeare: The Wide and Universal Theatre," *Alicante Journal of English Studies* 25 (2012): 5–17.

Bohanann's initial assumption that "*Hamlet* had only one possible interpretation and that one universally obvious" is undermined by the radically different "meanings" the Tiv extrapolated from her narrative.[3] That the Tiv arrived at such different conclusions about the various characters and their behavior reminded Bohanann to be on an anthropological alert for difference. We then read Martin Orkin's response to Bohannan which challenges and complicates the essay, its reception, and our understanding of its claims about "otherness" and "sameness." Orkin suggests that rather than focusing solely on the differences non-English speaking audiences and non-Western epistemologies bring to Shakespeare, we must also examine "points of connection" and "possible proximities."[4] Read together, these essays provide a useful framework for many of the formal, political, and theoretical questions that emerged in our discussions of the nature of global Shakespeares.

Second, we considered the aesthetic issues inherent in the process of re-visioning Shakespeare on stage or re-creating his work in other genres, particularly film or the novel. Gèrard Genette's theories of intertextuality advanced our thinking about the relationship between the hypo (originary or source) text and the hyper (or subsequent) text. We discussed the distinction between an adaptation, which signals a more explicit and conventional relationship with a source text, and an appropriation, which typically departs from the source text into a "wholly new cultural product and domain."[5] For example, students made a case for Kosintsev's *Lear* as an adaptation but Greenaway's *Prospero's Books* as an appropriation, while the nature of Kurosawa's films according to this paradigm was vigorously debated. The purpose was not to definitively pinpoint various works on an intertextual continuum, but to allow students to engage with the nuanced aesthetic questions raised by the revisionary process: what precisely is being transferred and transformed from one text to the next, by whom, and to what end? From the outset, it is also important to encourage students to be descriptive rather than evaluative, to be analytical rather than judgmental. In other words, students encountering a Japanese film inspired by *Macbeth* or an avant-garde response to *The Tempest* are encountering unfamiliar works, and they should be prepared and encouraged to embrace the strangeness of the new: it is not productive to focus on which work is superior or preferable or on how

[3] Laura Bohannan, "Shakespeare in the Bush," *Natural History* (Fall 1966): 56.

[4] Martin Orkin, *Local Shakespeares: Proximations and Power* (New York: Routledge, 2005), 28. See also Ania Loomba and Martin Orkin, *Post-Colonial Shakespeares* (New York: Routledge, 1998).

[5] Julie Sanders, *Adaptation and Appropriation* (New York: Routledge, 2006), 27. There is considerable scholarship on adaptation and intertextuality in Shakespearean studies; Sanders' text provides a useful overview of the theoretical concerns in adaptation studies. See also Gèrard Genette, *Palimpsests: Literature in the Second Degree*, trans. Channa Newman and Claude Doubinsky (Lincoln: University of Nebraska Press, 1982).

closely the adaptation adheres to the original—what Linda Hutcheon refers to as the pitfalls of "fidelity criticism."[6] Students should be encouraged to consider what each version accomplishes on its own terms rather than what is sacrificed from the source text or lost in translation.

Third, because this course focuses not just on Shakespearean revisions but particularly on works in languages other than English, issues such as translations, colloquial rewriting, and film subtitles demand attention. John Russell Brown's essay, "Foreign Shakespeare and English Speaking Audiences" is especially useful here. Brown notes that comparisons between "foreign Shakespeares" and the original plays will invariably notice the superficial differences "most open to manipulation"—for example, setting, casting against convention, deletion or addition of scenes. This comparative inquiry should, Brown argues, "go beyond this elementary accounting" of differences and ask more fundamental questions. Brown acknowledges our necessary appreciation of the subtleties of Shakespeare's poetry, but since accurate translations are impossible, he points to what is valuable in Shakespearean drama beyond "its English and metrical niceties." He reminds us that all performances of Shakespeare are in "some sense foreign to [his] intentions," that given the inevitable and continuous changes in language, "there is no one who can claim to present the plays in their own language." With non-English Shakespeares, as much can be gained in translation as lost: "in an unfamiliar language we pay more attention to visual signals. . .certain ideas and experiences will be more potent or probing, and some scenes more animated" a central point that he illustrates with accounts of various foreign performances.[7]

Brown also argues that in non-English revisions, Shakespeare often seems more political and polemical, a claim we returned to frequently throughout the course. Anthony Dawson's article, "Reading Kurosawa, Reading Shakespeare" was useful in articulating ways to analyze "foreign and political" Shakespeare. Dawson approaches this subject by addressing how the local versus global dichotomy in Shakespeare studies can be a limiting binary for political interpretations of his works. Instead, Dawson argues that to characterize Shakespeare as global means "that his plays are astonishingly plastic and adaptable. . .[and] appeal to so many different temperaments and cultures. It is the ground of his universality; too often, I think, especially in circles that distrust the very idea of the universal, this element is misinterpreted as a bland and homogenizing sameness, when

[6] Linda Hutcheon, *A Theory of Adaptation*, 2nd ed. (New York: Routledge, 2012).

[7] John Russell Brown, "Foreign Shakespeare and English-speaking Audiences," in *Foreign Shakespeare: Contemporary Performance*, ed. Dennis Kennedy (Cambridge: Cambridge University Press, 1993), 28–29. Since Brown's essay, the many successful OP (original pronunciation) performances of Shakespeare's works challenged his claim that it is impossible to recapture Shakespeare's own language in any performance.

what it really means is variety, scope, and difference. So if Shakespeare is global, it is because his work is able to inhabit so many different locals."[8]

Dawson points to the limitations of collapsing "global" and "local" into "glocal," a term "that carries with it a two-pronged political agenda." It is not that foreign Shakespeares cannot be political and polemical, but there is a tendency to assume that universal values "are suspect, mainly a screen for cultural or political domination" and that the local "is a potential antidote, resistant to hegemony." However, it is often the presumed "universal" values themselves that offer the lens and means of resistance: "in eastern Europe, for example, liberal ideas such as individual freedom in the face of state oppression have often marked productions of *Hamlet*. In such locations, the 'local' is the space of oppression, the 'global' of liberation."[9] Dawson's arguments opened up ways in which we could explore the strong and explicit political underpinnings of the various global Shakespeares we read and viewed together, particularly Kozintsev's Marxist *Lear* and Salih's postcolonial novel, as well as many of the subjects of the final projects.

Finally, since most of the adaptations or appropriations we considered are films, the course needed to accommodate the logistics of viewing and cinematic analysis. While students may acknowledge the genre of film as text, that requires critical attention as much as any literary work, and while they may be avid filmgoers, their critical apparatus for discussing films is often surprisingly undeveloped. Fortunately, a number of works are available that provide critical vocabulary and a conceptual framework for discussing film as text.[10] We also viewed the films together, which required additional class time but allowed for productive group discussion and analysis. Critical readings about the films were assigned in advance; these were a useful preparation for the viewing experience. As one student put it, "It was so helpful to bring a foundational vocabulary and previous analysis to the film; I learned to become a more sophisticated viewer."

In addition to the many general resources on Shakespearean film, Douglas Lanier's essay, "*Prospero's Books* and the Textual Shakespeare," offered a valuable

---

[8] Anthony Dawson, "Cross-Cultural Interpretation: Reading Kurosawa Reading Shakespeare," in *A Concise Companion to Shakespeare on the Screen*, ed. Diana Henderson (Malden, MA: Blackwell Publishing, 2006), 157.

[9] Dawson, "Cross-Cultural Interpretation," 158.

[10] There are a number of works on cinematic Shakespeare. Among the more useful are Richard Burt and Lynda E. Roose, eds., *Shakespeare, The Movie II: Popularizing the Plays on Film, TV, Video, and DVD* (New York: Routledge, 2003); Samuel Crowl, *Shakespeare and Film: A Norton Guide* (New York: W.W. Norton, 2007); Anthony Guneratne, *Shakespeare, Film Studies, and the Visual Cultures of Modernity* (New York: Palgrave Macmillan, 2008); Russell Jackson, ed., *The Cambridge Companion to Shakespeare on Film* (Cambridge: Cambridge University Press, 2007); Robert Shaughnessy, ed., *Shakespeare on Film: Contemporary Critical Essays* (New York: St. Martin's Press, 1998), 18–42; and Kenneth Rothwell, *A History of Shakespeare on the Screen: A Century of Film and Television* (Cambridge: Cambridge University Press, 2004).

lens for expanding the "tension between the textual and theatrical Shakespeare" to include cinematic revisions. Lanier argues that recent multimedia technologies have challenged the authority of the literary text since we can now mimic the practice of reading and rereading by viewing and re-viewing. *Prospero's Books* is but one example of a revision that engages directly with "the issue of the Shakespearean medium, raising anew the crucial question of what forms the Shakespearean book and the cultural capital it represents can take in a post-literate age."[11]

Culminating Shakespeare Around the World Projects

Eighteen students were enrolled in this class. Early in the semester, I offered twenty-four subjects as options for the final research project. Some of the choices were prescribed to ensure that particular subjects were covered, and others were general country assignments from which students could choose their focus area. Excerpts from the assignment:

> **First Step:**
> Your task is to explore your subject—which will include viewing and analyzing a film, reading available reviews about a noteworthy stage performance, or reading critical discussions of how Shakespeare has been appropriated by a particular country or culture. In other words, you will not all follow the same process: some of you will be focusing on a very specific subject—a micro-analysis—and some of you will be offering a broader perspective.
>
> **Research:**
> You are encouraged to explore resources on Netflix, YouTube, and MIT's Global Shakespeares Video and Performance Archive. Research of print sources through the MLA bibliography will lead you to appropriate journals of Shakespearean studies, film studies, and performance criticism; the online journal *Borrowers and Lenders: The Journal of Shakespeare and Appropriation* will be useful for many of you. For more recent performance reviews, more popular media will be useful.
>
> **Outcome/Oral Presentation:**
> 1: We will allow 25 minutes for each presentation: approximately 15 minutes for the presentation itself and 10 minutes for class response and questions. You must respect the time limit.

[11] Douglas Lanier, "Drowning the Book: *Prospero's Books* and the Textual Shakespeare," in *Shakespeare on Film: Contemporary Critical Essays,* ed. Robert Shaughnessy (New York: St. Martin's Press, 1998), 194.

2: Presentations must include a visual component—film clips, websites, or still images—but use of PowerPoints or Prezi must be used efficiently and be well integrated with your verbal presentation.

3: A one-page handout (front and back) should provide a brief overview of your project and an annotated list of 8–10 works you consulted for your project. This list is meant to demonstrate your research and to provide further information for your audience. This bibliography may include performance reviews, book reviews, and critical articles but it must show your thorough research on your topic.

4: Your presentation should be well-rehearsed, engaging, and animated; you should make connections, where appropriate, to the theoretical questions and issues we have discussed throughout the semester.

Grading/Peer Feedback Forms:
1: Quality of Research: (Was the subject carefully and thoroughly researched? Were the sources appropriate and relevant?) 5 points

2: Delivery/Presentation: (Was the speaker clear, concise, well-prepared, engaging?) 5 points

3: Overall Quality of information presented: (Was the subject presented in a clear, focused, and coherent manner?) 5 points

4: Handout: (Was the handout well-prepared, error-free, informative, visually appealing?) 5 points

Midway through the semester, I met with students individually to discuss their progress. Initially, most students approached the final project with skepticism: they were entering unfamiliar territory and they were certain they would not find any material on their assigned subject. By conference time, however, most students were excited and surprised by the embarrassment of riches they had uncovered; while the research component was challenging, students were empowered by their success and resourcefulness. As one student put it, "It's been exciting to move beyond the boundaries of the MLA sources."

A Brief Description of the Final Projects

Australia: Shakespeare Down Under focused on Bell Shakespeare, the national theatrical company founded in 1990 by director John Bell, with attention to the company's mission and ethos in transcending traditional British emulation into innovative and distinctly Australian Shakespeares.

Caribbean: Shakespeare of the Caribbean explored Nobel-prize winning poet Derek Walcott's *A Branch of the Blue Nile,* a play in which characters struggle to reconcile their Caribbean heritage with and against *Antony and Cleopatra.* Walcott's work engages with Shakespeare through the lens of postcolonial Antilles.

Caribbean: Francophonic Island Shakespeares discussed the 1969 play, *Une tempête,* Aimé Césaire's radical postcolonial response to *The Tempest.* Césaire's work has become one of the most visible global appropriations of Shakespeare, and this presentation situated the work within its dynamic tradition of critical reception.

China: The Banquet explored the 2006 film released in the United States as *The Legend of the Black Scorpion.* The presentation focused on the different ways this controversial film, a contemporary revision of *Hamlet,* was received by Chinese and Western audiences.

China: Wu Hsing-kuo. In 1986, popular Taiwanese actor Wu Hsing-kuo helped found the theatrical company, Contemporary Legend, with the intention of integrating traditional Chinese theatre with Western classical plays. Wu directed several Shakespearean adaptations, including a one-man *King Lear* in which he merges the Shakespearean narrative with autobiographical elements.

Germany: Shakespeare in Germany described productions of *The Merchant of Venice* in post-World War II Germany. The student examined the political challenges of the representation of Shylock and of his daughter Jessica, situating the performances in their historical moment and considering the ramifications of "political Shakespeare."

Hong Kong: Shakespeare in Hong Kong focused on a stage production of *King Lear* by the Hong Kong Repertory Theatre, which rotated Cantonese and Mandarin speaking casts to accommodate a hybrid audience; the presentation also described two film adaptations of *Romeo and Juliet: Crocodile River* (1965) and *Young Lovers* (1969).

Hungary: Shakespeare in Hungary explored Hungarian identity and subversive theatre during the Communist years, focusing on the decidedly political interpretation of various productions of *Hamlet*—particularly interesting since Stalin found fault with Hamlet's alleged naive intellectualism and individualism.

India: Maqbool analyzed the 2003 Bollywood film based on *Macbeth* by Indian director Vishal Bhardwaj. This presentation focused on issues of intertextuality and adaptation, beginning with Bhardwaj's acknowledgement of his debt to both Shakespeare and Kurosawa's *Throne of Blood.*

India: Omkara examined the 2006 film inspired by *Othello* and also directed by Vishal Bhardwaj. The film, in the genre of Indian crime thriller, won multiple international awards and was featured at the 2006 Cannes Film Festival. The presentation focused on the film as appropriation and on how the change in cultural dynamics specifically affects the gender politics of the play.

Italy: From Play to Score to Film examined Verdi's opera, *Otello,* and the filmed stage version by Franco Zefferelli. This presentation focused on the process of transforming drama to musical theatre and on the tensions between lavish spectacle and linear narrative.

Japan: Shakespeare in Japan focused on two recent adaptations: the 1993 *Hamlet* Rock Opera in which Hamlet was played by the famous vocalist of the heavy metal group X Japan, Toshi, and the 2012 filmed stage production in Tokyo of *Romeo and Juliet* starring popular actors Sato Takeru and Ishihara Satomi. The student also examined a Kabuki performance of *Twelfth Night* to demonstrate that Japan's adaptations of Shakespeare comprise both traditional and Western-inspired responses.

Mexico: Shakespeare in Mexico examined *A Soldier in Every Son: The Rise of the Aztecs,* a play by Mexico's leading playwright, Luis Mario Moncada. The play, commissioned by the Royal Shakespeare Company for the 2012 World Shakespeare Festival, recounts Mexico's fifteenth-century dynastic conflicts through parallels with Shakespeare's history plays.

New Zealand: The Maori Merchant of Venice. In 2002, *The Merchant of Venice* was filmed entirely in Maori, using primarily Maori actors. This was the first Shakespeare film to be produced in New Zealand and the first Maori-language feature film. The director, Don Selwyn, is an advocate for Maori art and culture and encourages inclusion of the Maori perspective in mainstream film and television.

Russia: Russian "Hamletism": What is Rotten in Elsinore. This project explored the presence of *Hamlet* in Russia, focusing on the influential 1912 stage production by Stanislavski and Craig and on Kozintsev's post-Stalin film of 1964, based on Boris Pasternak's colloquial but poetic translation. This project explored the many aesthetic and ideological challenges of representing *Hamlet* in various moments throughout Russian history.

South Africa: Shakespeare in Mzansi. In 2008, a popular four-part miniseries, *Shakespeare in Mzansi*, transformed *King Lear, Macbeth,* and *Romeo and Juliet* into contemporary South African settings. One part of the series, *uGugu noAndile* (based on *Romeo and Juliet*) was subsequently expanded into a feature film, which was well received throughout Africa and won awards at the African Movie Academy Awards in Nigeria.

South Africa: uMabatha. During the apartheid era, Welcome Msomi, a South African playwright and director, wrote a Zulu adaptation of *Macbeth. uMabatha* recounts the story of Shaka, a legendary nineteenth-century Zulu chief. After premiering in South Africa, the play travelled to Europe and the United States and was one of the six plays selected for the opening of London's rebuilt *Globe* theatre in 1997.

Spain: Shakespeare in the Spanish Theatre focused on the Shakespearean adaptations and appropriations of Spanish director Calixto Bieito. Known for his innovative and controversial transformations of classic literary works, Bieito has transformed *Macbeth, Hamlet,* and *King Lear.* His most recent response to Shakespeare is his play *Forests,* a bilingual mash-up based on references and plot strands involving the presence of forests in twenty of Shakespeare's plays.

Conclusion

Jacques Derrida, an avowed bardolater, described Shakespeare's ongoing global appeal: "Who demonstrates better that texts loaded with history offer themselves so well in contexts very different from their time and place of origin, not only in the European twentieth century, but in Japanese or Chinese transpositions?"[12] That Shakespeare offers endless potential for global transformations is undeniable, and the possibilities for incorporating "global Shakespeares" in the classroom are equally limitless. The adaptations, appropriations, and final projects listed here comprise a small number of the many Shakespearean transformations available for exploration. While the ability to travel to locations to view global Shakespeare performances is necessarily limited, the possibilities for research and creativity that digital technologies afford are legion and students are generally fluent in negotiating these resources.

At the graduate level, this course was theoretically driven, but the level of scholarly discourse could be adjusted to an undergraduate level. A course in global Shakespeares inevitably and appropriately transcends the boundaries of Shakespeare studies as it involves broader questions of cultural appropriation, intertextuality, authorship, genre, and textual stability—discussions that can enrich understanding of other literary studies as well.

The culminating projects comprised one of the best pedagogical experiences I have enjoyed in many years of teaching. The presentations created a rich learn-

[12] Jacques Derrida, *Acts of Literature*, ed. Derek Attridge (New York: Routledge, 1992), 62.

ing community in which all the students took satisfaction in their creativity and resourcefulness in introducing classmates to a new subject. Finally, a welcome result of this assignment was that each student was compelled to research and convey a historical and political understanding of the assigned country or culture. An understanding of Hong Kong's independence from Britain, or Aztec history, or the rich diversity of the Caribbean community emerged from what became an interdisciplinary inquiry. Global Shakespeares encouraged students to appreciate the ongoing and broad literary and theatrical appeal of Shakespeare, while also leading them to become more sensitive global citizens.

What Would Helen of Troy Say?: Premodern Schoolroom Practices and Modern Students' Creative Projects

Linda Shenk, Iowa State University

As a teacher of premodern literature, I am forever—like the Roman god Janus—looking simultaneously in different directions, hoping to take into a single view competing and sometimes contradictory impulses. I want students to appreciate and enjoy literary creativity and performance while learning the skills of sophisticated close reading; I want students to explore the philosophical relevance of literature's enduring, often open-ended questions while still acknowledging the alterity of the historical world that produced the texts we study. The figure Helen of Troy from Christopher Marlowe's *Doctor Faustus* helped bring together these competing impulses back in my first year of full-time teaching when I assigned a creative capstone project in my Shakespeare and His Contemporaries course.

For that final project, students could choose to perform a scene, rewrite an existing one, or write new lines /speeches for a character in any of the plays we had read that semester. One student chose to write a speech for Marlowe's Helen of Troy. In the student's project, Helen breaks the limpid silence Marlowe gives her and addresses Faustus in a speech archly full of reproach. This Helen mocks Faustus by praising him for all his learning and access to Christianity and intellectual culture: *he*, unlike she, has free will because of his connection to these traditions—traditions that have subjected Helen to the male gaze and used her as a scapegoat for human violence. The student took the play's questions of sin, faith, knowledge, and free will—added her own interest in gender—and engaged cruxes that Marlowe probes but leaves unresolved.

This student, without realizing it, had written an *ethopoeia* (piece written in the voice of another) inflected with both a *suasoria* (a speech of advice) and a paradoxical *encomium* (speech of ironic praise)—all forms of composition that Marlowe would have learned in school. In fact, Helen of Troy was one of the best-known prompts for the paradoxical *encomium*, with its tradition that extended back to the classical rhetoric of the Sophist Gorgias and his famous "Encomium of Helen."[1] These types of compositions, along with such exercises as the *controversia,* taught schoolboys like Marlowe to argue on either side of a question, to construct voices for fictional speakers, and to suggest an argument through the slippery medium of irony. As numerous scholars from Sister Miriam Joseph, Joel B. Altman, and Eugene M. Waith to Victoria Kahn and Peter Mack have demonstrated, [2] Marlowe and his contemporaries, including Shakespeare, Ben Jonson, John Donne, Sir Philip Sidney, Sir Walter Ralegh, and John Lyly, learned to think and write like Januses, facing two directions at once. Their training in rhetoric taught them to acknowledge the possibility for competing viewpoints and truths and, as Altman explains, helped these writers create literary works that "did not merely raise questions, in the general sense, but literally were questions—or rather fictional realizations of questions."[3]

Over the years, I have tapped increasingly into the rhetorical tradition and its manifestations in the premodern schoolroom to give modern students strategies for turning the analytical precision of close reading into practices that lead to the glamor of performance and creative projects. In addition to and in keeping with Janus's simultaneous views into the past and the future, I work toward taking in both the world of premodern literature as well as modern applications for these skills. Beginning on the first day of the semester, I quietly layer in elements of the premodern schoolroom, such as teaching students to identify rhetorical figures and to see how the literary texts we study are steeped in the rhetorical practice of arguing "in either part," *in utramque partem.* Essentially, I use tools once thought to be rather "old-school" but that have recently received renewed interest as scholars re-remember how the premodern interest in rhetoric and oratory unlocks clues to character, dramatic structure, and performance itself.[4] I use

---

[1] For more on the tradition of the paradoxical *encomium* and its popularity in early modern and Restoration England, see Henry Knight Miller's "The Paradoxical Encomium with Special Reference to Its Vogue in England, 1600–1800," *Modern Philology* 53, no. 3 (1956): 145–78.

[2] Sister Miriam Joseph, *Shakespeare's Use of the Arts of Language* (New York: Columbia University Press, 1947); Joel B. Altman, *The Tudor Play of Mind: Rhetorical Inquiry and the Development of Elizabethan Drama* (Berkeley: University of California Press, 1978); Eugene M. Waith, *The Pattern of Tragicomedy in Beaumont and Fletcher* (1952; repr., Hamdon, CT: Archon Books, 1969), especially 87–98 in the Archon edition; Peter Mack, *Reading and Rhetoric in Montaigne and Shakespeare* (London: Bloomsbury Academic, 2010); and Victoria Kahn, *Machiavellian Rhetoric: From the Counter-Reformation to Milton* (Princeton: Princeton University Press, 1994).

[3] Altman, *The Tudor Play of Mind,* 3.

[4] For recent scholarship on rhetorical training and drama, see, for example, Ira Clark, *Rhetorical Readings, Dark Comedies, and Shakespeare's Problem Plays* (Gainesville: University Press of Florida, 2007); William L. Davis, "Better a Witty Fool than a Foolish Wit: The Art of Shakespeare's Chiasmus," *Text and Performance Quarterly* 23, no. 4 (2003): 311–30; Jane Freeman, "'Fair Terms and a Villain's Mind': Rhetorical Patterns in

these same elements to lay the foundation for engaging in performance-related exercises as well as for opening doors to the interpretative cruxes that will spark students' creative projects at the end of the term.

Over the years since I first assigned this type of creative project, many students have composed *ethopoeiae* by doing such things as writing the letter Shakespeare's Cressida sends to Troilus (the one he shreds before reading it) or crafting a speech of advice from Queen Elizabeth (in Shakespeare's *Richard III*) to her daughter on the eve of marrying Richmond. Such a project, with its direct link to the early modern schoolroom, remains an option in my current creative assignment; however, I have realized that the deeper philosophical structures taught in these exercises can lead to an array of options that typically do not look anything like an *ethopoeia* or a *suasoria*. Now, the students' options for creative projects are endless. Students paint, make films, write novellas, perform scenes (sometimes in both English and American Sign Language), take photos, blow glass, make video blogs, devise architectural designs, write detailed unit-lesson plans, construct life-size puppets, sew costumes, make stained-glass pieces, do digital animation, write and perform music. I tell them to play a little, experiment a little, dream a little, say something important.[5]

The key criterion is that the creative project must respond to and take a stand on one of the original text's questions, and, to showcase how it engages with the polyphonic perspective of the original, the student writes a seven-page companion paper.[6] In many ways, this leap from questions to "taking a stand" responds to the concept of art's participation in social change. As Theodore Leinwand observes, stopping at the notion of (Shakespeare's) art posing questions, allows us to "confine Shakespeare to the realm of analysis. It hardly gets students or teachers up on their feet and it stops conveniently short of action. Real citizens, like their fictional counterparts, make choices and then act on them."[7] In this essay, I will describe how I build to an action-focused, interpretative, open-

---

The Merchant of Venice," *Rhetorica* 20, no. 2 (2002): 149–72; Stefan D. Keller, "Combining Rhetoric and Pragmatics to Read *Othello*," *English Studies* 91, no. 4 (2010): 398–411; and Jenny C. Mann, *Outlaw Rhetoric: Figuring Vernacular Eloquence in Shakespeare's England* (Ithaca, NY: Cornell University Press, 2012).

[5] Just as Carole Levin discusses in this volume, I find that these creative projects often give students a different kind of venue to engage with the material and succeed; some students have skills that translate better into creative work than traditional analysis.

[6] For additional approaches to combining open-ended creative projects with written work, see Anna Riehl Bertolet's and Karolyn Kinane's essays in this volume. Like Kinane, I also encourage students to create projects that connect to their individual majors as well as to consider how ideas in the assigned texts can be transformative and therefore relate to real-world situations.

[7] Theodore Leinwand, "Afterword," in *Shakespearean Educations: Power, Citizenship, and Performance*, ed. Coppélia Kahn, Heather S. Nathans, and Mimi Godfrey, 277 (Newark: University of Delaware Press, 2011).

ended creative project and final paper as the culmination of a trajectory of exercises steeped in premodern schoolroom traditions. Because I assign the creative project mostly in my upper division Shakespeare courses (enrollment: 35), I will focus my examples on Shakespeare's plays, using them essentially as a *synecdoche* for premodern texts in general, but I will give nods to other works along the way.

The Creative Project Assignment

The following text begins my assignment sheet for the creative project and final paper:

> In several of the activities and assignments for this class, we have considered how Shakespeare's plays themselves give space for multiple interpretations because of the way Shakespeare learned, in school, to construct arguments that acknowledged the possibility of multiple, even conflicting, truths. His plays do more than raise questions; they *are* questions—questions that expose gaps in both logic and truths through the very fact that plays are dialogic, offering a plurality of voices.
>
> In addition, we have thought about Shakespeare across media—thinking about how directors use visual elements of space to shape an interpretation; thinking about how designers use costume, lighting, and/or color to emphasize certain elements; thinking about how speaking Shakespeare's language aloud affects interpretation.
>
> For this final assignment, produce a creative piece that responds with an answer to a question that arises in one of Shakespeare's characters, relationships, or plays. Essentially, create a piece that takes a stand on an idea or issue so that it puts forward a possible *interpretation* of a scene, play, or character. In your academic career and personal life, many of you engage in some type of creative activity, such as music, graphic design, fiction/poetry writing, theatrical performance, film animation, lesson plan creation, photography, web design, pottery, sewing, puppetry, architectural design, sculpture, etc., so here is your chance to design a project that engages your specific interests. Your options for what this piece can be are wide open, so play a little, experiment a little, dream a little, say something important.
>
> To help ensure that you are on a good path that will lead to an interpretation of some aspect of Shakespeare's play(s) and that you are taking on an appropriate-size endeavor, let me know as soon as possible what you are thinking of doing for your project. Look on the Schedule of Assignments for the deadline for contacting me. (You may email me, talk to me in person, or write me a short, informal description.) Feel free to contact me *especially if* you are stuck on what to do. Devising a creative project might not be as difficult as it may seem; some of the best projects have come from students who initially thought they had no inkling of creativity!

The First Day of Class and the First Assigned Texts: Introducing the First Rhetorical Figures

Keeping in mind that this creative project is the capstone for the course, I introduce those Janus impulses of creative playfulness, precise reading, and rhetorical tools on the first day of class, saving work with the texts as questions for the second week (or later) in the term. I want the first day to give a peek into the allure and relevance of close reading with an eye toward character analysis and relationship. My foray into these worlds is a simple technique related to what linguists call discourse analysis: I introduce the technique as characters "speaking a same language." I ask students to notice when characters literally "speak each other's language" (i.e., repeat each other's words) and then how these words get passed back and forth. I use this technique as the foundation on which I teach rhetorical practices, techniques of staging power dynamics, and some surprising real-world connections.

Before we analyze anything from Shakespeare, I ask the class the generic question: "What individuals or groups in real life speak the same, sometimes specialized, language?" Students note people in the same country or geographic location, in similar professions or activities, with similar backgrounds or interests (families, friends, lovers), and we talk about the fact that most intimate sharing typically happens between lovers. . .and twins. Because there are not too many sets of twins in literature, I then ask, "Who are the most famous lovers in all of literature?"—to which students always respond (thank heavens): "Romeo and Juliet!" At this point, I have the students get with a partner and read aloud Romeo and Juliet's first exchange in act 1 and then go through this pair's dialogue, circling all the words that these characters share. Romeo and Juliet do indeed speak the same language. When we come back together as a large group, the students and I begin to explore the complicated layers of this simple tool of speaking the same language. We make a list of all the main words Romeo and Juliet share—such as pilgrim(s), lips, hands, touch, kiss, prayer, sin, saint, palm, palmer's, grant—noticing that the words these two characters share relate to physical contact and to religion. This linguistic common ground reveals in very concrete terms the mixture of hormones, spirituality, and courtly love tradition that students intuitively sense in the scene.

As the next step, we move from discussing the shared words to noting the way the characters pass words back and forth. Do the characters mean, or refer to, the same thing when one of them repeats a word? By examining shared words in Romeo and Juliet's first exchange, we watch how this "love at first sight" moment involves delicate negotiation: Juliet gently takes Romeo's words and twists their referent and context to delay the kiss. For example, the first substantive word they share is "pilgrim/pilgrims." Romeo refers to his lips as "pilgrims"; Juliet picks up this word but uses it to refer to *him* as a pilgrim. In one deft move, her shift of referent takes the focus off his lips moving in on hers (made playful rather than sexual with his description of them as religious followers) and makes him the pilgrim. She thus gives him a claim to virtue, which he must now accommodate and find a new way to move in on her again. Juliet continues the religious imagery by introducing the idea of palmers and a palm-to-palm kiss. As the students analyze how Juliet cleverly introduces a different, more modest kind of kiss, I introduce the rhetorical figure *polyptoton* (repeating a word but in a slightly different form, often a cognate such as "palm" and its cognate "palmers").[8] We note that Juliet's wit prompts Romeo to worry that he will not get to kiss her, and there follows a moment of light tension when they have a brief series of one-liners, which illustrates the rhetorical figure *stichomythia*.

I introduce only these two rhetorical figures on the first day because I am layering in an attention to prose versus verse and rhyme alongside the technique of "speaking the same language." Through Romeo and Juliet's exchange, we talk about how the shared language (and the rhetorical figures) show flirtation and intelligence, even as the words themselves clearly show the mixing of spirituality and surging hormones that makes this scene so famous. Then of course, we put the icing on the cake by noting that Romeo and Juliet share a sonnet. . .and that knowing these things can translate into a performance far more nuanced than the basic theater objective for the subscene: "love at first sight."

The first full text I assign for the term in the Shakespeare course is often *The Taming of the Shrew* because, quite literally, Petruchio requires Katherine to speak his language to the extent that, in act 4, he gets her to call the sun, the moon. Watching how Katherine and Petruchio speak the same language serves as a nice counterpoint to Romeo and Juliet. In Katherine and Petruchio's first exchange (2.1),[9] they share words but often through either *polyptoton* or changes in a word's referent or meaning, and these linguistic disagreements demonstrate their combative relationship. Their shared words center on physical movement or aggression (*sting, move, sit*) and common domestic creatures or items (*crab, stool, buzzard*)—a far cry from the lofty, courtly love and evident physical attraction in Romeo and Juliet's shared language. Students always notice that Petruchio often twists words to their sexual meanings (*bear* and *tail*, for example), and sometimes I show them this same scene from Franco Zeffirelli's film version (starring Elizabeth Taylor and Richard Burton) to illustrate, in part, how Zeffirelli downplays the crass sexuality of these moments. When Burton delivers the line about his tongue in her tail, he is under a trap door, and she is on top of it, dragging bags to weigh him down. In this way, I begin to show how students can use close reading to identify a director's interpretative choices.

---

[8] A wonderful resource for rhetorical figures and their definitions is Silva Rhetoricae; all definitions used here come from its website at http://rhetoric.byu.edu/.

[9] All references to and quotations from Shakespeare's plays will be from *The Riverside Shakespeare*, ed. G. Blakemore Evans (Boston: Houghton Mifflin Company, 1974); parenthetical in-text citations will be to act, scene, and line.

Even as I use the strategy of "speaking the same language" pointedly in the opening few class sessions, this technique remains a central tool we will use as we study other Shakespearean plays throughout the semester. Using this approach, students can watch how Richard, Duke of York (later Richard III) ensnares Lady Anne by moving her away from her language of heaven and hell (her power over Richard comes from this moral high ground) and into that of the physical and earthly; students can explore the specifics of Iago persuading Othello (3.3) that Desdemona is unfaithful by taking nebulous notions of *thought* and *seem* and replacing them with *proof* and *satisfaction*. In addition, students can hear Iago take the language of love for Othello and shift it from Desdemona to himself—a transfer that culminates in the exchange of vows between the two men at the end of this same scene.

This technique of speaking the same language also works well in my British literature survey courses. In the fourteenth-century *Sir Gawain and the Green Knight*, students can explore how Sir Gawain and the lady essentially compete to see who can speak the chivalric language of subservience and fidelity better; in Geoffrey Chaucer's "Wife of Bath's Tale," the students can analyze how the young knight learns humility and trust from the old hag during their "pillow talk." This notion of "speaking the same language" is a simple, effective way of moving into close reading that has clear character-relationship and performance goals. It also occurs in real life, which is why linguists study shared language in discourse analysis. In fact, a colleague with whom I team-taught a Shakespeare course for a class of Bachelor of Fine Arts acting students noticed the playful real-world application right after I shared it with our students. The next class session, she came in and whispered that she had noticed this technique during the episode of Star Trek she had watched the night before. We enjoyed a good laugh over it, and it is true: I tell students that they will use this technique not only in examining fictional characters (in all contexts) but also in real-world situations. I tell them it can, for example, help them land their first job (by lightly speaking the language of an employer in their job letter and interview) and also create stronger, more cohesive written work for this class and in other disciplines. (Their introduction should set up the language of a writer's argument—a series of keywords that the writer then uses strategically in the rest of the paper). My colleagues in the STEM (science, technology, engineering, math) disciplines with whom I have shared this technique have commented that this strategy will help them in writing grants.

Students love the technique of speaking the same language for its simplicity, sophistication, and far-reaching applications. It also gets us, as a class, moving swiftly into close reading in ways that lend themselves to introducing rhetorical figures of repetition while providing a window into strategies of manipulation and articulations of extreme emotion.

While working on the first few texts early in the semester, I teach rhetorical figures related to repetition not only because they are easiest to identify but also because they are associated with the high style, which is the rhetorical style associated with arousing emotion. I teach *anaphora*, *epistrophe*, *symploce*, *epizeuxis*, *diacope*, *climax*, *anadiplosis*, and *gradatio*. Quite often, students have heard instances of *anaphora* and *epistrophe* (the same word beginning or ending a series of clauses or sentences, respectively) in political campaign speeches but never knew these patterns had names. I often use examples from past campaigns to drive home the point and then note that the candidates strategically use the high style to stir our emotions with the hope of gaining votes. In Shakespeare's works, Bottom in *A Midsummer Night's Dream* draws attention to his (over)use of the high style when he boasts that his acting can "move storms" (i.e., move the audience to tears, 1.2.27), and he whips out his "raging rocks" speech in the vein of a tyrant's rant after which he notes its high style, proclaiming, "This was lofty!" (1.2.39). Likewise, students have additional evidence to note the intensifying emotion in the Anglo-Saxon poem "The Wanderer" when they encounter the anaphoric repetition of "*Ubi sunt*."

By analyzing such rhetorical strategies, students gain concrete tools to talk intellectually about the structure of language and its intended effects. They also are encouraged to see literary texts as individual parts that can be named in much the same spirit that they learned (if they were lucky) about language through diagramming sentences. This same focus on parts translates nicely into deconstructing speeches and character representations into specific moments and strategies to see how a poet creates ambiguity and paradox—skills already present in the premodern classroom exercises that required students to be able to argue on either side of a question.

Arguing Multiple Sides of a Question

At the end of the first play in the Shakespeare course—and as initial preparation for the first paper assignment—I begin to introduce exercises inspired by the premodern-schoolroom activity called the *controversia*. For centuries extending back to classical rhetorical training, students were given a complicated, usually fantastical legal case and were assigned to argue on one side or the other. This assignment served as the apex of a student's rhetorical training, and the drama of the declamations prepared for this exercise gained such popularity that *controversiae* were often conducted before large audiences. As Joel B. Altman and Eugene M. Waith have analyzed at length in regard to Tudor plays,[10] this academic activity, with the way it acknowledges multiplicity of argument, serves as a useful lens through which to examine many pre-modern literary works.

10 Altman, *The Tudor Play of Mind*, especially chapter 2; Waith, *The Pattern of Tragicomedy in Beaumont and Fletcher*, 87–98.

In the Shakespeare course, I use the philosophies inherent in *controversiae* to create activities that require students to argue *in utramque partem*, on either side of a question. It is particularly effective to use this approach in relation to Katherine's long monologue at the end of *The Taming of the Shrew*: Is Katherine tamed? Or is she playing a game? I assign one of these perspectives to each side of the class, and students work in small groups to devise their answer and support it with specifics from the speech. We use these conflicting arguments to discuss not only how Shakespeare includes contradictory moments in a speech (and how performance choices further allow for complexity) but then also how these contradictions can allow a speech or an entire play to become unsettling because the issue never becomes fully resolved. With the final monologue in *Shrew,* we consider how the idea of taming a woman addresses questions of domestic abuse. Before reading the play, students print off the Wheel of Power and Control, distributed by the Center for Domestic Abuse and Violence. While the students read the play, I have them note places of physical, psychological, and emotional abuse. Even when we consider how Katherine is upholding patriarchy in her final speech, we consider how the play, like life, makes these power dynamics occasionally difficult to categorize solely as abuse. The speech has moments that can easily be read otherwise.

The exercise with Katherine's final speech approaches the issue of arguing on both sides of a question from more of a textual perspective, even as we, in class, also layer in an attention to performance noting that how a director stages Katherine's speech affects interpretation. One particularly nice moment is the placing of Katherine's hand beneath Petruchio's foot. I have students experiment with different ways of staging that moment to support their assigned position of tamed or "playing the game."[11]

Within the first few plays we study in the Shakespeare class, I want to move more clearly into territories of performance and creative activity, so I have an in-class exercise that links arguing on either side of a question to director's interpretation. I call it "the director's exercise," and I typically introduce it with Shylock from *The Merchant of Venice.* Here is the simple prompt for the activity:

> In groups of 4 or 5, work on one of the two following scenes from MV (1.3 or 3.1), and edit it as if you are a team of directors preparing a production of the play. As we have noticed in the presentations for film versions of Shakespeare, directors often cut lines in order to shape interpretation. For your particular production, you want to create a Shylock who is clearly more evil or more sympathetic than the one Shakespeare creates. First decide: Do you want your Shylock to gain the audience's empathy, or do you want

[11] For more ideas regarding using staging to explore Katherine and Petruchio's relationship (as well as other character relationships), see Mary Ellen Lamb's essay in the volume.

> Shylock, "the cur"? Feel free to edit not only Shylock's lines but also those of the other characters to create your desired portrayal. (A limitation: You may cut a few lines at a time but NOT lengthy speeches.)

When we discuss the exercise as a whole class, we go over some of the specific lines the groups eliminated, but I structure most of the discussion around the idea of what this activity revealed about the way Shakespeare constructs Shylock and other characters. Many students express that they found the strands of Shylock-the-cur tied more tightly than they expected to the places that arouse sympathy. They could see that these portrayals often rest side-by-side, and the "Hath not a Jew eyes" speech usually becomes a telling example to watch Shakespeare arguing on different sides of the question all within the confines of one speech. The speech opens and concludes with Shylock's vindictiveness, but the central portion where he addresses common humanity and introduces the whimsical idea of tickling evokes tenderness.

An exercise like this one can be useful for teaching all philosophically complex literature—I have used it in teaching the Anglo-Saxon *Beowulf*, for example, by asking students to go through and eliminate lines that call Beowulf's pure heroism into doubt. I also use it when examining Marlowe's questions of free will in *Doctor Faustus*, and then I echo this exercise when considering free will in John Milton's *Paradise Lost*. When teaching medieval and, definitely, early modern texts, I draw particular attention to the schoolroom exercise of the *controversia*, which is designed to get individuals arguing *in utramque partem*, and I have students read Russ McDonald's chapter "In Other Words" from *The Bedford Companion to Shakespeare.*[12]

As a follow-up to this reading, I elaborate on the *controversia* and draw attention to how the trial scene in *The Merchant of Venice* comes directly from this tradition. We examine how Portia succeeds in the trial precisely because she uses rhetorical dexterity to argue on both sides of the case—a dexterity made even more visible when we know that she argues the case through the argumentative approach of *concessio* (conceding one point in order to make a stronger one). Shylock, on the other hand, loses the trial, in part, because he uses the repetitive rhetorical strategy *commoratio* (frequently returning to one's strongest argument). Students can then link Shylock's repetitive style of argumentation to aspects they have already recognized in his speech patterns. Shakespeare consistently has Shylock use such repetition-driven rhetorical figures as *epizeuxis*, in which the same word is repeated with no other words in between, or *diacope*, when the same word is repeated with one or more intervening words. Examining the trial scene in *The Merchant of Venice* makes clear not only how premodern cultures celebrated rhetorical dexterity but also how the author's own nimble ability to argue

[12] Russ McDonald, *The Bedford Companion to Shakespeare: An Introduction with Documents*, 2nd ed. (Boston: Bedford/St. Martins, 2001).

on more than one side of a question (that students examined with the representation of Shylock) creates artistic ambiguity.

To solidify this notion of intellectual complexity in literary texts (premodern and otherwise), I want students to begin using this approach in their writing—an inclusion that will continue to inform class discussion as well as pave the way for the creative project. In the Shakespeare class and in the first half of my British literature survey, I have just started including a gentle refutation paper assignment. A focus on the refutation exercises in the premodern schoolroom is the inspiration for this first paper, an assignment new to my pedagogy—added after I read Joanne E. Gates's essay.[13]

First Paper Assignment: Gentle Refutation

To give students concrete territory for examining the philosophical complexity of the texts they are reading, I find that an early step for seeing premodern texts as philosophical questions comes with comparing a work we have studied alongside one idea from an editor's introduction to that text's historical period. In the survey course, students use the introduction to the period found in their anthology; in the Shakespeare course, they use Russ McDonald's *The Bedford Companion to Shakespeare*.[14] I ask students to take a passage from one of these introductory sources and demonstrate how the literary text creates a more nuanced picture than the broad introduction can possibly acknowledge. I make clear that the editors of the survey anthology and McDonald's introduction must necessarily be general, which is why I call the assigned refutation a "gentle" one.

This assignment not only integrates text with historical context but it also invokes the idea that art can go beyond reality. Art naturally has the freedom to expose faults, ask questions, and imagine new ways of interacting with and in the world. This paper assignment draws attention to literature's flexibility to probe and reimagine. It allows us, as a class of individual writers, to explore imagination as a call to reflection and to the action of citizenship without necessarily prescribing what path we ought to take.

---

[13] Joanne E. Gates, "Introducing Students to Effective Refutation," in *Approaches to Teaching Shakespeare's* Hamlet, ed. Bernice W. Kliman (New York: Modern Language Association of America, 2002), 216–17. Gates has her students refute some aspect of Kermode's introduction to *Hamlet* found in the Riverside edition.

[14] See note 12.

Mind the Gaps

As a philosophical ideal, the notion that art and its questions are important is absolutely true but also, in my opinion, too general. I want students to see the mechanics of exactly how art provokes by creating gaps or dissonance, by incorporating multiple perspectives. How does a text's structure, a speech's elements, a speaker's phrasing, a juxtaposition of moments create ideological polyphony? Peter Mack, in his book *Reading and Rhetoric in Montaigne and Shakespeare*, provides a window into one rhetorical avenue for examining such tools. By knowing the forms of argumentation that early modern writers learned, Mack notes that Shakespeare did not always draw a great deal from these forms, and when Shakespeare does not use these strategies, it makes it more clear how the text has gaps in logic that, in turn, resist resolution. Mack explains that Shakespeare actually "avoids (or when working from a source even suppresses) the logical connectives which explain the links between ideas or seek to force the listener's assent to particular conclusions."[15]

Examining how Shakespeare's plays have gaps in logic or places where Shakespeare withholds logic provides concrete moments to help students see not only the questions a text raises but also how these examples show interpretative silence in very specific places and in relation to very specific ideas. I often begin this movement into noticing these silences by looking at moments where we see characters asking questions of themselves or making decisions based on other characters' comments. We can watch Brutus decide to assassinate Caesar through Cassius's influence in Brutus's soliloquy in act 2 where he cements his decision by reasoning through analogy, which is false reasoning. We can watch Hamlet repeatedly question whether or not to act in this famously question-filled play. As Maynard Mack explains, *Hamlet* is set in "an interrogative world,"[16] and Terry Reilly uses the approach of questions in this play to help his students explore "knowledge as pluralistic rather than hierarchical."[17]

To examine this plurality, I often begin with the exercises described earlier that focus on just one character and then, as the term progresses, to discuss how the multivocality of numerous characters creates gaps regarding an issue. How does Iago's description of Othello match this character when we meet him in the

---

[15] Mack, *Reading and Rhetoric,* 84.

[16] Quoted in Robert H. Ray, "A World of Questions: An Approach Indebted to Maynard Mack," in Kliman, *Approaches to Teaching Shakespeare's* Hamlet, 97 (see note 13).

[17] Terry Reilly, "Decentering *Hamlet*: Questions and Perspectives Concerning Evidence and Proof," in Kliman, *Approaches to Teaching Shakespeare's* Hamlet, 157. Other helpful essays in this collection also provide question-driven approaches to *Hamlet*, especially Ray's "A World of Questions: An Approach Indebted to Maynard Mack," 97–101; David George's "Groups Debating Issues," 233–34; and Alan R. Young's "Existential Questions," 234.

next scene? How does the old hag's pillow lecture in the "Wife of Bath's Tale" match what the Wife herself says in the final moments of this section? What does Milton's Satan say about freedom in Hell, and how does the Council scene in Hell—including Belzebub's decision as to which action to take—reflect these values? In the Anglo-Saxon poem "The Dream of the Rood," how do images of Christ's humanity compete with images of His divinity? This approach of conflicting moments also works well, as James S. Baumlin demonstrates, with the tension between the ideals of Neoplatonic love and the pull of carnal desire in early modern love poetry such as in Sir Philip Sidney's *Astrophil and Stella* and John Donne's love poems. Baumlin maps this tension succinctly by analyzing the moment in Baldassare Castiglione's *The Book of the Courtier* when Lord Cesar Gonzaga and Lord Gaspar respond doubtfully to Pietro Bembo's rhapsodic exposition of Neoplatonic love.[18]

Staging the Art of Questions: Moving from Text into Multi-modal Creativities

This notion of plurality becomes even more concrete when explored through performance and the infinite number of choices directors and actors make. Certainly, any exercise that involves having small groups devise staging for a particular moment can help show differing interpretations, but here are two exercises I use that build added attention to cruxes in a text—approaches to texts that will continue to pave the way for the creative project.

Staging a visual representation: Although I often do standard staging exercises, sometimes I have groups take a more abstract approach. I ask students to use every member of their group (and they may ask other classmates to join in later) to create an abstract visual representation that encapsulates either the layers of a particular character or a comparison between two different characters or ideas in a text. For example, I have had groups look at the multiplicity of roles that Cressida or Desdemona adopt in their first scenes on stage. Students identify layers in Cressida's sly wit yet girlish hope and in Desdemona's obedient duty yet assertive strength. In premodern literature classes, I could have students create visual representations of the competing strands of sexual and transcendent love in Donne's "A Valediction: Forbidding Mourning" or the dif-

[18] In addition to his discussion of using a rhetorical dialogic approach to early modern love poetry, Baumlin opens his essay with an extremely clever analysis of both Raphael's fresco "The School of Athens" in the Vatican and another fresco—just across from it—"Dispute on the Sacraments" as visual representation of dialogic versus monologic approaches to truth; James S. Baumlin, "Dialogue and *Controversia* in English Renaissance Literature: Historicizing the Reader's Response," *Publications of the Missouri Philological Association* 19 (1994): 1–20.

fering representation of Catholicism and Protestantism in book 1 of Edmund Spenser's *The Faerie Queene*. By identifying multiple and sometimes conflicting strands within a character (and sometimes creating a visual representation that shows the interchange between them), students begin to see how interpretations will work with these shifting dynamics—a discovery that then can move into a later class discussion of how these dynamics address central questions in the text overall. Likewise, when I have students work on visual representations of a pair of characters in the Shakespeare course, I often use such duos as the battle oration of Richard III versus that of Richmond or something more esoteric such as the different approaches to language we see between Berowne and Armado in *Love's Labour's Lost*. Overall, this exercise that moves students away from staging a scene allows them to identify more swiftly the tensions within and among characters, using physicality in space to explore underlying cruxes.

Companion scenes or moments: In a more traditional staging vein, I have students stage what I call companion scenes—scenes that a writer clearly wants us to use as comparisons: the opening scenes set in Egypt and Rome in Shakespeare's *Antony and Cleopatra*; Richard's and Richmond's battle orations in *Richard III*; Brabantio's act of joining Desdemona's and Othello's hands in act 1 versus Iago's and Othello's kneeling in act 3; Beowulf-poet's stories of Hildeburh in comparison to Wealtheow in the mead-hall; the Gawain-poet's three bedroom and hunt scenes; Spenser's House of Pride versus that of Holiness. I use staging (or analyzing) these moments to have us explore specifically what questions and interpretations such juxtapositions might prompt.

Back to the Creative Project

Throughout the term, I have used identifying rhetorical devices and examining the texts through the approach of arguing *in utramque partem* to help students see layers and possibilities of interpretation. The creative project then becomes the space for students to make their own response to a question fictionalized in one or in a very limited number of the texts we have read together. Framing the creative project as an interpretation rooted in a question, I have found, helps not only to create more pointed creativity but also ensure that less confident students do not slink back and do something too much like mere summary or paraphrase. Likewise, the paper they write along with the creative project shows how this creative exploration engages directly with the specifics in the text. This way, students keep their work rooted in the text even as they may create an interpretation that, like the student who worked on Christopher Marlowe's Helen of Troy, voices a critique found in the original text but puts forth a more modern "answer" to that piece's questions. This approach lets the original premodern text speak relevance to us today while not trying to make it be modern. And all this creative work springs from the same set of tools many premodern writers learned in school—practices that merge composition with creativity as well as evoke exploration rather than proclaim a single-minded truth.

Back when the student wrote her speech for Helen, I was a new teacher more focused on surviving the semester than on creating an archive for this current essay's publication, but in some ways I am glad I no longer have her speech in my possession. The student's work responded to cruxes in Marlowe's play, but, like stage performance, this artistic piece evaporated, leaving the questions in Marlowe's play still unanswered—preserving that clever silence that gives space for other artist-students to enter and create their own responses that draw attention to Marlowe's questions even as they sometimes acknowledge the alterity of the premodern world and its practices.

Is There an Editor in This Text?: Renaissance Drama and Bibliographical History

Jonathan Walker, Portland State University

When teaching a graduate seminar titled Renaissance Drama, Bibliography, and Textuality, I assign a term-long project that helps teach students about early modern printing practices as well as modern editorial procedures by asking them to become experts on both the early imprints and the publication history of a non-Shakespearean play text. The project consists of five separate components, which students assemble into mini-editions of their chosen plays. Three of these components can be classified as descriptive bibliography insofar as they require students to exercise their powers of detailed observation while resisting their impulses to analyze, which they perform in the final portion of the project. The seminar itself is organized as a conversation between two critical paradigms: the New Bibliography, which to a great extent codified editorial principles for Renaissance drama during much of the twentieth century, and the New Textualism, which revised those principles through its poststructural critique of the New Bibliography. Using key readings from these two schools as well as research of their own, graduate students come to understand the purpose and idiosyncrasies of early textual features, such as signatures and catchwords; they learn the optimistic goals and unexamined assumptions of the New Bibliography, whose tenets and judgments (not always exercised with care) largely reigned over the editing of Renaissance drama for more than half a century; the major critiques leveled by the New Textualism as a fresh set of literary critical values rose to prominence; and, finally, the intimate details of early printings of their selected plays, which they describe and analyze using the techno-critical languages of bibliography and textual studies. In this essay, I would like to spell out the specific demands and aims of the assignment, to provide some examples from a couple of especially shrewd student projects, and to conclude by reflecting on some of the assignment's limitations.

Because all parts of the project revolve around a single non-Shakespearean play, students' first task is to choose an early modern dramatic text, several printings of which must be accessible in photographic facsimile editions or in the

Early English Books Online database. As simple as it may seem, this initial selection must consider a variety of factors to ensure that the text will yield rich enough results to complete sufficiently the later portions of the assignment. For instance, the 1633 printing of *The Famous Tragedy of the Rich Ievv of Malta* is the only extant text of Christopher Marlowe's play, which would make it a problematic choice when a student comes to produce an early publication history for the play and to account for textual variants between editions. On the other hand, a student choosing *The Spanish Tragedie* as her play would be faced with ten separate printings plus two variant editions between [1592] and 1633, resulting in too much information for her reader to digest. The selection of an appropriate play, then, requires students to conduct initial research in light of the latter portions of the assignment, striking a balance between a rich but not overabundant history of publication and collection of textual variants. The logic of restricting texts to non-Shakespearean drama is to try to discourage students from seeing authorial control as the dominant question—or, more precisely, the solution—to the myriad differences in textual materials they encounter. The question of authorship is certainly an active one throughout our class discussions, but with Shakespeare's habit of evoking the image of solitary genius, it is useful to subtract him from the equation from the outset. Incidentally, I also restrict students' choices to popular drama of the period since the process of publication that academic and court plays followed was often significantly different from those appearing in London's open-air and indoor playhouses.

The next portion of the assignment asks students to utilize two different reference books in order to locate as many copies as possible of the first impression of their plays: the A. W. Pollard and G. R. Redgrave *Short-Title Catalogue* (STC) and W. W. Greg's *Bibliography of the English Printed Drama to the Restoration.*[1] When locating copies of their plays, students must list the repositories where they are housed while also noting cases in which institutions own multiple copies and whatever variations or imperfections they exhibit, such as missing leaves or uncorrected states of the copies. For some of the plays that students choose, the Pollard and Redgrave *STC* suffices for finding all of the first imprint copies, but since the *STC* limits the number of copies it lists to ten—five in the United Kingdom, five in the United States—I ask students to crosscheck their findings with Greg's *Bibliography*, which lists all of the institutional and private collections in which surviving copies reside. Questions inevitably arise about why students must consult both reference books when Greg's seems to provide the

[1] *A Short-Title Catalogue of Books Printed in England, Scotland, & Ireland and of English Books Printed Abroad, 1475–1640*, 3 vols., 2d ed., comp. A. W. Pollard and G. R. Redgrave, rev. and enl. by W. A. Jackson and F. S. Ferguson, compl. by Katharine F. Pantzer (London: Bibliographical Society, 1976–1991); and W. W. Greg, *A Bibliography of the English Printed Drama to the Restoration*, 4 vols. (Oxford: Oxford University Press, 1939–1959).

readier information here. My response is that crosschecking facts between the reference books is itself a form of research because it constitutes due diligence on the students' part to verify the information that they find. But it is also important because the *STC* and Greg's *Bibliography* were published during different periods and therefore may reflect changing circumstances as copies of early printings change hands or, in rare cases, are newly discovered. The format of the individual entries in the two reference books is also rather dissimilar, so one of my aims in this component of the assignment is for students to acquire literacy in reading the particular conventions of each. The larger aim is for my students to gain a sense of the relative scarcity of many early modern printed plays as well as a sense of geographical or other factors that might affect their accessibility and thus the editing of modern editions.

After having gotten some practice reading the entries in the *STC* and Greg's *Bibliography*, students are more equipped to produce a publication history of their selected plays up to the year 1700, which is their next task to accomplish in the project. Because the Pollard and Redgrave volume extends only to 1640, I introduce students to the Donald Wing *Short-Title Catalogue*, which allows them to account for printings of their plays to 1700.[2] For each entry in their publication history, students must include the play's title, which should record variants in phrasing, spelling, generic identification, and so forth; the author or authors, if identified, as well as any variants appearing between editions; the printer's name; the publisher's name; the places of publication; and the years of publication. Although much of this information may be similar, even identical, between editions, creating such a publication history is productive, I argue, not only because it acts as a kind of index to a play's popularity, marketability, and relevance to later generations in the seventeenth century, but also because the variations that frequently appear between editions affirm the New Textualist precept about the fundamental instability of the text. Considering "the textual and titular diversity of these early publications," as Margreta de Grazia and Peter Stallybrass write, "How is the very name of a text to appear? In the case of multiple-text plays, how many variants between texts of a given play warrant the reproduction of the play in multiple forms? In short, how can [modern editorial] reproduction be true to either a title or a text when that title or text is not—to our eyes, at least—true even to itself?"[3] By paying careful attention to the sometimes minimal, sometimes exorbitant differences between imprints of their chosen plays—by learning about the plays' historicity, in other words—students have the opportunity to question the notion that a text exists as a Platonic ideal (a position commonly

[2] *A Short-Title Catalogue of Books Printed in England, Scotland, Ireland, Wales, and British America, and of English Books Printed in Other Countries, 1641–1700*, 3 vols., comp. Donald Wing (New York: Modern Language Association of America, 1982–1998).

[3] Margreta de Grazia and Peter Stallybrass, "The Materiality of the Shakespearean Text," *Shakespeare Quarterly* 44 (1993): 260.

attributed to the New Bibliography) and to consider instead that what we call a singular play or "work" is usually a conflation of many, often contradictory material manifestations that are similar without at all being the same.

The fourth component of the project is a descriptive bibliography of a single copy of the first impression of their plays. Before getting this section underway, however, I have students read Terry Belanger's essay "Descriptive Bibliography" as well as William Proctor Williams' and Craig S. Abbott's chapter, also titled "Descriptive Bibliography."[4] These essays are useful for helping students to focus on the descriptive process of accounting for a book's physical construction, which they must do, unfortunately, within the limitations of facsimile editions. In addition, we spend time reading and discussing excerpts from Philip Gaskell's *A New Introduction to Bibliography*, which gives students technical knowledge about composition, imposition, and presswork in printing houses during the hand-printed book period.[5] For the descriptive bibliography, the first description that they tackle is that of the title page, which must provide all of its text verbatim—small capitals, italic, roman, and so on—with lines divided as they appear on the page; were I not teaching on the quarter system and had more flexible time, I would also require students to locate printers' marks using Ronald B. McKerrow's *Printers' & Publishers' Devices in England & Scotland, 1485–1640*.[6] After the title page, students reproduce the half-title (if present); the running-titles, along with any variations occurring therein; the collation, including the book's format, its sequence of gatherings, and the number of leaves; any special front matter that might be present, such as a dedicatory epistle or poem, or a prologue to the play; the signature on which the play opens; and a notation about whether act and/or scene divisions are marked in the text. A short note should follow indicating any interesting anomalies or observations that do not fall into the descriptive categories above. Finally, students should note the specific copy under consideration.[7] Although some readers might find this kind of work outmoded or an exercise in antiquarianism, I believe that the process of creating a

[4] Terry Belanger, "Descriptive Bibliography," *Book Collecting: A Modern Guide*, ed. Jean Peters (New York: R. R. Bowker Company, 1977), 97–115; and William Proctor Williams and Craig S. Abbott, "Descriptive Bibliography," in *An Introduction to Bibliographical and Textual Studies*, 4th ed. (New York: The Modern Language Association of America, 2009), 36–56.

[5] Philip Gaskell, *A New Introduction to Bibliography* (Oxford: Clarendon Press, 1972).

[6] Ronald B. McKerrow, *Printers' & Publishers' Devices in England & Scotland, 1485–1640* (London: Chiswick Press, 1913).

[7] I should point out that Greg's *Bibliography* furnishes exactly the sort of descriptive bibliographies that I ask students to produce, which runs the risk of inviting temptation. I usually inform my graduate students about this, however, and appeal to their scholarly integrity, encouraging them to create their own descriptive bibliographies first, and then to compare and even modify their own in relation to Greg's.

descriptive bibliography slows students down by asking them to examine a text's material features and not simply to read for information, which hopefully fosters in them observant and detail-oriented habits of reading.

The last and by far the most elaborate section of the project involves students editing 100–200 lines of text from an early impression of their selected plays. The foregoing sections will have prepared them for this editorial task by familiarizing them with the plays' various imprints and the major variants that exist between them. Moreover, the secondary readings that the class completes by roughly midterm include some major statements within the New Bibliography as well as within the New Textualism, giving students at least two perspectives on how they might approach their editing work. Whereas the earlier portions of the project had been restricted to the description of historical and material facts within highly conventional models of presentation, this last portion encourages students to be creative with their editorial choices while exercising the sort of intellectual rigor that they have encountered in the secondary readings. Students, in other words, are welcome to adopt whatever editorial method that appeals to them, which allows them to produce innovative, even radical editions of their plays, just as they might take a conventional or conservative stance and produce an edition that has no interest in being pioneering. Yet, whatever approach that students take, they must articulate their editorial rationales—both on theoretical grounds and in terms of their choices about spelling, punctuation, and any other interventions they might make in their texts—by writing the kind of formal introduction and "Note on the Text" found in modern critical editions of their plays.

The first choice I encourage students to make is the audience for whom they will be editing their plays, and the best way to assess how different approaches appeal to a variety of audiences is to examine as many modern editions of their plays as they can find. Because some plays that students choose have only been published in a few modern editions, I provide them with a list of Shakespeare series that target a range of scholarly, actor, high school, and college audiences in order to compare introductions, page-layouts, glosses, and other features that help the reader to navigate a difficult or unfamiliar text. For their own mini-editions, students must decide whether to retain a text's original spelling or to modernize it; wrestle with the deceptively simple issue of punctuation; figure out how extensive their glosses will be and whether they will place them in the margin, in footnotes, after the conclusion of the play, or in some combination of these—most of which depends upon the target audience; choose how to approach lineation, how to differentiate the text of stage directions and speech headings from the dialogue and where to position them on the page, and whether to use running titles. Even when they have a solid grasp on all of the textual components that are in play—from the primary dramatic text to the various parts of the critical apparatus—students often have difficulty determining what information goes where in their editions. What kind of problem or topic warrants a discussion in the introduction, for instance, and what can be handily addressed in a gloss? Is it wise simply to follow the lead of previous editors who have determined the field of salient problems in a play, or might one pursue an issue that others seem to have overlooked? And what is an acceptable amount of redundancy of information in the critical apparatus?

This is the point in the project when many students become overwhelmed by the sheer number of decisions facing them, and while a high school, an acting, or especially a print facsimile edition might seem to offer a simpler format and, it is assumed, less work for students to produce, I remind them that the apparent simplicity in such publications is a result of a great deal of work, so whichever audience they aim to reach, their mini-editions will require a substantial investment of time and effort. I often set aside some class time at this point in the term so that students can get into groups and discuss the problems they are encountering, which gives them an occasion to share ideas and solutions with one another. I also emphasize repeatedly that audience is the key that will determine most of the other decisions they will make, and that once they make this choice they can significantly narrow the number of previous editions from which they draw inspiration or models for their own. On one hand, I explain that, in most instances, modern editions have been peer-reviewed, and so the dominant questions that editors raise about textual cruxes and literary topoi derive from a community of the most seasoned scholars, which means that students should give respectful consideration to those scholars' positions through the process of creating their own editions. On the other hand, I stress that individual scholars make intellectual advancements through disagreement with their scholarly communities, which should encourage students to pursue their own interests in the project, to be mindfully eclectic in the ideas and models they borrow from other editors, and to be creative or even experimental in the method and goals they adopt. Above all, I underscore that the students are the editors of their chosen plays, which presumes that they have a great deal of freedom, but which likewise assumes an equal amount of responsibility to their readers to specify the reasons for the editorial decisions they will make.

While many students opt to produce conventional—though, I hasten to add, perfectly respectable—mini-editions of their plays, some have taken large risks in order to create something quite novel and to reimagine the assignment itself. In imagining writing this essay, two particular student projects came to mind, and both former students have been kind enough to allow me to discuss their work here. The first, a project completed by Erin Stevanus, makes the issue of textual instability the hinge around which the entire mini-edition turns. The play she edited is *A Looking Glass for London and England* by Robert Greene and Thomas Lodge, which she transformed into a dynamic "reading experience" complete with an "Owner's Guide" to help her ideal high school or college reader navigate the difficult terrain of both an unfamiliar textual experience and an obscure Renaissance play. The play itself is an elaboration of the Book of Jonah, providing spectacular background about the sinful corruption of the people of Nineveh, who eventually repent when Jonah arrives, *ex cetacean*, and preaches to them. The "looking glass" of the title comes in the form of a concluding monologue by Jonah, who encourages the theatergoers to reflect on the events of the play and especially the unrepentant state of the Assyrians as a representation of their own historical moment and lives. The conceit is that the play takes the role of a prophet to warn the people of London and England about their god's imminent judgment, as the character Jonah beseeches:

> London awake, for feare the Lord do frowne,
> I set a looking Glasse before thine eyes.
> O turne, O turne, with weeping to the Lord,
> And thinke the praiers and vertues of thy Queene,
> Defers the plague which otherwise would fall.[8]

The problem of textual instability that Stevanus foregrounds in her mini-edition becomes not simply an issue addressed in the introduction and glosses, but one embedded in the reading process itself. The entire project she fashioned into two codices, one the "Owner's Guide," which contains most of the critical apparatus, and another the "Reading Experience" of the play, which includes the edited text and glosses. In the edited segment she alternated standard white paper with transparencies (which she calls "vellum"), both of which contain printed text. Her description of this layered construction and the reading experience it produces offers guidance on how to approach the text's complex materiality, but it also encourages readers to make interpretive decisions on their own. Stevanus writes:

> The vellum overlay that you see dispersed throughout the mini-edition is called the layer prima and bears most of the text of the printed play. The text is not printed as dark as traditional text in order to create a veil-like effect for this layer of text. When the layer prima is lifted up, the text printed upon the vellum's surface loses some of its substance (or substantiveness) and, when placed under bright light, might even appear as a mere watermark. The printed text of the layer prima represents how the text works as an unstable marker of potential meaning, which is only realized when worked/played upon.
>
> Underneath this veil of text lies the layer secunda, which appears to be a typical leaf of paper. Printed on the recto side of the leaf are possibilities of meanings, in the form of variants between the five quartos and including [Alexander] Dyce's emendations and your constructor's [Stevanus'] readings. Though the vellum layer prima needs this layer secunda underneath it

[8] Thomas Lodge and Robert Greene, *A Looking Glasse for London and England* (London: by Thomas Creede, 1594), sig. I4^{v}.

> in order to be read as a complete page, this stabilizing layer contains nothing stable in itself. By itself it, too, is only another layer of possible meaning and the raw potentiality of decontextualized and sometimes deconstructed meaning should be arresting in its stark nakedness.[9]

On the transparencies, the reader confronts the dramatic text largely unaltered from the copy-text except for having been selectively modernized in its spelling and punctuation, but several words on each transparent page are absent and only appear on the white page beneath as textual variants printed interlinearly. Stevanus has chosen these specific words as particularly problematic for the editor who attempts to stabilize their meanings, and their material separation from the transparent pages emphasizes that their meanings—both individually and in the context of the play's action—are free-floating as opposed to possessing solid, incontrovertible values; she also recognizes that the specific words she has chosen to highlight are not the only textually unstable ones available, which helps to lay bare her own editorial agenda. The text's fluctuating materiality thereby encourages the reader to engage in a kind of literary interpretation that claims neither to be entirely objective nor subjective, but that rather considers the multiple possibilities of meaning in order to enhance the experience of reading. The point, in other words, is not to settle on textual stability but to revel in its complexity.

The source for these multiple possibilities of meaning is a series of glosses that Stevanus provides on the verso of the white paper. In the "Owner's Guide," she makes clear how the reader must access these glosses and why extra procedural levels are built into the reading process itself:

> On the verso side of the layer secunda the constructor's glosses are printed backwards. These glosses explain the variants printed on the recto side and explain vocabulary based on the possibilities suggested in the *Oxford English Dictionary*. Thus, rather than clarify and reduce meaning, the verso of the layer secunda contains glosses that further contribute to potential interpretation. The backwards text on the verso side will appear to have absorbed the recto's words and its possible meanings. They now must be worked or played upon. Thus, to access these glosses, to get in(sight)to the second layer, (your) illumination upon the constructor's illuminations is required. When held up to a light, you will be able to read through the possibility of meanings printed on the recto side to the glosses printed on the verso side. Alternatively, you may wish to employ a mirror to read the glosses.[10]

---

9 Erin Stevanus, "Owner's Guide to A Reading Experience of *A Looking Glass for London and England*," unpublished paper, 9–10.

10 Stevanus, "Owner's Guide," 10–11.

Here, Stevanus has thematized the looking glass of the play's title both as a way to read the backward-printed text of the glosses and in an effort to encourage student-readers to reflect on the process by which they come to conclusions about dramatic meaning in the play—in the box that contains the whole project, she supplies a small mirror to enhance the reader's experience. Editors intent on stressing textual instability in modern editions of Renaissance plays will often multiply a word's or a passage's meanings by discussing the polysemy in glosses, but Stevanus has done this by modifying how the reader interacts with the material text. This interaction is designed to be somewhat labor-intensive, which means that it is potentially alienating to readers, yet such alienation might also serve to disrupt conventional or lazy reading practices, which create blindspots through their familiarity. That an actual publisher would probably not invest in this kind of edition is irrelevant to its success as a conceptually fascinating exercise, which grounds the reader in the material conditions of the text and its instability, and which invites the reader to make informed interpretive decisions instead of passively consuming the conclusions of an all-knowing editor.

The second graduate student project I would like to discuss was written by Lisa Sibbett, who not only produced a mini-edition of Ben Jonson's *Epicoene*, but created an alter ego with whom she engages in a fictional critical controversy. The controversy regards the question of whether there is a difference between "editing" and "translating." That is, where do we draw the line between making a text intelligible to an inexperienced reader through modern editorial interventions and making a text a fundamentally different object that in fact obscures the early modern copy-text? To stage this controversy, Sibbett the student first invents Sibbett the "translator," who employs T. S. Eliot's remarks in his essay "Ben Jonson" as a theoretical justification for her edition of *Epicoene*. There, Eliot writes that "to enjoy him [Jonson] at all [. . .] we must see him unbiased by time, as a contemporary," and to appreciate him as such "does not so much require the power of putting ourselves into seventeenth-century London as it requires the power of setting Jonson in our London."[11] To make *Epicoene* accessible to the modern reader, then, the fictional Sibbett sets Jonson's play in New York City, substituting his three wits with "lazy and indolent heirs to old money" and "render[ing] his fools foolish in twenty-first century terms, casting them as no-talent teen idols."[12] Yet Sibbett goes on to invent the scholar Thaden Gaines, who critiques the liberties that Sibbett the translator has taken with Jonson's text and who meditates on the limits of editorial power—indeed, on the limits of what actually counts as editing.

[11] T. S. Eliot, "Ben Jonson," *Selected Essays, 1917–1932* (New York: Harcourt, Brace and Co., 1932), 128.

[12] Lisa Sibbett, "De-Authorizing Jonson: Modern Translations and the Ethics of Authorship," unpublished paper, 6.

The context in which Sibbett the student plays out this controversy is a mock book by Thaden Gaines, including a title page, a table of contents, an introduction, and several appendices where Gaines excerpts act 4, scene 5 of Sibbett the translator's edition and also provides the corresponding scene from the 1620 quarto of *Epicoene*, descriptive bibliographies for both A- and B-issues of that quarto, and the play's publication history. The "translation" of *Epicoene* into modern English, first of all, moves the action to luxury hotels in contemporary New York City, altering the characters' names and retaining only the storyline of Jonson's play. Clerimont becomes Clarence, Truewit becomes Einstein, Dauphine becomes Kingsley, Jack Daw remains Jack Daw, Sir Amorous La Foole becomes Loverboy, and the status of knighthood is replaced with the dubious honor of the Teen Choice Awards. The idioms that the characters use are thoroughly modern and coded with the braggadocio of masculine youth, which are larded with both moneyed pretension and aggressive acquisitiveness. Sibbett the translator adds plenty of stage directions to help her reader follow the general action, but otherwise there are no glosses or notes to distract from the story's unfolding, which results in a much more visually streamlined text than one might expect from, say, a critical edition of the play. Sibbett's dramatic dialogue is in prose like Jonson's original text and, although it reads like a teleplay from an afterschool special aimed to encourage bullying and manipulative behavior, she manages to capture the spirit of Jonson's action with none of Jonson's language.

For instance, when Truewit dupes Jackdaw into believing that he is engaged in a deadly quarrel with La Foole, Jonson's text reads:

> [*Enter Jackdaw*]
> *Daw*. Which is the way into the Garden, trow?
> *Tru*. O, *Iack Daw*! I am glad I haue met with you. In good faith, I must haue this matter goe no furder betweene you. I must ha'it taken vp.
> *Daw*. What matter, Sir? Betweene whom?
> *Tru*. Come, you disguise it---Sir *Amorous* and you. If you loue me, *Iack*, you shal make vse of your Philosophy now, for this once, and deliuer me your Sword. This is not the Wedding the *Centaures* were at, though there be a shee-one here. The Bride has entreated mee I will see no bloud shed at her Bridall, you saw her whisper me ere-while.
> *Daw*. As I hope to finish *Tacitus*, I intend no Murder.
> *Tru*. Doe you not wait for Sir *Amorous*?
> *Daw*: Not I, by my Knight-hood.
> *Tru*: And your schollership too?
> *Daw*: And my schollership too.[13]

[13] B.I., EPICOENE, OR *The silent VVoman* (London: by William Stansby, 1620), sig. K4r.

In contrast, Sibbett the translator completely modernizes the text:

> —ENTER JACK DAW—
> JACK: Which way to the reception, do you know?
> EINSTEIN: Hey, Jack! Dude, I'm so glad to see you! Seriously, man, you guys need to knock this stuff off. It's wigging me out.
> JACK: What are you talking about? What guys?
> EINSTEIN: Hey, no need to hide it from me: you and Loverboy. If you're really my friend, you'll wise up for once and agree not to fight him. Give me your gun. This isn't some gangster wedding here, even if the bride is Italian. She asked me to make sure nobody got hurt at her wedding reception; you saw her talking to me earlier, right? *[Takes Jack's gun].*
> JACK: I can't kill anybody. I'm trying to finish *War and Peace*!
> EINSTEIN: So you aren't waiting around for Loverboy then?
> JACK: No, I swear by my Teen Choice Award.
> EINSTEIN: And your PhD, too?
> JACK: And my PhD.[14]

This is clever stuff, which I imagine Sibbett had great fun in writing, but it is the critique she devises and puts in the mouth of Thaden Gaines that gives the project more theoretical heft. The choice of a Jonson play for this project is also especially apt since he asserted authority over his printed texts in a way that no other contemporary playwright did, so the line between editorial intervention and editorial invention is an especially delicate one. As Gaines writes:

> Sibbett's modern translation proposes, in effect, to reverse the formula that preserves the so-called original text: she drops Jonson's signifiers in favor (theoretically) of rehabilitating his signifieds. Altering the author's very words, she aims to "recuperate Jonson's meanings" as they operated at the time of the play's performance. Although her attempt to bring new life to an archaic idiom frequently falls flat—Sibbett is no poet—the critical apparatus she suggests raises some important questions about the location of authority in a text.[15]

Yet Sibbett the translator is also no straw-woman set up for a sound trouncing by Gaines, who after sincere deliberation actually concludes that such translations of literature into contemporary language might have some limited pedagogical appeal, though she rightly questions at what cost. Gaines furthermore concludes that Sibbett the translator enacts not only Roland Barthes' declaration about "the death of the Author," but also his dependent statement about "the birth of the reader"—at least to an extent:

---

14 Sibbett, "De-Authorizing Jonson," 10–11.
15 Sibbett, "De-Authorizing Jonson," 3–4.

> If, as Barthes argues, "the birth of the reader" is the payoff, Sibbett's modern translation seems to spell, not the birth of *the* reader, but the birth of *a* reader: of Sibbett herself as a reader of Jonson. If modern translation often seems to both alienate and pander to the reader, perhaps the deeper implication is that each reader must write his or her own "translation," in order to fulfill his or her own critical and literary needs. And indeed, a continual re-writing of the text is precisely what Sibbett proposes.[16]

For me, this fictional critical controversy ended up staging the birth of Sibbett the reader, who grappled with the difficult questions posed by Jonson's text as well as modern editorial theory in order to fulfill her own critical and literary needs. Moreover, both Sibbett and Stevanus managed to transform the assignment itself, turning their projects into robust intellectual exercises about how early modern dramatic texts and modern editorial practices might fruitfully intersect.

Erin Stevanus and Lisa Sibbett produced some of the strongest responses to this assignment that I have read, though there have been plenty of other graduate students whose projects have likewise exceeded my expectations, and for these reasons I plan to use the assignment again when I teach the seminar in the future. The assignment is not without its limitations, however, and I should like to detail its more problematic aspects here for those who might want to adopt the assignment. The primary issue that my students have faced is the degree of specialization in the field of textual studies, which always results in a very steep learning curve that some students never manage to summit. My suspicion is that doctoral students might have less trouble than master of arts students in acquiring the necessary fluency with the material in so short a time, if only because they tend to have more experience in graduate seminars, but this of course does not make the field any less specialized or complex. Every time I have taught the course, there has been at least one student whose interest in the material remains nominal at best and whose work follows the path of least resistance. Such students there will always be, yet I still believe that part of my job is to elicit interest even from those disinterested graduate students, and this I have not always been successful at doing with this assignment. What has prevented me from actively working on this issue are the pedagogical demands that I have to meet with those students who are already highly invested, whose success often depends on my careful guidance through the thickets of the field. As they currently stand, the seminar and assignment favor those students who are already enterprising and self-motivated, but it comes at the expense of those who are not.

---

[16] Sibbett, "De-Authorizing Jonson," 7, her emphases. The line in Barthes reads: "the birth of the reader must be at the cost of the death of the Author," Roland Barthes, "The Death of the Author," in *Image Music Text*, trans. Stephen Heath (New York: Hill and Wang, 1977), 148.

Another problem that aggravates this dynamic is the quarter system on which I teach. To be sure, ten weeks is scarcely enough time for most of the courses in my repertoire, but this graduate seminar in particular has suffered as a result of inadequate time, which I am sure would be partially alleviated during the fifteen weeks or so of a semester. With 50 percent more class meetings and time to work on their projects, students would doubtlessly benefit not only intellectually, since they could digest the readings and critical debates in a less accelerated way, but also in terms of their projects, since they could contemplate and formulate their work in a more deliberate manner. One solution to this problem with time would be to trim the assignment of some of its components, such as the descriptive bibliography or publication history, but at the same time these feel to me to be central activities in a project such as this.

In spite of these problems, the assignment has been effective, I have found, at teaching graduate students about how both early modern printing practices and modern editorial procedures have shaped the Renaissance dramatic texts that we study. It is a demanding project, and even those who are equal to the challenge often remark that they wish they had had more time to pursue ideas they could not quite flesh out before the end of term, or even that it was only at the end of the term that they felt prepared enough to undertake the project sufficiently. Perhaps there is a pedagogical benefit for students to finish a course with the feeling of having not quite mastered the material, which might encourage continued thinking about it instead of fostering a sense that there is little left to learn about the subject. In any event, most students—even those who struggle to maintain a nominal interest—find that by the end of term their presumptions about textual stability and the simple givenness of textual artifacts are shaken to the core by the seminar and its work, which is knowledge that they can take with them to any other field or period regardless of their affection for Renaissance drama.

The Issue of Relevancy: Contemplative, Subjective, Affective

Karolyn Kinane, Plymouth State University

The main hurdles in assigning creative projects in my medieval and Renaissance literature classes have been developing clear evaluation guidelines and provoking the creation of robust, thoughtful, transformative experiences and projects from my students. Despite my own experience as a college student with deeply meaningful and inspiring creative projects and activities, these hurdles stemmed from my private fear that creative projects were anti-intellectual, perhaps more suitable to middle school than college. For years I have waffled, occasionally assigning or offering creative projects as final options for students. While my students and I experienced varying degrees of satisfaction with the process and outcomes of such assignments, I nonetheless nursed a vague sense that creative projects can be not only fun but deeply valuable, loaded with potential for effective learning. Inspired by work in medieval studies that encourages attention to the affective domain and supported by the broad movement of contemplative pedagogy, I have spent the past couple of years attempting to articulate this sense.[1] My teaching now draws more upon contemplative values and less upon postmodernist and New Historicist perspectives, which had guided my teaching and scholarship for the previous decade.[2] Creative projects are more thoroughly embedded in my courses, which privilege students' experiences, reflections, and transformations alongside course content; we focus on *making* rather than deconstructing meaning. In addition to my own increased confidence in the intellectual (as well as emotional and spiritual) benefits of this new direction, which is itself in fact,

---

[1] "Contemplative pedagogy" involves contemplative, reflective, and meditative practices as well as attention to subjectivity and questions of meaning. www.contemplativemind.org.

[2] I discuss this shift in Kinane, "Contemplative Pedagogy, Enchantment, and the Medieval Past," *postmedieval Forum IV: Pedagogy*. Mary Dockray-Miller, ed. (October, 2013). http://postmedieval-forum.com/forums/forum-iv-pedagogy/contemplative-pedagogy-karolyn-kinane/.

quite old,[3] such clarity has led to developing clear evaluation criteria on my part and a steady improvement in the quality of creative work on the part of students.

Referring obliquely to several projects and assignments in two classes I regularly teach—a general education course on Arthurian legends and an early British literature survey for junior and senior English majors—this essay describes the pedagogy that has emerged from my exploration of the value of creative projects.[4] My goal here is not to offer tips and tricks for developing assignments that involve creation or creativity. Rather, I hope to encourage college teachers to consider their own deeply felt sense of purpose for their teaching and to allow that sense to pervade their own courses and assignments. At a more practical level, I would also encourage instructors to attend to the particular needs of their own schools, departments, and curricula as they articulate their pedagogy. What follows works for me in my rural, public institution of roughly 4,000 undergraduates, and in my department, which fosters a strong foundation in critical theory; it may not be appropriate to all teachers in all settings.

Creative projects, such as those offered at the end of this chapter, work better now that they are thoroughly embedded in the larger pedagogy of my courses rather than introduced as anomalous, refreshing, or jarring breaks from routine. Over the course of fifteen weeks, through assignments, discussion, and activities, students in Arthurian Legends and Currents in British Literature I learn that their personal and creative responses to literature are valuable springboards for further reflection. Of *course* students' ideas and experiences (not just their "lenses") shape the way they encounter texts; I endeavor to make that process explicit and visible in the class by bringing those ideas and experiences to the fore. I will take a bit of time at the start of this article to explain some of the broad contours of how this process works, lingering on reading practices in particular, because it is the course experience as a whole, not the particular assignment, which has made for creative projects that feel meaningful to me and to students and that suggest students' sensitivity to, curiosity about, and investment in the texts, the past, themselves, and their broader world.

Due to my own graduate training as well as our undergraduate program's emphasis on critical theory, I have been aware of the charges against reader-response: that it adopts a quaint and naïve position of joy, or, perhaps worse, that

---

[3] James Rhem, Executive Director of the National Teaching and Learning Forum, notes that, "to skeptical ears, 'contemplative pedagogy' may sound like the latest franchiseable insight into better teaching, something new perhaps. But contemplation and meditation have ancient histories and as they have always been seen as teaching some of the most profound lessons, they have always been pedagogies," "Contemplative Pedagogy, Part 1," *National Teaching and Learning Forum* 21, no. 2 (2012): 1.

[4] For a practical description of creative projects in Arthurian Legends see Karolyn Kinane, "Arthurian Legends in General Education: An Example of Student-Centered Pedagogy," *Studies in Medieval and Renaissance Teaching* 20, no. 2 (Fall 2013): 85–104.

it is a self-centered and apolitical way of reading. But I believe that facility with thinking about and through emotions and existential questions in the company of others is essential to the development of a person willing and able to contribute to a democratic society. For me, the greater challenge of reader-response has been navigating the space between *connecting* the past to the present, which suggests that there are enduring qualities or themes across time and space, and demonstrating the *alterity* of the past, which highlights how we can never really know the Other and encourages recognition of historical and cultural diversity. And so, in our class discussions, I encourage traditional reader-response to texts by inviting those evocative, instant, initial responses and then encouraging students to explore the significance of their own observations, explicitly noting how encountering a text invites us to encounter ourselves in new ways or from a new perspective.

In *Teaching Literacy for Love and Wisdom*, Jeffrey D. Wilhelm and Bruce Novak expand upon three stages of reading outlined in Wilhelm's *You Gotta Be the Book*, a text often used in college courses for K-12 teacher preparation. These stages are "evocative," "connective," and "reflective." The "evocative" tends toward the present as students notice what calls out to them from a text here and now—what they initially are drawn to or repulsed by. The "connective" tends toward the past as students then consider the experiences and ideas they have brought to the text, those their peers bring to the text, and the experiences and ideas the text brings *to them* from the historical and implied author's context. Students do "connective" work by explicitly engaging with several forms of questions: What do I want to ask my peers about this text and why? What do I still wonder about the context and implied-author and why? How do these contexts relate to one another or nuance my understanding of this text, myself, the past, the present? "Connective" work requires research, conversation, and collaboration. The third stage, "reflective" reading, tends toward the future as students ask: How has my encounter with the text and others impacted the way I see the world? How will it affect my thoughts and actions from here on out? How have I been transformed through this interaction with the text and others? As I practice them in my college classrooms, these stages of reading merge reader-response and New Historicism, tapping into students' curiosity and encouraging connection with the past through explorations of social and historical differences. These ways of reading also provoke reflection upon what emerges when one openly and curiously experiences literature from a desire to learn *from* it, not simply *about* it. In these courses, we do not often deconstruct a text to determine, with suspicion, the designs it has on us, unless student inquiry takes us that way. More often, while we know texts are products of their culture as much as we are products of our own, we nonetheless try to allow for communication across time and space that could help us enrich the experience of living.

For example, at the start of Arthurian Legends, a 1000-level general education course that enrolls students from a variety of majors with a range of reading and writing skills, before our first reading assignment, I ask students to do several free-writes in their notebooks. First, they choose one of the follow four prompts to write about:

1. Have you ever been a stranger in a strange land?
2. Have you ever felt instantly drawn to someone?
3. Have you ever broken a promise?
4. Has your pride ever gotten you in trouble?

What was the situation? What did you do, think, and feel?

These responses are kept private. Students then write down three essential qualities of a good friend, of a good leader, and of an ideal romantic interest (not husband or wife). These qualities should be abstract, like "honesty," not concrete like "red-headed." Then they write three *concrete* qualities of an ideal romantic interest for themselves and three they think are the "mainstream" qualities that society in general values. After students discuss in small groups their responses, I tell them to write "Gawain," next to the "friend" qualities, "Arthur" next to "leader," and "Lanval/Fairy" next to "romantic interest." I tell them we will be reading a romance written by a woman in the 1100s and I handout a copy of *Lanval*, with these homework prompts:

Evocative: (Remember—Use specific examples (quotations) from the text to support your point.)

a. Write a paragraph or so: What strikes you about this story? What stands out most; what are your initial reactions to it? (This could be a memorable moment, a strong feeling about a character, a question about something. . .Whatever you notice or feel or think)

b. Make note of one "that's cool" moment you have while reading. (Underline or highlight it, write page #)

c. Make note of one "what the heck?" moment that provokes confusion or elicits surprise from you.

Connective: (Remember—Use specific examples (quotations) from the text to support your point.)

a. What would you like to ask other students about this story? Why?

b. What would you like to know about the author? Why?

c. What would you like to know about the time period? Why?

d. What about this story strikes you as similar to entertainment we have today?

e. What about this story strikes you as different from entertainment we have today?

These preparations before reading allow for initial responses to the story such as "Arthur is weak," "They're so materialistic," and "Who *is* this imaginary woman?" yet quickly bring us deeper into our own connections and disjunctions with the world of the story; the story lets us see our world in new ways. We can interrogate the notion of "love at first sight" from a subjective place rather than an objective, critique-oriented position. We cannot very easily criticize the past as being materialistic and "backwards" if our own prewriting confirms that we and our culture are pretty similar or that there may be a broader culture around this story about which we have questions. After small and large group discussions, students then engage in the "reflective" portion of the reading process, considering what this story suggests to us about lies, shame, intimacy, generosity, and friendship, revisiting their initial writings from the previous class. The reflection stage illuminates that the student now knows something more or different about the story as well as about those pressing topics.

The "evocative," peer-"connective" and "reflective" pieces of this process take valuable class time, but I believe they are the pieces that students should engage in with others in community. Therefore, for the historical-"connective" stage, I make use of the "flipped classroom" and post mini-lectures on our online course management (Moodle) site for students to watch as homework. They view these lectures on social and historical contexts and take online or in-class quizzes to test for completion and retention. We can then, in class, elaborate upon those initial "evocative" responses in "connective" ways, noticing similarities and differences across time and space and suggesting ways they can speak to one another. The "reflective" piece, explored in informal writing, student papers, projects, and large assignments, suggests action taken in the world as a result of transformative reading experiences. For example, after our *Lanval* activities, one student noted that he would make an effort to reach out to exchange students on campus—he had never thought about being a "stranger in a strange land." Another reflected upon how she was going to pay more attention to the role that promises and secrets play in her friendships and relationships. These are admittedly anecdotal and subjective "proofs" that I offer of transformation; nonetheless, I believe that such reflection saves reader-response from being apolitical and self-centered; it also saves critical inquiry from being a loop of continual questioning with no ground from which to act.

A course climate that recognizes and invites subjectivity, affective responses, and playful curiosity about the past, ourselves, and others is essential for building trust among students and between me and individual students, which prepares us for risk-taking and creativity that is personally meaningful and academically rigorous as we approach larger projects and assignments. Framing this climate is a core question at the heart of my own beliefs about literature: how can my encounter with this literature help me learn to be a better person? I leave it up to students to determine what "better" means for them, though ideally, for me, these encounters with literature would broaden their perspectives, boost their confidence, deepen their empathy, increase their joy, and provoke ethical action on behalf of themselves and others. Do not get me wrong: I know that well-read people can be evil. The point is not how much or even what people read; the point is how we approach and what we do with (not just *to*) literature.

To enhance the potential impact of the reflective stage in our readings and build a scaffolding upon which larger creative projects can be built, I draw from Wilhelm and Novak as they encourage the pursuit of existential questions. Many college teachers may already be familiar with "essential questions," as often many of us frame our courses around "issues" or "critical problems." Essential questions are those that are up for debate and are "about the way the world works in general." As examples, Wilhelm and Novak offer, for civics, "what is a responsible community?" For history, "what makes a great leader?" For English, "what makes and breaks relationships?" In a historical survey of literature, we have the opportunity to explore this latter question quite broadly, exploring relationships among men, women, lovers, families, nations, friends, and the like. *Existential* questions, on the other hand, are about "how each one of us should best live," and we answer existential questions by applying essential questions to our own lives.[5] I believe that framing the course not around "issues" but around essential and existential questions can be as useful in a major as well as a general education course where students are at various stages of academic careers and from different majors. All students share a common interest in and experience with themselves. Existential questions allow teachers to tap a (latent) interest in not only how the world works but how one can best live in it. To tap this interest, on the very first day of class, students in Arthurian Legends rank the following statements from 1–13 in order of their interest.

What is love?
What is friendship?
Why do people do bad things?
How can I be happy?
What is my purpose in life?
Why are family dynamics so difficult?
Do I control my emotions or do they control me?
Is it possible to enhance my own happiness and not hurt others?

[5] Jeffrey D. Wilhelm and Bruce Novak, *Teaching Literacy for Love and Wisdom* (New York: Teachers College Press, 2011), 11.

> How does my own past shape who am I today?
> Can I be my *true* self and yet fulfill what other people need from me?
> What makes and breaks relationships?
> Is there a God?
> Are duty and obligation good things or bad things?

They then write about their top three and share their musings in groups of three or four. I collect, respond to, and hand back these lists and students staple them into their notebooks. We revisit the rankings throughout the semester; such revisiting reminds me to foreground the relevance of course material to these questions and reminds students of the goal of their inquiry, which works well with quest and romance narratives of the Arthurian tradition over time.

I now turn to three examples of framing canonical early British literature with essential and existential questions in the context of evocative, connective, and reflective reading processes.

Not only are the language and form of medieval and Renaissance texts difficult for students; the *content* is sometimes inaccessible. I teach many texts that have to do with religion in one way or another, and whether it is *Everyman*, *Dr. Faustus*, or *Paradise Lost*, students who have no interest in or outright hostility towards Christianity or the idea of God struggle to engage with these texts. At some point, I found myself wondering, if students do not care about the *questions* such texts wrestle with and work through, what can they hope to learn from them? Certainly there are ways to make ideas from the past relate to contemporary debates. For example, the question of a priest's morality in *Everyman* can be fruitfully positioned next to that of K–12 teachers in our own climate: many of my students are in a Teacher Certification program and are highly aware that what they post on Facebook could jeopardize their career. One could also position medieval texts on courtship and chivalry alongside contemporary dating rules and codes of conduct. But I have found that essential and existential questions—more so than pat analogies to the present—effectively tap student curiosity and heighten their engagement and interest in literature from the past.

One semester, when students encountered *Beowulf*, many of them offered "evocative" responses to the elaborate descriptions of arms and armor. They wondered why so much attention is paid to these external objects while readers get relatively little insight into the inner-world of the characters. Of course, such "evocative" responses offer the occasion to explain to students large shifts in literary style, to talk about the invention of the novel (the aesthetics of which they have been weaned on), to contrast the epic's focus on exchanges and actions *among* people with the novel's focus on the inner, private world of one person's mind, and to examine the implications of these differences. But additionally, that semester I focused the "connective" stage of reading on *gift-giving*. We spent time writing, thinking and talking about how gift-giving works in students' own lives, making visible an aspect of their lived reality that had, it seemed, heretofore gone unanalyzed. Fascinating confessions of guilt and obligation on the part of the giver, of embarrassment and frustration on the part of the receiver, emerged from class discussion. With some careful questioning, students also shared the joy they have felt when they found the perfect gift for someone else, how elated they were to commemorate their appreciation of their friend or family member through the gift, and how loved they felt when they received such a thoughtful gift. I was then able to focus my social and historical contexts mini-lecture on ring-givers, thanes, and *comitatus*, but with particular attention to how ritual and ceremony can create bonds, how public exchanges of goods link people through both love and obligation. Suddenly, Beowulf and Hrothgar are no longer long-dead heroes who did some cool stuff; their story provides ways for contemporary humans to tap into the feelings and needs underlying relational exchanges. Here, the "reflective" stage of reading foregrounded existential and action-oriented questions students could choose to pursue in their larger writing assignments or creative projects: What do we do with this information (about gifts, ritual, kinship) moving forward as individuals living in society? What opportunities do we have to praise and honor one another, to be honored and not embarrassed by love and appreciation?

Part of the beauty in this approach, for me, is that each semester is different, which keeps my own enthusiasm and curiosity fresh and genuine. In an earlier semester students' "evocative" responses to the poem constellated around Beowulf's boasting. "He seems arrogant;" "The biggest jerks in movies are always the rich, boastful brats;" "Everyone loves the underdog," they told me. Students' resistance to Beowulf's boasting threw into relief the mixed messages that broadcast from their own culture, which tells them they must simultaneously be humble and yet also compete and advocate for themselves in a harsh economy. I was shocked and saddened to hear how these young people had grown accustomed to minimizing their own "awesomeness." As a class we could only think of two contemporary venues where individuals are encouraged by other individuals to be fabulous: team sports and drag shows. That semester I staged an intervention by throwing a mead-hall boasting ceremony. Students brought to class a treasured object that had a story. I brought in sparkling cider and hand-thrown mugs and played re-created medieval folk music. Students introduced themselves by their family name, stated a past deed of greatness, and made a formal boast of future greatness. Students then presented one another with their treasured object, telling its story and encouraging the individual in her or his formal boast, whether that be to study abroad, hike the Presidential Range, or call mom every Sunday. To some professors this may sound like middle school. To me, it felt and sounded like young adults coming into their own voices, playfully exchanging with one another in the spirit of generosity and encouragement. I believe that once we have an *experience* of something, we know it better than if we simply read or hear about it. The world of *Beowulf* was now connected to students' emotions and the exploration of Anglo-Saxon England rooted in these stirrings. As Tobin Hart reminds us, "Emotion awakens attention, which drives learning and memory. Relevance and resonance activate interest."[6] Such awakening and interest should be as much a part of an adult's life as a child's life. In fact, in light of the social, environmental, and economic challenges facing graduating seniors, it is perhaps even more pressing that they have emotionally impactful experiences and learn how to process and use them in collaboration with others.

Near the middle of the semester we encounter Marlowe's *Dr. Faustus.* I must confess, I never know what kinds of reactions students will have to this play. Some semesters it is a favorite. One semester I found students singularly bored by it. (Interestingly, that semester I did not provide any preparatory free-writing before we launched into the reading.) Their evocative responses focused on how stupid Faustus is, selling his soul. "We all know that's wrong," they claimed. "There is no new message here." To recoup the value of this work, I encouraged students to look at the times our own lives are filled with contradiction. When are we making Faustian bargains, sacrificing future benefit for instant gratification (partying on a Thursday night and missing class Friday)? Or, sacrificing that which we most deeply treasure and value (clean water, love, nature) for cheaply made, mass produced trinkets that destroy the environment and bring only temporary elation? These conversations allowed us to dive into theories of theatre and performance, to explore how the omniscient yet immersed perspective of an audience member allows us to feel a false sense of superiority as our own actions are played out before us. The next time I teach this play I will lead with brainstorming prompts about instant gratification and long term value with the hope that students' evocative responses and connective questions may be more nuanced, generous, and creative as well as critical.

At the end of the semester, we encounter Milton's *Paradise Lost*. It is difficult. We are tired. I offer overviews and outlines so students can follow the plot line easily and dig into the poetics of the work. I created audio files so they could hear me and other faculty volunteers speak the poetry. (The beloved chair of our small department was the voice of Satan, which elicited some joy and surprise from those who made use of the files). But students have responded most profoundly to the text when I have framed it with what I called "Meta-Milton" questions. Before reading the poem, I asked students to respond to the following prompts:

1. Love requires some form of surrender, a loss or lack of control, a willing giving of power to the beloved.

2. Knowledge can bring pain but it is essential to intimacy.

[6] Tobin Hart, *From Information to Transformation* (New York: Peter Lang, 2009), 8.

3. Seeing (i.e., "sight") can both help us to know a thing and prevent us from knowing it.

4. Pride in excess is the most dangerous "excess" to humanity.

5. Gods and devils are externalized manifestations of internal human states.

6. People in power can interact with their underlings either from a position of confident compassion or anxious fear. That choice dictates whether the person is a good (benevolent, reverent) leader or a bad (malevolent, irreverent) leader.

7. Humanity can possess free-will within a system overseen by an omniscient, omnipotent God-force.

(Ontology) Do you consider the statement(s) true or false? Why? Explain.
(Epistemology) On what do you base your decision? Experience (your own), received wisdom (learned from an authority), or faith (intuition, hunch)? Or some combination?

We spent a full class period hashing out these responses in small groups and continually returned back to "Meta-Milton" as we worked through the books of the epic. Once a text like *Paradise Lost* becomes as much about the power of love, the pain of surrender, humility, reverence, and the transformative power of knowledge as about civil wars, monarchy, God, and the Bible, I have found students more open to and curious about the text before us and the past behind us. Milton's social and historical contexts do not disappear entirely from the survey course; they are just no longer what I *lead* with. The quality of writing and discussion improved as students worked through their own ideas about knowledge, collaborated with others to build coherent responses, and parsed the poem to see how Milton resolved or muddied the issue. Students first needed to see that they had opinions, ideas, and questions about these topics before they could fully "appreciate" what *Paradise Lost* could bring to them and analyze what they bring to it. In this way, students learn not only *about* the past but how thinking *with* and through the past can enhance and clarify their present and future.[7]

Many of us invite such essential or existential inquiry into texts without realizing it: open-ended activities such as brainstorming and free-writing are common in some college classrooms as teachers begin units. We often do such

[7] Nicholas Watson, "Desire for the Past," *Studies in the Age of Chaucer* 21 (1999): 59–97.

activities so we may "meet students where they're at," as these activities expose to us what students already know or assume about the content at hand. However, we can invest these activities with additional purpose and meaning if we come to think of them as "frontloading" or "gateway activities" that not only evaluate but also tap into students' existing interests and perceptions, which may be carried throughout the course. As in the *Lanval* example above, rather than asking students to brainstorm on what they know about King Arthur in order to assess prior knowledge, I might ask students to write about betrayal, identity, journeys, community, or friendship in order to stir emotions, incite curiosity, and suggest personal investment in the matter at hand. These free-writes become contemplative practices when we attend to their content, when we offer students time and space to be deeply reflective about their experiences, feelings, and attitudes, when we return to those free-writes in subsequent class meetings. On the other hand, when we invoke then dismiss free-writes as simple springboards to the course content, we miss the opportunity for students to craft their experience with the material, to create their own sense of relevancy, which is an essential skill for approaching the world as a place of potential meaningfulness, as worthy of engagement.[8] The return to the free-write exposes what has been evoked, what connections can be made, and highlights the value of reflection and receptivity within a cultural climate that privileges the consumption of data and focused attention.[9] With so much anxiety expressed in the popular press about "distraction" and lack of attention among digital natives, I would urge fellow educators to hone students' abilities to not only "pay attention" but to remain in open-awareness so that flashes of insight may arise, engendering creativity.[10]

By focusing our inquiry on not simply essential questions but *existential* questions, I have found students' dispositions to be much more generous and open, which allows for the improved retention of content and honing of skills. This shift to making students' *dispositions* just as central to learning as the text, the history, and reading/writing/critical thinking skills are, has greatly improved the efficacy and experience of creative projects and also helps my majors advocate for the use and benefit of the humanities in a climate that allows (and even advocates for) historical and cultural amnesia. Scientific advancements proceed as a result of building on previous knowledge. Human "advancements" in wisdom, compassion, and joy can proceed as a result of engagement with the hundreds

[8] Jane Bennett, *The Enchantment of Modern Life: Attachments, Crossings, and Ethics* (Princeton, NJ: Princeton University Press), 2001.

[9] Arthur Zajonc, *Meditation as Contemplative Inquiry* (Great Barrington, MA: Lindisfarne Books), 2009.

[10] Ellen Langer, *The Power of Mindful Learning* (Reading, MA: Addison-Wesley), 1999; Jennifer L. Roberts, "The Power of Patience: Teaching students the value of deceleration and immersive attention" *Harvard Magazine* (November-December 2013), http://harvardmagazine.com/2013/11/the-power-of-patience.

(and thousands) of years of experimentation and questioning that literature and other texts provide. I urge that scientific "progress" be paired with progress in other realms of knowing, doing, and being. Historical and cultural amnesia can atrophy key ways of knowing and being that encourage a sense of purpose and connection to the world.

Thinking *with* and not just *about* the past usefully undermines progressivist thinking—the idea that things are always getting better and better. It encourages a more generous disposition towards the Other, be it a past or contemporary culture or person. Rather than dutifully respecting the Other as something we cannot fully know, students turn that respect into actionable feelings about the present. Of course, we do not want to romanticize the past as a hazy halcyon era when things were better, deeper, or more authentic. Instead, I would propose that what students learn from the past is not necessarily that culturally specific things like laws, dress, and poetry were better, and not even that "people were just like us back then," falling in love and fearing death, but rather that the question of ethics is deeply important. The process of thinking about why we do things and how we relate to the world is an essential piece of education on what it is to be human. Those processes are expressed in particular ways through art, music, and literature and we (students) should be jazzed up to participate in that legacy, to create and not solely critique texts.

I offer this background on my pedagogy because creative projects had been less successful in classrooms where I had trained students over fourteen weeks to sit quietly and listen to lectures or to adopt a disembodied "objective" stance to critique material through discussion. To create meaningfully, my students needed to have experienced rigorous and thorough explorations of their opinions and interpretations in community. In my early years of assigning creative projects, students would deconstruct, analyze, and evaluate a text and then create an object or text that displayed those skills—all actions rooted in the cognitive domain. But, particularly in an English department where Creative Writing is assigned to all majors, attention to the affective domain and "creation" as a process, not solely a product or means of demonstrating skill and content acquisition, could be quite valuable as students consider how to explain the power and value of imagination to themselves, potential employers, and concerned parents.

Creation should be guided by inquiry and reflection. I ask students before, during, and after the creation process to answer such questions as the following: What provoked your curiosity in the raw materials? What happens when you imaginatively encounter something strange or foreign? How do you make something your own while respecting its difference from you? What problems did you encounter while tapping into creativity and how did you deal with them? How does your own attitude (disposition) towards yourself, others, situations, and texts help or hinder the creation of something valuable? The creation of a project can be transformative for a student's inner life but can also be articulated as a rigorous experience and demonstration of character. A student needs to be encouraged to see the making of, say, a puppet show, as something that could actually be talked about in a job interview: it is proof that one has self-starting curiosity, problem-solving skills, follow-through, the capacity for respectful engagement, a sense of audience, and, of course, creativity. These are the skills and dispositions that make one a "good citizen" as well as "marketable."

Now I'll turn to the differences between how I situate creative projects in my 1000-level general education course, Arthurian Legends, and how I situate them in my 3000-level early British literature survey for English majors. In Arthurian Legends, the semester is peppered with "fun" activities such as debates, mock trials, scavenger hunts, and reenactments, and students, on the whole, are comfortable engaging in such "play" with our course materials. They dive into the activity and, *afterwards*, I do the work of connecting their actions and responses to broader questions the course examines: What do these texts and authors value? What do *we* expect from them and why? How do we envision the past? How does that vision reflect or affect our present? Students pursue these lines of inquiry through discussion and writing, having had their own kinesthetic and emotional ways of knowing tapped through activity. As we build trust over the semester, students—from first-year business majors to seniors in meteorology—can begin making such connections themselves as we embark upon a new activity. For some students it becomes a fun challenge to try to guess how I am going to make our activity relevant to the texts, context, and broader themes of the course. By the time I ask them to, say, make a shield that reflects their values, or to review their notebooks for themes that can help them craft a meaningful and relevant creative final project, they have had several solid experiences of connecting with material creatively, contemplatively, and critically, of reflecting on meaning-making.

The development of a final project for Arthurian Legends is a thorough, collaborative, and labor-intensive process. I ask students to return to their early writings in the semester and find genuine questions or links to their own major or interests outside of the classroom. They brainstorm, process, and refine with other students. They write a proposal and meet with me in small groups or one-on-one. We lay out a plan guidelines for evaluation and clarify expectations. As mentioned above, evaluation of creative projects can be tricky; I have found this focus on *process* rather than product useful. When I had assigned creative projects without all of this apparatus, students had focused on word-count and length. *With* this apparatus, they can craft something that fulfills my expectations for breadth, depth, rigor, and creativity while enabling their own curiosity and strengths to take the lead. It takes time and trust to lead people through a process rather than demand a product. But that is what I most deeply value about education and therefore that is where I put my energy. To draw from Ben Morgan in his discussion of the relationships among medieval and modern notions of the self: "Growth and a sense of purposive unfolding can be acknowledged without the claim being made that the end point is known. Indeed, one aspect of real growth is that we don't know where it's going; it's an expansion that takes us beyond what we're used to and forces us to improvise new habits and ways of acting."[11] Creation is a process that can enable growth, not simply a product that demonstrates content mastery.

On the other hand, the junior and senior English majors who attend my survey course are considerably more resistant to such play at the start of the semester than General Education students. They often identify as writers, have mastered the literary analysis essay, and have had a healthy dunking in critical theory. They are either reticent to strike out and take risks with a new approach or they simply do not see the value in creative, active, playful engagements with the texts. To mitigate these resistances, I swap the order in which I present the activity and the connections discussed just above. Here, I instead *lead with the connections*. I explicitly tell these English majors about my pedagogical perspective, about my goals for the activity, about why I value experience and emotional engagement as springboards to inquiry. These English majors need to know why we are doing something out of the norm—such as "making" a medieval manuscript page—before they will relax into the engagement, whereas my General Education students leap into activities and are then (pleasantly) surprised by the larger purpose and meanings of them.

Such risk taking throughout the semester prepares English majors to be experimental and creative in any final projects they choose to undertake. (Students also have the option of writing traditional literary analysis papers for their final). Here I present creative final projects as an "honor's option" that would require significant time, energy, and thought. As with Arthurian Legends, students write proposals and I meet with them individually or in small groups. By the end of their process, students should be able to answer, in a reflective essay, any of the following questions: How has your creation process been a meaningful experience with the potential to transform you or the world you live in? or: How has your creative project/process facilitated your growth cognitively and/or affectively? Or: How has your creative project/process demonstrated key aspects of your attitude, disposition, and character as well as skills and content mastery from our Course Goals? Since many of our English majors are in our Teacher Certification program, many of them are eager to draw on materials I provide regarding learning domains and learning styles; from their own practice with developing lesson plans for other courses, they are also comfortable linking activities and projects to clearly articulated goals and outcomes (which, in this instance, we take from our course syllabus).

By inviting students to reflect upon and create testimonies to their lived experiences with the past, I have found that contemplative and creative pedagogies help course materials "come alive" for students, enrich the sense of community in the classroom, and achieve course goals in memorable, unconventional,

[11] Ben Morgan, *On Becoming God: Late Medieval Mysticism and the Modern Western Self* (New York: Fordham University Press), 2013.

and unpredictable ways. In pedagogical shorthand, we may know the importance of linking new concepts to students' existing knowledge base. That is, when introducing content or skills to students, teachers should root them in something students already know or with which they have experience. We can also root the new knowledge in something they are already *curious* about to enliven the creation process. Overall, the relevance of the medieval text is, quite simply, how it becomes meaningful for the reader. Giving students the opportunity to explore and create that relevancy, and enhancing their ability to advocate for the process, is priceless in terms of experience and valuable in terms of the market. When students can "respond and [. . .] cause response in another through experiencing and creating art," I hope that they can, by extension, consider the value of "living in artful, feeling discourse with one another."[12]

Rather than getting distracted by ahistorical and presentist ideas of "relevance" that permeate the discourse of teaching-techniques or that dominate the discourse of program assessment, I've zoomed out my perspective to essential questions and existential questions and tended to students', and my own, dispositions. At some point I asked myself: Can I continue to teach from a disembodied, unfeeling attitude towards literature and my students? to pretend at objectivity? to worship skill-acquisition? I have decided that I do not want to teach in a way that contributes to a diminishment of feeling; I want to *heighten* sensitivity and offer people the tools to connect and reflect on that sensitivity, to consider it a strength to be channeled to ethical action. If feeling connected to one another in the classroom through discussion or to the past through a poem, is seen as soft, so be it. The way I see it, softness is not bad; it is necessary. The more often we can provide safe spaces for people to be open and receptive, to be moved by something and then reflect on the effects of that exchange, the better. Opening students to feeling the thrill (or "enchantment," "reverence," or "joy"[13]) of the simultaneously familiar and strange (or "uncanny") means we need to work on students' disposition and curiosity—and to do that we need to engage emotions and experiences.

When we ignore students' inner landscapes in the classroom, we contribute to the disconnect between "school" and "the rest of my life." True, we want students to get beyond themselves, but we never truly leave ourselves behind and being asked to do so in the classroom might be precisely what makes it seem so different than the "real world." By allowing for the personal and affective to be part of the course content and stating that the deliberate cultivation of a disposition of openness and curiosity is a course goal, I believe that existential inquiry, contemplative methods, and creative projects can contribute to the sense that

[12] Wilhelm and Novak, *Teaching Literacy for Love and Wisdom*, 57.

[13] See Bennett, *The Enchantment of Modern Life*; A. G. Rud and Jim Garrison, eds. *Teaching with Reverence* (New York: Palgrave Macmillan), 2012; Wilhelm and Novak, *Teaching Literacy for Love and Wisdom*, respectively.

what happens in the classroom matters and is "real." The classroom can be a lively place where issues of pressing personal as well as social and professional concerns can be reflected upon, sorted through, and creatively expressed in community and through dialogue with the past. Relevance can be felt.

I would like to note again here that I am not advocating for a wholesale adoption of my pedagogy by everyone. Rather, I urge college-level instructors to view their courses and pedagogy in the context of their program's whole curriculum to ensure that there is diversity among the approaches students are invited to take with texts. As I mentioned at the start of this essay, I currently teach in a program where students receive a strong introduction to critical theory in their Studies in English course and where Critical Theory is a required course. Our majors come to my survey class with a hermeneutics of suspicion pretty well practiced and the hermeneutics of faith rejected.[14] If it were the other way around, my teaching would probably look very different right now. Within a curriculum that lacks critical theory, the recouping of reader-response that I outline above might not be necessary or valuable to students. Diversity of approaches is particularly important in a program with a large Teacher Preparation component. Current students/future teachers should, I think, be invited to think with and through different critical and creative perspectives, to explore why some approaches resonate with them, which can help them be better teachers who recognize and encourage such resonance with their own students.

Learning through creative projects is not just joyful and fun (though we should not totally disqualify joy and fun as valuable); "creating" has been granted the highest rung on Bloom's Taxonomy of Educational Objectives and helps people retain and apply information. But "creating" is also an opportunity for students to participate in cultural processes of influence and re-creation. Creative projects in historical classrooms help students not only feel like *consumers* of culture but like participants in a broader human culture and exchange across miles and centuries. From reenacting a gift-giving ceremony and creating "speaking objects" (like the Ruthwell Cross or Bayeux Tapestry), to designing shields, quests, and alternative histories, students engage creatively, critically, intellectually, and affectively with course material in ways that invite rigorous exploration of their own personal goals, values, and purposes. Such explorations go a long way toward "educating the whole person," exemplifying "student-centered learning," and demonstrating the value of art, literature, and history in the ordinary life. These goals are explicitly invoked by my university and seem essential to living our motto, *Ut Prosim* (that I may serve). Educators in the humanities and social sciences can tap into and develop aesthetic (that is, *feeling*) responses, promote reflection upon them, and thereby provoke action in students so that they may serve. As Wilhelm and Novak note, "responsiveness *to* life, at larger

[14] Paul Ricoeur, *Freud and Philosophy: An Essay on Interpretation*, trans. D. Savage. (New Haven, CT: Yale University Press), 1970.

and larger levels of it, leads us. . .to take larger and larger responsibility *for* it.[15] Students must *feel* something towards and about the world and others in order to be inspired to serve. *What could be more relevant?*

[15] Wilhelm and Novak, *Teaching Literacy for Love and Wisdom*, 16.

Appendix

Currents in British Literature I
Fall 2013
Professor Kinane
Plymouth State University

Final options

From the syllabus:

Course goals: I hope this course inspires students

- to consider the varieties of uses for literature over time [Why do people read and write the things they do in various eras? How do technology, literacy, access, and social/historical contexts impact the construction and consumption of texts in different eras?]
- to consider how language works dramatically, poetically and/or rhetorically, and to what effect [Close readings]
- to gain familiarity with the basic narratives of literary history and to find ways of questioning those narratives [Which genres were popular when, with whom, and why? Or, we can consider a basic narrative—like, "women had no power in the Middle Ages"—and consider how literature illuminates this idea differently—perhaps in the writings of Marie de France and Margery Kempe, for example. Or, we can unravel the idea of the Anglo-Saxon warrior ethos by exploring the tenderness expressed by Anglo-Saxon elegies.]
- to ask significant questions of texts to develop arguments about them [What is interesting, why, and what do you make of it?]
- to write an engaging and clearly argued, thesis-driven, original essay on a topic of their choice

Your final project should demonstrate your facility with **at least two** of these course goals.

Your final project will be **accompanied by a statement** noting your goals and describing how you have achieved them.

Any final project should incorporate texts, genres, and/or themes **from across the semester,** with representation from the Anglo-Saxon, Anglo-Norman, medieval, 16th century, and 17th century units.

All written documents should be in 12 point Times font, one inch margins, heading as the top of this paper with your name, stapled.

1. **Creative option:** Make a film, write a few skits, create musical scores, craft games, etc. Consider creative and playful (or serious) ways to explore themes, genres, characters, and authors we've encountered this semester. Some further suggestions:

Diary entries. Choose several character or authors we've studied this semester and create a series of journal entries written from that point of view. You may want to include entries from different points of his/her life or a series of daily entries from one specific phase of life. Be sure you demonstrate your thorough familiarity with texts, genres, themes, characters, and social and historical contexts through this creative project. Be as descriptive as possible.

Mash up. Choose characters from or authors of different texts we've studied this semester and put them together in a series of scenarios or one extended scenario. How would they meet up? What is the setting? What would each say? How would they behave towards one another? This could be presented as a filmed theatrical play, as a script, or as a short story. Be sure you demonstrate your thorough familiarity with texts, genres, themes, characters, and social and historical contexts through this creative project. Be as descriptive as possible.

Contemporary movie. Modernize the texts we've studied this semester and turn that idea into a movie. What would be the title? Who would star in it? Create a movie poster, soundtrack, and tag line. Create a preview for the film that illustrates your dramatization of several scenes, or write a scene or two from the movie. Be sure you demonstrate your thorough familiarity with texts, genres, themes, characters, and social and historical contexts through this creative project. Be as descriptive as possible.

2. **Take home essay** questions (~7 pages of response excluding quotations). Choose one of the following and write a well-organized, thesis-driven essay in response:

A. Close reading, explication and analysis.
   a. Choose 15–45 lines from John Milton's Paradise Lost and brief passages from two works of two other different eras we've covered this term in this course. You may want to choose passages that touch on gender, the nature of knowledge, inner and outer states

of being, or the relationship between the spiritual and earthly or the individual in society, but the choice is yours.

b. Compare and/or contrast the passages in terms of themes/issues addressed, tone towards the subject, formal features (verse, rhyme, imagery, metaphor, repetition, etc.).
c. Discuss how historical context informs the different choices of the authors. You may want to discuss the political climate, the role of the author in society, and/or the class/gender of the author.
d. Consider how these different/similar treatments can illuminate some aspect of your contemporary life, world, or understanding.

B. Stereotypically, the medieval and Renaissance past are seen as uniformly oppressive patriarchies. Using texts we've studied this semester and any research you'd like, craft an essay that nuances this stereotype and explores evidence for women's voices and autonomy in this era and through the Christian Church. Be sure to use specific examples from texts across a variety of eras.

3. **Philosophical inquiry** (~7 pages of response excluding quotations)

Write a final paper that responds to this claim, which I have synthesized from a variety of notions:

> The Humanities are dead. Art, literature, and other cultural pleasantries have no practical value in today's economic climate and therefore precious educational resources should not be spent on such frivolities. Instead, students today need to learn how to think rationally and logically, how to cultivate business skills that will help them get jobs. Reading old, dusty books might have been a nice past-time for wealthy gentlemen in the nineteenth century, but our era needs a new way of thinking and new ways of preparing students for success. 'The appreciation of literature' not only can't be taught; it *shouldn't* be taught. Such subjective and 'soft' thinking certainly has no place in today's educational system or broader society. Further, English professors themselves profess that there is no inherent meaning in texts, that nothing can ever be known, and that all positions are subjective and faulty. Why, then, should we bother with literature? What good can come from such a 'discipline'?

How would you respond to this claim by invoking texts, themes, and experiences from this course this semester? Revisit the "Communion of Strangers" article, the "Setting the Course" discussion Forum, the "Beowulf: Manifesto" questions and postings. Review your own and other students' postings in other Forums, our class activities (mead hall/boasting, making riddles, coloring manuscripts, Socratic seminars, etc.), the discussion prompts I've provided, and your general notions about medieval and Renaissance texts. Consider what you thought at the beginning of the course (about the purposes of literature, how and why we read, the value of the past) and compare it to your thinking on these subject now. Review your experiences in other classes within and beyond your English major. Bring in specific examples from readings and discussion boards over the entire semester that help you articulate a thesis about how and why literature matters to you personally, how and why it should matter to the university, how and why it should matter to people outside of the university. Or how and why it doesn't and shouldn't.

4. **Unit plan**. Craft a unit plan using the guidelines at the end of this packet. Option available only to Teacher Certification majors who have worked with such a plan before.

Selected Bibliography

Ahearn, Kathleen A. "'I'm Not a Feminist But. . .': Liberatory Approaches to Teaching Margaret Cavendish's *The Blazing World*." *Women's Writing* 14, no. 2 (Aug 2007): 215–31.

Altman, Joel. *The Tudor Play of Mind: Rhetorical Inquiry and the Development of Elizabethan Drama*. Berkeley: University of California Press, 1978.

Augar, Naomi, Ruth Raitman, and Wanlei Zhou. "Teaching and Learning Online with Wikis." In *Beyond the Comfort Zone: Proceedings of the 21st ASCILITE Conference*, edited by R. Atkinson, C. McBeath, D. Jonas-Dwyer, and R. Phillips. Perth, Australia, December 5–8, 2004), 95–104. http://www.ascilite.org.au/conferences/perth04/procs/augar.html.

Bamford, Karen, and Alexander Leggatt, eds. *Approaches to Teaching English Renaissance Drama*. New York: Modern Language Association of America, 2002.

Barta, Tony, ed. *Screening the Past: Film and the Representation of History*. Westport, CT: Praeger, 1988.

Barthes, Roland. "From Work to Text." In *Image Music Text*, 155–64. Translated by Stephen Heath. New York: Hill and Wang, 1977.

Bate, Jonathan. *The Genius of Shakespeare*. New York: Oxford University Press, 1998.

Baumlin, James S. "Dialogue and *Controversia* in English Renaissance Literature: Historicizing the Reader's Response," *Publications of the Missouri Philological Association* 19 (1994): 1–20.

Bennett, Jane. *The Enchantment of Modern Life: Attachments, Crossings, and Ethics*. Princeton, NJ: Princeton University Press, 2001.

Berger, Jr., Harry. *Imaginary Audition: Shakespeare on Stage and Page*. Berkeley: University of California Press, 1989.

Blocksidge, Martin, ed. *Shakespeare in Education*. London: Continuum, 2005.

Bohannan, Laura. "Shakespeare in the Bush." *Natural History*, (Fall 1966): 53–57.

Borja, Rhea R. "Educators Experiment with Student-Written Wikis." *Education Week* 25 no. 30 (2006): 10.

Bourdieu, Pierre. *Outline of a Theory of Practice*. Translated by Richard Nice. Cambridge: Cambridge University Press, 2005.

Boyd, Barbara Weiden, and Cora Fox, eds. *Approaches to Teaching the Works of Ovid and the Ovidian Tradition*. New York: Modern Language Association of America, 2010.

Brayman, Heidi Hackel, and Ian Frederick Moulton, eds. *Teaching Early Modern Literature from the Archives*. New York: Modern Language Association of America, 2015.

Brennan, John, and Ruth Williams. *Collecting and Using Student Feedback: A Guide to Good Practice*. York, UK: Higher Education Academy, 2004.

Brown, John Russell. "Foreign Shakespeare and English-speaking Audiences." In *Foreign Shakespeare: Contemporary Performance*, edited by Dennis Kennedy, 21–35. Cambridge: Cambridge University Press, 1993.

Bulman, James C. "Shylock, Antonio, and the Politics of Performance." In *Shakespeare in Performance: A Collection of Essays*, edited by Frank Occhiogrosso, 27–46. Newark, DE: University of Delaware Press, 2003.

Butler, Judith. *Gender Trouble: Feminism and the Subversion of Identity*. New York: Routledge, 1990.

———. "Performative Acts and Gender Constitution: An Essay in Phenomenology and Feminist Theory." In *Performing Feminisms: Feminist Critical Theory and Theatre*, edited by Sue-Ellen Case, 270–82. Baltimore, MD: Johns Hopkins University Press, 1990.

Carnes, Mark C. *Minds on Fire: How Role-Immersion Games Transform College*. Cambridge, MA: Harvard University Press, 2014.

Chazelle, Celia, Simon Doubleday, Felice Lifshitz, and Amy G. Remensnyder, eds. *Why the Middle Ages Matter: Medieval Light on Modern Injustice*. London: Routledge, 2012.

Cheney, Patrick, ed. *Approaches to Teaching Shorter Elizabethan Poetry*. New York: Modern Language Association of America, 2000.

Clark, Ira. *Rhetorical Readings, Dark Comedies, and Shakespeare's Problem Plays*. Gainesville: University Press of Florida, 2007.

Coby, Patrick. *Henry VIII and the Reformation of Parliament*. New York: Norton, 2013.

Cohn, Ruby. *Modern Shakespeare Offshoots*. Princeton, NJ: Princeton University Press, 1976.

Conroy, Derval, and Danielle Clarke. *Teaching the Early Modern Period*. New York: Palgrave Macmillan, 2011.

Crowl, Samuel. *Shakespeare and Film: A Norton Guide*. New York: W. W. Norton, 2007.

Cummings, Robert E., and Matt Barton, eds. *Wiki Writing: Collaborative Learning in the College Classroom*. Ann Arbor: University of Michigan Press, 2008.

Cutchins, Dennis, Laurence Raw, and James M. Welsh, eds. *Redefining Adaptation Studies*. Lanham, MD: Scarecrow Press, 2010.

Davis, Lloyd, ed. *Shakespeare Matters: History, Teaching, Performance*. Newark, DE: University of Delaware Press, 2003.

Davis, William L. "Better a Witty Fool than a Foolish Wit: The Art of Shakespeare's Chiasmus." *Text and Performance Quarterly* 23, no. 4 (2003): 311–30.

de Grazia, Margreta, and Peter Stallybrass. "The Materiality of the Shakespearean Text." *Shakespeare Quarterly* 44 (1993): 255–83.

Derrida, Jacques. *Acts of Literature.* Edited by Derek Attridge. New York: Routledge, 1992.

Desmet, Christy, and Robert Sawyer, eds. *Shakespeare and Appropriation.* London: Routledge, 1999.

Dupuis, Margaret, and Grace Tiffany, eds. *Approaches to Teaching Shakespeare's* The Taming of the Shrew. New York: Modern Language Association of America, 2013.

Ebner, Martin, Michael Kickmeier-Rust, and Andreas Holzinger. "Utilizing Wiki-Systems in Higher Education Classes: A Chance for Universal Access?" *Universal Access in the Information Society* 7 (2008): 199–207. doi:10.1007/s10209-008-0115-2.

Emmerson, Richard K., ed. *Approaches to Teaching Medieval English Drama.* New York: Modern Language Association of America, 1990.

Erickson, Peter, ed. *Approaches to Teaching Shakespeare's* Othello. New York: Modern Language Association of America, 2005.

Ferris, S. Pixy, and Hilary Wilder. "Uses and Potentials of Wikis in the Classroom." *Innovate: Journal of Online Education*, 2, no. 5 (2006). http://www.learntechlib.org/d/104294.

Fischlin, Daniel, and Mark Fortier, eds. *Adaptations of Shakespeare: A Critical Anthology of Plays from the Seventeenth Century to the Present.* London: Routledge, 2000.

Flaherty, Kate, ed. *Teaching Shakespeare beyond the Centre: Australasian Perspectives.* Basingstoke, UK: Palgrave Macmillan, 2013.

Freeman, Jane. "'Fair Terms and a Villain's Mind': Rhetorical Patterns in *The Merchant of Venice.*" *Rhetorica* 20, no. 2 (2002): 149–72.

Fries, Maureen, ed. *Approaches to Teaching the Arthurian Tradition.* New York: Modern Language Association of America, 1992.

Furco, Andrew, and Shelley H. Billig, eds. *Service-Learning: The Essence of the Pedagogy.* Greenwich, CT: Information Age Publishing, 2002, 23–50.

Genette, Gerard. *Palimpsests: Literature in the Second Degree.* Translated by Channa Newman and Claude Doubinsky. Lincoln: University of Nebraska Press, 1982.

Gibaldi, Joseph. *Approaches to Teaching Chaucer's* Canterbury Tales. New York: Modern Language Association of America, 1980.

Goldfarb, Brian. *Visual Pedagogy: Media Cultures in and Beyond the Classroom.* Durham, NC: Duke University Press, 2002.

Gottlieb, Sidney, ed. *Approaches* to *Teaching the Metaphysical Poets.* New York: Modern Language Association of America, 1990.

Gregory, Marshall. "From Shakespeare on the Page to Shakespeare on the Stage: What I Learned About Teaching in Acting Class." *Pedagogy: Critical Approaches to Teaching Literature, Language, Composition, and Culture* 6, no. 2 (2006): 309–25.

Grobman, Laurie, and Roberta Rosenberg, eds. *Service Learning and Literary Studies in English.* New York: Modern Languages Association of America, 2014.

Guillory, John. *Cultural Capital: The Problem of Literary Canon Formation.* Chicago: University of Chicago Press, 1993.

Hackel, Heidi Brayman, and Ian Frederick Moulton. *Teaching Early Modern English Literature from the Archives.* Modern Language Association of America, 2015.

Hansen, Matthew C. "Learning to Read Shakespeare: Using Read-Throughs as a Teaching and Learning Strategy." *Working Papers on the Web 4: Teaching Renaissance Texts* (2002). Accessed 1 April 2014. http://extra.shu.ac.uk/wpw/renaissance/hansen.htm.

———. "'O Brave New World': Service-Learning and Shakespeare." *Pedagogy* 11, no. 1 (2011): 177–97.

Hart, Tobin. *From Information to Transformation.* New York: Peter Lang, 2009.

Healey, Mick, and Alan Jenkins. "Developing Students as Researchers." In *Linking Research and Teaching in Higher Education: Proceedings of the Newport NEXUS Conference,* edited by Simon K. Haslett and Heflin Rowlands, 7–11. Newport: University of Wales, 2009.

Herman, Peter C., ed. *Approaches to Teaching Milton's* Paradise Lost. New York: Modern Language Association of America, 2012.

———. *Approaches* to *Teaching* Milton's Shorter Poetry and Prose. New York: Modern Language Association of America, 2007.

Hickey, Dona, and Donna Reiss, eds. *Learning Literature in an Era of Change: Innovations in Teaching.* Sterling, VA: Stylus, 2000.

Higgins, Marilyn, Fiona Grant, Pauline Thompson, and Alicia Montarzino. "Effective and Efficient Methods of Formative Assessment: CEBE Innovative Project in Learning and Teaching." Edinburgh, UK: Heriot-Watt University, 2010. http://www.cebe.heacademy.ac.uk/projects/funding/pdf/Formative%20assessment%20final%20report.pdf.

Hiscock, Andrew, ed. *Teaching Shakespeare and Early Modern Dramatists.* Basingstoke, UK: Palgrave Macmillan, 2007.

Hodgdon, Barbara, and W. B. Worthen, eds. *A Companion to Shakespeare and Performance.* Malden, MA: Wiley-Blackwell, 2008.

Hunt, Maurice, ed. *Approaches to Teaching Shakespeare's* Romeo and Juliet. New York: Modern Language Association of America, 2000.

———. *Approaches* to *Teaching Shakespeare's* The Tempest *and Other Late Romances.* New York: Modern Language Association of America, 1992.

Jackson, Russell, ed. *The Cambridge Companion to Shakespeare on Film*. Cambridge: Cambridge University Press, 2007.

Jorgens, Jack J. "Realizing Shakespeare on Film." In *Shakespeare on Film,* edited by Robert Shaughnessy, 18–42. New York: St. Martin's Press, 1998.

Joseph, Sister Miriam. *Shakespeare's Use of the Arts of Language*. New York: Columbia University Press, 1947.

Jurgens, Eric. "Finding the Artist Within: Student Projects in the Humanities." *Tribal College Journal of American Indian Higher Education* (May 1, 2014). http://tribalcollegejournal.org/finding-artist-within-student-projects-humanities/.

Kahn, Coppélia, Heather S. Nathans, and Mimi Godfrey, eds. *Shakespearean Educations: Power, Citizenship, and Performance*. Newark, DE: University of Delaware Press, 2011.

Katz, Lillian G., and Sylvia C. Chard. *Engaging Children's Minds: The Project Approach*. Norwood, NJ: Ablex, 1989.

Keller, Stefan. "Combining Rhetoric and Pragmatics to Read *Othello*." *English Studies* 91, no. 4 (2010): 398–411.

Kidnie, Margaret Jane. *Shakespeare and the Problem of Adaptation*. London: Routledge, 2009.

Kinane, Karolyn. "Arthurian Legends in General Education: An Example of Student-Centered Pedagogy." *Studies in Medieval and Renaissance Teaching* 20 (Fall 2013).

———. "Contemplative Pedagogy, Enchantment, and the Medieval Past." *Postmedieval Forum IV: Pedagogy*. Mary Dockray-Miller, ed. (October, 2013). http://postmedieval-forum.com/forums/forum-iv-pedagogy/contemplative-pedagogy-karolyn-kinane/.

Kliman, Bernice W., ed. *Approaches to Teaching Shakespeare's* Hamlet. New York: Modern Language Association of America, 2002.

Landy, Marcia. *The Historical Film: History and Memory in Media*. New Brunswick, NJ: Rutgers University Press, 2001.

Langer, Ellen. *The Power of Mindful Learning*. Reading, MA: Addison-Wesley, 1999.

Lloyd-Jones, Roger, and M. J. Lewis. "Integrating Information Technology into the History Curriculum." In *The Practice of University History Teaching,* edited by Alan Booth and Paul Hyland, 70–84. Manchester, UK: Manchester University Press, 2000.

Loehlin, James N. "Teaching Through Performance." In *A Companion to Shakespeare and Performance*, edited by Barbara Hodgdon and W. B. Worthen, 627–43. Malden, MA: Blackwell, 2005.

MacFarlane, A. "Teaching and Learning in an Expanded Higher Education Section (The MacFarlane Report)." Bristol, UK: HEFCE [Higher Education Funding Council for England], 1992.

Mack, Peter. *Reading and Rhetoric in Montaigne and Shakespeare*. London: Bloomsbury Academic, 2010.

Mallin, Eric S., and Paul E. Sullivan. *Stages of Power: Marlowe and Shakespeare, 1592*. New York: Norton, 2016.

Mann, Jenny C. *Outlaw Rhetoric: Figuring Vernacular Eloquence in Shakespeare's England*. Ithaca, NY: Cornell University Press, 2012.

McCloskey, Susan. "Teaching Dramatic Literature." *College English* 46 (1984): 385–91.

McDonald, Russ. *The Bedford Companion to Shakespeare: An Introduction with Documents*. 2nd ed. Boston: Bedford/St. Martins, 2001.

McKerrow, Ronald B. *Printers' & Publishers' Devices in England & Scotland, 1485–1640*. London: Chiswick Press, 1913.

Michaelsen, Larry K., Arletta Bauman Knight, and L. Dee Fink, eds. *Team-based Learning: A Transformative Use of Small Groups*. Westport, CT: Praeger, 2002.

Miller, David Lee, ed. *Approaches to Teaching Spenser's* Faerie Queene. New York: Modern Language Association of America, 1994.

Miller, Miriam Youngerman, ed. *Approaches to Teaching* Sir Gawain and the Green Knight. New York: Modern Language Association of America, 1986.

Mills, Dan. "Mind the Gap: Teaching *Othello* through Creative Responses." *Pedagogy: Critical Approaches to Teaching Literature, Language, Composition, and Culture* 8, no. 1 (2008): 154–59.

Monta, Susannah Brietz, and Margaret W. Ferguson, eds. *Teaching Early Modern English Prose*. New York: Modern Language Association of America, 2010.

Morey, James H., "The 'Cultour' in the *Miller's Tale*: Alison as Iseult," *Chaucer Review* 29 (1995): 373–81.

Naremore, James, ed. *Film Adaptation*. New Brunswick, NJ: Rutgers University Press, 2000.

Ober, Josiah, Naomi J. Norman, and Mark C. Carnes. *The Threshold of Democracy: Athens in 403 B.C.* 4th ed. New York: Norton, 2015.

Oberdorfer, Richard. "Pursuing the White Boar: Approaches to Teaching *Richard III*." *Studies in Medieval and Renaissance Teaching* 6, no. 1 (Spring 1998): 67–85.

Orkin, Martin. *Local Shakespeares: Proximations and Power*. New York: Routledge, 2005.

Parker, Andrew, and Eve Kosofsky Sedgwick, eds. *Performativity and Performance*. New York: Routledge, 1995.

Parker, Kevin R., and Joseph T. Chao. "Wiki as a Teaching Tool." *Interdisciplinary Journal of Knowledge and Learning Objects* 3 (2007): 57–72.

Pearlman, Edith. "*Macbeth* on Film: Politics." In *Shakespeare and the Moving Image*, edited by Anthony Davies and Stanley Wells, 250–60. Cambridge: Cambridge University Press, 1994.

Petty, Geoff. *Teaching Today: A Practical Guide*. 3rd ed. Cheltenham, UK: Nelson Thornes, 2004.

Popper, Karl. *The Logic of Scientific Discovery*. London: Routledge, 2002.

Pugh, Tison, ed. *Approaches to Teaching Chaucer's* Troilus and Criseyde *and the Shorter Poems*. New York: Modern Language Association of America, 2007.

Race, Phil. *The Lecturer's Toolkit*, 3rd ed. London: Routledge, 2006.

Ray, Robert H., ed. *Approaches to Teaching Shakespeare's* King Lear. New York: Modern Language Association of America, 1986.

Reynolds, Candyce, Dannelle D. Stevens, and Ellen West. "'I'm in a Professional School! Why Are You Making Me Do This?' A Cross-Disciplinary Study of the Use of Creative Classroom Projects on Student Learning." *College Teaching* 61, no. 2 (2013), 52.

Richardson, Will. *Blogs, Wikis, Podcasts and Other Powerful Web Tools for Classrooms*. Thousand Oaks, CA: Corwin, 2010.

Riggio, Milla Cozart, ed. *Teaching Shakespeare through Performance*. New York: Modern Language Association of America, 1999.

Roberts, Jennifer L. "The Power of Patience: Teaching Students the Value of Deceleration and Immersive Attention," *Harvard Magazine*, November-December 2013. http://harvardmagazine.com/2013/11/the-power-of-patience.

Rollins, Peter C., ed. *Hollywood as Historian: American Film in a Cultural Context*. Lexington: University Press of Kentucky, 1983.

Rosenstone, Robert. *Visions of the Past*. Cambridge, MA: Harvard University Press, 1995.

Rothwell, Kenneth. *A History of Shakespeare on the Screen: A Century of Film and Television*. Cambridge: Cambridge University Press, 2004.

Rud, A. G., and Jim Garrison, eds. *Teaching with Reverence*. New York: Palgrave Macmillan, 2012.

Sanders, Julie. *Adaptation and Appropriation*. New York: Routledge, 2006.

Selke, Mary J. Goggins. *Rubric Assessment Goes to College: Objective, Comprehensive Evaluation of Student Work*. Lanham, MD: Rowman & Littlefield Education, 2013.

Semler, Liam E. *Teaching Shakespeare and Marlowe: Learning versus the System*. London: Bloomsbury, 2013.

Shand, G. B., ed. *Teaching Shakespeare: Passing It On*. Malden, MA: Blackwell, 2009.

Smith, Paul, ed. *The Historian and Film*. Cambridge: Cambridge University Press, 1976.

Strage, Amy. "Long-Term Academic Benefits of Service-Learning: When and Where Do They Manifest Themselves." *College Student Journal* 38, no. 2 (2004): 257–62.

Taylor, Gary, and John Jowett. *Shakespeare Reshaped, 1606–1623*. Oxford Shakespeare Studies. Oxford: Oxford University Press, 1993.

Thompson, Ann. "'King Lear' and the Politics of Teaching Shakespeare," *Shakespeare Quarterly* 41, no. 2 (1990): 139–46.

Thompson, Ayanna. "Unmooring the Moor: Researching and Teaching on YouTube." *Shakespeare Quarterly* 61, no. 3 (2010): 337–56.

Toplin, Robert Brent. "The Filmmaker as Historian." *American Historical Review* 93, no. 5 (Dec 1988): 1210–27.

Watson, Nicholas. "Desire for the Past." *Studies in the Age of Chaucer* 21 (1999): 59–97.

Weller, Toni, ed. *History in the Digital Age.* London: Routledge, 2013.

Wells, Stanley, and Gary Taylor, eds. *William Shakespeare: A Textual Companion,* rev. ed. 1987. Reprint, Oxford: Oxford University Press, 1997.

Wilhelm, Jeffrey, and Bruce Novak. *Teaching Literacy for Love and Wisdom: Being the Book and Being the Change.* New York: Teachers College Press, 2011.

Williams, Joanna. *Consuming Higher Education: Why Learning Can't Be Bought.* London: Bloomsbury Academic, 2013.

Wilson, Richard. "Global Shakespeare: The Wide and Universal Theatre." *Alicante Journal of English Studies* 25 (2012): 5–17.

Woodcock, Ben, Andrew Middleton, and Anne Nortcliffe. "Considering the Smartphone Learner: An Investigation into Student Interest in the Use of Personal Technology to Enhance their Learning." *Student Engagement and Experience Journal* 1, no. 1 (2012): 1–15.

Worthen, William B. *Drama: Between Poetry and Performance.* Malden, MA: Wiley-Blackwell, 2010.

———. *Shakespeare and the Authority of Performance.* Cambridge: Cambridge University Press, 1997.

Yeager, R. F., ed. *Approaches to Teaching the Poetry of John Gower.* New York: Modern Language Association of America, 2011.

Zajonc, Arthur. *Meditation as Contemplative Inquiry.* Great Barrington, MA: Lindisfarne Books, 2009.

Notes on Contributors

Charles Beem is a professor of history at the University of North Carolina at Pembroke, where he teaches courses in World Civilizations, Early Modern Europe, all aspects of British History, and the History of Sexuality. He is the author of *The Lioness Roared* (2006) and the editor of *The Royal Minorities of Medieval and Early Modern England* (2008), *The Foreign Relations of Elizabeth I* (2011), *The Name of a Queen: William Fleetwood's Itinerarium ad Windsor* (2013), and *The Man Behind the Queen: Male Consorts in History* (2014). He is also, with Carole Levin, the editor of the book series Queenship and Power for publishers Palgrave Macmillan. He is currently at work on the monograph *Queenship in Early Modern Europe.* Beem was the recipient of an excellence in teaching award in 2006 and 2015, two Folger Shakespeare Library fellowships in 2007 and 2011, and the Adolph Dial Award for Scholarship and Creativity in 2008. In 2012 he was elected a fellow of the Royal Historical Society.

Anna Riehl Bertolet is an associate professor in the Department of English at Auburn University. She is the author of *The Face of Queenship: Early Modern Representations of Elizabeth I* (Palgrave, 2010) and a coeditor, with Thomas Betteridge, of an essay collection, *Tudor Court Culture* (Susquehanna University Press, 2010). She is a coeditor, with Carole Levin and Jo Eldridge Carney, of *A Biographical Encyclopedia of Early Modern Englishwomen 1500–1650: Exemplary Lives and Memorable Acts* (Routledge, 2016) and the editor of *Queens Matter in Early Modern Studies* (Palgrave, 2018). She won the Auburn University College of Liberal Arts teaching award in 2011, Department of English Faculty Excellence in Teaching Award (2017), and Folger Shakespeare Library fellowship in 2014–15. Her essays on Queen Elizabeth I, early modern poetry, drama, and needlework have been published in various journals and essay collections.

Craig E. Bertolet is a professor of English at Auburn University. His area of specialty is Medieval English Literature with an emphasis on Geoffrey Chaucer, John Gower, and their late fourteenth-century contemporaries. His essays on medieval literature have appeared in *Chaucer Review*, *Studies in the Age of Chaucer*, and *Studies in Philology*, among others. He is the author of *Chaucer, Gower, Hoccleve and the Commercial Practices of Late Fourteenth-Century London* (Ashgate, 2013). He has published an essay on teaching selections of the works of

John Gower with Chaucer's *Canterbury Tales* in *Approaches to Teaching the Poetry of John Gower*, ed. Brian Gastle & R. F. Yeager (MLA, 2011).

Renee A. P. Bricker is an associate professor of history at the University of North Georgia (UNG) and earned her doctorate at Wayne State University in 2010. In 2015 she received an award from UNG for the Scholarship of Teaching and Learning, and in 2016 received the Faculty Scholarship of Engagement Award. She is also the Principal Investigator of an NEH Enduring Questions Award to codevelop the course, "Enduring Questions of Peace in Western and Eastern Cultures."

Regina Buccola is a professor and chair of the Department of Humanities and of Literature and Languages at Roosevelt University in Chicago, where she also serves as core faculty in Women's and Gender Studies. She has published several books on early modern British drama and culture, most recently as editor of *A Midsummer Night's Dream: A Critical Guide* and coeditor, with Peter Kanelos, of *Chicago Shakespeare Theater: Suiting the Action to the Word*. Her recent journal publications include *Medieval and Renaissance Drama in England* and *Borrowers and Lenders: The Journal of Shakespeare and Appropriation*. She serves as the scholar in residence at Chicago Shakespeare Theater and is one of the Midwest American reviewers for the online journal *Reviewing Shakespeare*.

Jo Eldridge Carney is a professor in the Department of English at The College of New Jersey. Her most recent book is *Fairy Tale Queens: Representations of Early Modern Queenship* (Palgrave, 2012). She is a coeditor, with Carole Levin and Anya Riehl Bertolet, of *A Biographical Encyclopedia of Early Modern Englishwomen 1500–1650: Exemplary Lives and Memorable Acts* (Routledge, 2016). She has also published articles on Shakespeare, early modern queens, and Renaissance and contemporary fairy tales and edited essay collections on early modern queenship. She teaches courses in Shakespeare, early modern British literature, the literary fairy tale, and contemporary literature.

Matthew C. Hansen is a professor of English at Boise State University and researches and publishes on Shakespeare, the teaching of Shakespeare, and early modern English drama and poetry. Also an actor and director, he has most recently directed productions of Shakespeare's *The Taming of the Shrew* and a stage adaptation of Jane Austen's *Pride and Prejudice* and appeared as Mozart in a production of Peter Shaffer's *Amadeus*. He is currently at work developing plans to measure the long-term impacts on elementary-student learning and community engagement of his "Shake It Up After School" project.

Nancy Hayes is a professor in the English Department at St. Ambrose University in Davenport, Iowa. Her scholarly publications include "Negativizing

Nurture and Demonizing Domesticity: The Witch Construct in Early Modern Germany" in *Maternal Measures: Figuring Caregiving in the Early Modern Period* (Ashgate, 2000), entries in *Encyclopedia of Women in the Renaissance: Italy, France, and England* (ABC-CLIO, 2007), and reviews in *Renaissance Quarterly* (Winter 2006) and *Sixteenth Century Journal* (Winter 2012). She has published numerous poems including translations and sonnets in *Quercus*. Her recent research focuses on Shakespeare and the medieval and Renaissance lyric.

Kimberly Jack is an assistant professor of English and Drama at Athens State University, where she teaches Medieval and Renaissance English Literature, Early World Literature and Mythology, as well as Drama Production and Costume Design. She also designs and produces costumes for three plays a year for the Athens State theatre program. Her scholarship focuses on costume rhetoric in Middle English Literature, especially the works of the *Pearl*- or *Gawain*-Poet.

Karolyn Kinane is a professor of English and organizer of the Contemplative Communities Project at Plymouth State University with teaching and research interests in saints, mysticism, medievalism, contemplative pedagogy, and New Religious movements. Among other publications, she edited and contributed to "New Age and Neopagan Medievalisms," *Relegere: Studies in Religion and Reception* 3, no. 2 (2013) (http://relegere.org); coedited with Meriem Pagès *The Middle Ages on Television: Critical Essays* (McFarland Press, 2015); and coedited with Michael A. Ryan *End of Days: Essays on the Apocalypse from Antiquity to Modernity* (McFarland Press, 2009).

Jonathan P. Lamb is an assistant professor of English at the University of Kansas, where he writes and teaches about Shakespeare, early modern literature, form, and book history. He recently published a book, *Shakespeare in the Marketplace of Words* (Cambridge, 2017), about Shakespeare's use of peculiar formal features of language to interact with the world. He is now at work on a project about how early modern writers used the vocabulary of the printed book to talk about life, death, sex, gender, damnation, old age, and capitalism.

Mary Ellen Lamb is a professor of English (emerita) at Southern Illinois University Carbondale. She is the author of *Gender and Authorship in the Sidney Circle* (1990) and *The Popular Culture of Shakespeare, Spenser, and Jonson* (2006), co-editor of *Oral Traditions and Gender in Early Modern Literary Texts* (2007) and *Staging Early Modern Romance: Prose Fiction, Dramatic Romance, and Shakespeare* (2009). She has authored numerous essays on women writers and on Shakespeare in such journals as *English Literary Renaissance, Shakespeare Quarterly, Shakespeare Survey, Review of English Studies,* and *Criticism*, as well as in numerous collections. She is currently on the editorial board of *English Literary Renaissance* and is the editor of the *Sidney Journal*. She is currently collaborating on an edition of poetry by William Herbert, third Earl of Pembroke, for the Renaissance English Text Society.

Carole Levin is Willa Cather Professor of History and was Director of the Medieval and Renaissance Studies Program at the University of Nebraska-Lincoln. She has won awards for her teaching from SUNY/New Paltz and the University of Nebraska. She is the author or editor of seventeen books, including *The Heart and Stomach of a King: Elizabeth I and the Politics of Sex and Power* (University of Pennsylvania Press, 2013; 2nd ed.) and *Dreaming the English Renaissance* (Palgrave, 2008). She is also a coeditor, with Anna Riehl Bertolet and Jo Eldridge Carney, of *A Biographical Encyclopedia of Early Modern Englishwomen 1500–1650: Exemplary Lives and Memorable Acts* (Routledge, 2016). She has held long-term fellowships at both the Newberry Library in Chicago and the Folger Shakespeare Library in Washington, DC, and in 2015 she was a Fulbright Scholar at the University of York in England.

Linda Shenk is an associate professor and the Director of Graduate Education in the Department of English at Iowa State University where she teaches Shakespeare and early modern drama. She has received Iowa State University's Early Achievement in Teaching Award as well as the College of Liberal Arts and Sciences' Jerry Shakeshaft Master Teacher Award, and her teaching has prompted students to give her the nickname "Shenkspeare." Professor Shenk is the author of *Learned Queen: The Image of Elizabeth I in Politics and Poetry* as well as articles on Elizabeth I, early modern drama, and court entertainment.

Nathanial B. Smith is an associate professor in the Department of English Language and Literature at Central Michigan University. He has published essays on humoral medicine and rhetoric in Shakespeare's *Taming of the Shrew* and Spenser's *Faerie Queene*, and he coedited a collection of essays, "Teaching Medieval Literature Off the Grid," for the journal *Pedagogy*. His current research draws on affect theory to explore conceptions of the body and soul in late medieval and early modern dream vision literature.

Jonathan Walker is professor of English at Portland State University, where he teaches Renaissance drama and critical theory. He has coedited a collection of essays titled *Early Modern Academic Drama* (Ashgate, 2008) and published in *Renaissance Drama*, *Theatre Survey*, *Comparative Literature*, and elsewhere. Jonathan's new book is titled *Site Unscene: The Offstage in English Renaissance Drama* (Northwestern, 2017).

Elena (Ellie) Woodacre is a specialist in medieval and Early Modern queenship and a senior lecturer in Early Modern European History at the University of Winchester. Her publications include her monograph *The Queens Regnant of*

Navarre; Succession, Politics and Partnership (Palgrave, 2013) and she has edited or coedited several collections including, *Queenship in the Mediterranean* (Palgrave, 2013), *The Image and Perception of Monarchy in Medieval and Early Modern Europe* (Cambridge Scholars, 2014), *Royal Mothers and their Ruling Children* (Palgrave, 2015) and *Virtuous or Villainess? The Image of the Royal Mother from the Early Medieval to the Early Modern Eras* (Palgrave, 2016). Elena is the organizer of the Kings & Queens conference series and the founder of the international Royal Studies Network (www.royalstudiesnetwork.org), a resource that aims to bring together scholars who work on monarchical topics. She is also the editor-in-chief of the *Royal Studies Journal* (www.rsj.winchester.ac.uk or www.royalstudiesjournal.com), an academic, peer-reviewed, multilingual, and fully open-access publication that was launched in 2014.

Plate 1: Photo of King Charles I on his knees.
Class of Carole Levin.

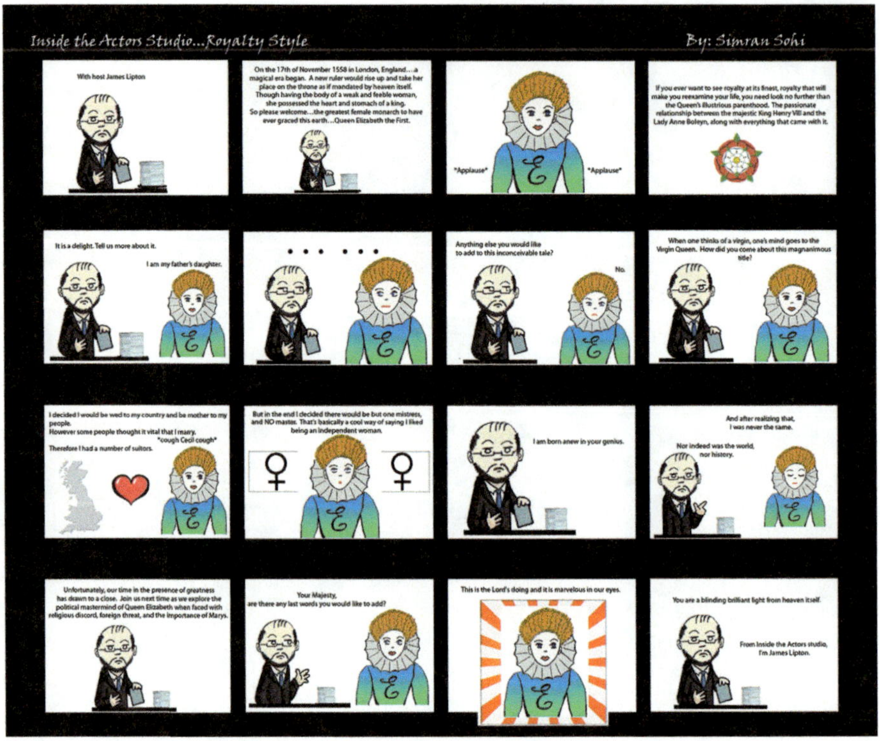

Plate 2: Queen Elizabeth Retelling.
Cartoon by Simran Sohi. Class of Carole Levin.

Plates 3, 4, 5: Elementary students perform *A Midsummer Night's Dream* as part of "Shake It Up After School."
Class of Matthew Hansen.

Plates 3, 4, 5: Elementary students perform *A Midsummer Night's Dream* as part of "Shake It Up After School."
Class of Matthew Hansen.

Plate 6: *Othello* Cupcakes, featuring the Othello cupcake (left), the Iago cupcake (center), and the Desdemona cupcake (right).
Class of Jonathan Lamb.

Plate 7: *Paradise Lost*: The cake of Eden.
Caitlin Sheridan and Scott Dukes. Class of Anna Riehl Bertolet.

Plate 8: *Paradise Lost*: Book XI Quilt.
Spenser R. Keel. Class of Anna Riehl Bertolet.

Plate 9: "Cookham" (based on the poem by Aemilia Lanyer).
Anna Mehta. Class of Anna Riehl Bertolet.

Plate 10: "A Dialogue Between Two Shepherds" (based on the poem by Mary Sidney Herbert).

Jordan Mollineux. Class of Anna Riehl Bertolet.